BARRON'S

HOW TO PREPARE FOR THE

AP*

MICROECONOMICS/MACROECONOMICS ADVANCED PLACEMENT EXAMINATIONS

Frank Musgrave
Chair and Professor
Department of Economics
Ithaca College
Director
Southern Tier (NY) Center for
Economic Education
Ithaca College

Elia Kacapyr
Associate Professor
Department of Economics
Ithaca College

BARRON'S

* AP and Advanced Placement program are registered trademarks of the College Entrance Examination Board, which was not involved with the production of and does not endorse this book.

Acknowledgment

We thank Tina Bennett, Department Assistant, for her many hours of superb services on behalf of the production of this manuscript. She worked diligently and was able to offer suggestions that were always helpful. Her patience, understanding and skillful assistance were more than sufficient as stress reducers and aids to the completion of the task.

Dedication

To Eva Mae Gifford Musgrave

All inquiries should be addressed to:
Barron's Educational Series, Inc.
250 Wireless Boulevard
Hauppauge, New York 11788
http://www.barronseduc.com

Library of Congress Catalog Card No. 00-051886
International Standard Book No. 0-7641-1164-7

Library of Congress Cataloging-in-Publication Data

Musgrave, Frank.
    Barron's how to prepare for the AP micro/macro economics advanced placement
examination / Frank Musgrave and Elia Kacapyr.
        p.   cm.
    Includes index.
    ISBN 0-7641-1164-7
    1. Microeconomics—Examinations, questions, etc.   2. Macroeconomics—Examinations,
questions, etc.   I. Title: How to prepare for the AP micro/macro economics advanced placement
examination.   II. Title: AP micro/macro economics advanced placement examination.
III. Title: Micro/macro economics advanced placement examination.   IV. Kacapyr, Elia, 1956–
V. Barron's Educational Series, Inc.   VI. Title.
HB172 .M87   2001
330′.076—dc21

                                                                00-051886

PRINTED IN THE UNITED STATES OF AMERICA
9 8 7

CONTENTS

INTRODUCTION

CHAPTER

1 Preparing for the Advanced Placement Exams in Microeconomics and Macroeconomics

The Exams

Advanced Placement (AP) exams are given each May to qualified secondary school students who wish to complete coursework equivalent to a one-semester college introductory class. There are two separate exams in economics; one in microeconomics and one in macroeconomics. Basically, the AP exam determines whether a student understands enough of the subject matter to be given college credit.

The AP exams in economics are both set up the same way. There is a multiple-choice section of 60 questions with a time limit of 70 minutes, and an essay section of 3 questions with a time limit of 50 minutes. One of the essay, or free-response, questions is typically more involved than the other two. The essay section is preceded by a 10-minute reading period where the essays can be outlined. The multiple-choice questions are graded by computers and the essays are evaluated by professional graders. Each exam is then given an overall score of 1 through 5.

College policies on granting AP credit vary. Generally, a score of 4 or 5 is required to obtain college credit. Anyone preparing for an AP exam should visit the web site of the College Board (*www.collegeboard.com/ap*).

The Design of This Book

This book is designed to prepare you for the AP exam in microeconomics, the AP exam in macro-economics, or both. The College Board is very specific about what material will appear on each exam and the extent to which specific topics are emphasized. For instance, 60 to 70 percent of the AP exam in microeconomics concerns "the nature and function of product markets." On the macroeconomics exam, "national income and price determination" is emphasized. This study guide takes into consideration the coverage and emphases of recently administered AP exams.

This chapter goes on to give general study guides and tips for doing well on either of the AP economics exams. Chapters 2 and 3 cover material that appears on both the microeconomics and the macroeconomics AP exams. Students preparing for the microeconomics exam should then continue on with Chapters 4 through 13. After Chapter 13 there is a full-sized sample AP exam in microeconomics for you to try.

Students preparing for the AP exam in macroeconomics should continue with this chapter and Chapters 2 and 3, then skip to Chapter 14 and continue straight through Chapter 21. After Chapter 21 there is a sample AP exam in macroeconomics.

Multiple-Choice Questions

There are any number of suggestions that have been made regarding the art and/or science of answering multiple-choice questions. If the student is thinking of "multiple-guess" questions, the student is not destined for greatness on the examination. Pure guessing will likely result in 20 percent correct (one out of five odds) on the multiple-choice section.

Indeed, on the Advanced Placement examinations there is an assigned penalty for random or haphazard guessing. The computerized process will record the number of correct answers and then will subtract one-fourth of the number of incorrect answers from the number of correct answers, based on five choices for each question. Therefore, pure guessing will most likely result in a score of zero on the multiple-choice section of the AP exam. You want to maximize the number of correct answers and minimize the number of guesses.

STRATEGY

A suggested strategy would be to avoid making any answer when you do not have "a clue" about the question or any of the choices (a blank answer is not recorded as an incorrect answer). However, if you have a reasonable knowledge about the question, and if two of the five choices appear to be feasible answers, then your odds have been considerably improved if you choose an answer.

Time is a factor in all of this, therefore, the questions that are the most difficult or are causing you to spend a lot of time should be either completely avoided or, at least, delayed until you have answered those questions with the least difficulty. Remember to take a watch with you to the exam in the event that the clock is difficult to see from your seat.

A good approach to answering multiple-choice questions would be to first read the question and any related graph and decide your answer before looking at the choices. Otherwise, you will find yourself checking each of the five choices for accuracy, which will consume too much time, a relatively scarce resource!

Some clues can be obtained by looking at the structure of the five choices for any "pairing," modifying clauses, or "far-out" (such as, apparently irrelevant even if true) statements.

The "pairing" of choices can involve two or four choices. If there are two pairings, for instance, two of the five choices are paired, then the odds are that one of them is the correct answer. For example:

Which of the following is correct?

A. The law of diminishing returns applies to the long run.
B. The law of diminishing returns applies to the short run.
C. The law of diminishing returns explains how total output decreases as inputs are added.

D. The law of diminishing marginal productivity applies to consumer demand.

E. The law of diminishing marginal utility applies to production of output.

The correct answer is **B**, "the law of diminishing returns applies to the short run." Since choices **A** and **B** did *not* contain the word "only" after "applies" so that the law might apply to both the long run *and* the short run, the answer to the question has to be **A** or **B**. In other words, the law of diminishing returns *must* apply to either the short run or the long run, you have effectively eliminated the other three choices! Of course, you now must choose between **A** or **B**. Your study of economics and your review of this book (see Chapter 8: Costs, Production, Supply) should indicate to you that the correct answer (**B**) reflects that in the short run, supply has not fully adjusted to changes in demand. This means that the quantity of at least one input, say capital, remains fixed, while the quantity of another input, say labor, varies. The law is framed in these terms of "allowing" labor (input) to vary while holding capital (input) constant. At some level of production, the addition of labor to this fixed quantity of capital will mean each additional unit of labor has less capital with which to produce (additional labor must "share" the fixed capital with the previous units of labor). This leads to diminishing returns or smaller and smaller additions to produce (marginal physical products of labor) with additional units of labor. The law of diminishing returns does *not* hold in the long run since all inputs vary in the long run. That is, the time frame for the long run is whenever supply fully adjusts for changes in demand; all inputs are variable in the long run.

Incidentally, as indicated above, choices **C**, **D**, and **E** are incorrect by process of limiting the choices to **A** or **B**. However, we have provided a basic reason for each of these choices being incorrect in their own way, as follows:

C—The law of diminishing returns explains how additions (marginal products) to total product decrease.

D—The law of diminishing returns applies to production.

E—The law of diminishing marginal utility applies to consumer demand.

Remember, we provide these reasons for rejecting **C**, **D**, and **E** only for information and instruction on diminishing returns. However, you should not have to examine these other choices too carefully for want of time.

The "pairing" may involve four of the five choices. Be careful of the structure of the choices, particularly if absolute terms, such as *always* or *never* are used. For example, which of the following is *true* about the relationship of the average product (AP) curve and the marginal product (MP) curve?

A. AP and MP are always equal.

B. AP and MP are never equal.

C. The AP curve intersects the MP curve at the minimum point of the MP curve.

D. The MP curve intersects the AP curve at the minimum point of the AP curve.

E. The MP curve intersects the AP curve at the maximum point of the AP curve.

Absolutes

If you look at the structure and pairing of the choices, you might find some revealing differences. First, beware of absolutes, such as *always*, *never*, *every*, *none*, *forever*, etc. This is especially noteworthy, as in this question, since *two* absolute terms are used in a question about relationships. If there is any significant or defining mathematical relationship, it is rarely *always* or *never*. Knowing this, you should figure that choices **A** and **B** can be eliminated. You should *not* expect that the mathematical or conceptual "relationship" between AP and MP would be either *always equal* or *never equal*. Now, you are left with choices **C**, **D**, and **E**. You should have a clue that **C** can be eliminated since one of **D** and **E** are contrasting points—either MP intersects AP at its minimum or its maximum point. Choice **C** has no contrasting choice. Conceptually, you should know that since MP is the addition to total product (TP), when MP is greater than AP, AP must be rising. Conversely, when MP is less than AP, AP must be decreasing. Therefore, when MP = AP the average product curve is neither rising nor decreasing. In other words, the addition (MP) to total product is equal to the average product (AP). Thus, **E** is the correct answer: "The MP curve intersects the AP curve at the maximum point of the AP curve."

You may see the symmetry between this MP/AP relationship and the MC/AC relationship; however, the marginal cost curve intersects the average cost curves (average variable cost *and* the average total cost curve) at the minimum of the average cost curve (see Chapter 8: Costs, Production, Supply) for graphs depicting MP/AP and MC/AC.

Two Similar Answers
Some multiple-choice questions will offer two answers that are identical except that one contains a clause that modifies the statement. If you do not have another substantive clue, choose the response with the modified statement. For example:

Which of the following *best* expresses the profits-maximizing condition for a firm that uses labor and capital?

A. The marginal physical product of labor equals the marginal physical product of capital.
B. The marginal physical product of labor is greater than the marginal physical product of capital.
C. The marginal physical product of labor is less than the marginal physical product of labor.
D. marginal revenue product of labor = marginal revenue product of capital
   marginal factor cost (price) of labor = marginal factor cost (price) of capital
E. marginal revenue product of labor = marginal revenue product of capital = 1
   marginal factor cost (price) of labor = marginal factor cost (price) of capital

You will observe that none of the first three choices relate directly to the question primarily since one cannot establish the most profitable combination of labor and capital without any revenue data, so, toss away choices **A**, **B**, and **C**.

You are left with choices **D** and **E**, which are identical except that choice **E** modifies choice **D** by adding =*1*. If you have no further clue, you might figure that choice **E** is correct. The knowledge you need to answer this correctly would start with your attempt to sketch the answer without looking at the choices. The modification, =*1*, suggests that $MRP_L = MFC_L$ and that $MRP_K = MFC_L$ where L = Labor, K = Capital, MRP = Marginal Revenue Product, and MFC = Marginal Factor Cost. If we had been considering profit maximizing for the firm separately for labor and for capital, we would need $MRP_K = MFC_L$ for profit maximizing in the hire of capital and we would need $MRP_K = MFC_L$ in the hire of labor. Therefore, each of the ratios in the profit-maximizing condition for the hire of both inputs (labor and capital) would have to be =*1*. Then, the correct answer is **E**. If each ratio is =*1*, then we must establish that the two ratios would equal 1. Without the *equals 1* modification, you could have something such as $MRP_L = 8$, $MFC_L = 4$; $MRP_K = 20$, $MFC_K = 10$. Thus, 8/4 = 20/10 or 2 = 2. This would not represent the most profitable combination of the two resources.

Another step in the process of reducing the choices to a few instead of five is to see how many of the choices are on "the same page" or, better yet, which choices are on "the same correct page." We can use the above example to illustrate this point. As we explained above, if the question refers to profits we need to have revenue data. No revenue data exists for choices **A**, **B**, **C**. Only choices **D** and **E** include the word "revenue." Thus, you need to select as choices those options that are relevant, or, "on the same page."

Another approach is to sketch a graph if one applies to the question and is not provided on the test. This would be particularly useful when seeing if your answer matches one of the choices. For example, a shift in aggregate demand may produce an effect on the price level and real GDP that is much more easily identified on your graph than trying to visualize the answer in your head. Similarly, on the micro side, shifts in demand and supply are much better identified in their effects on equilibrium price and quantity if you sketch a graph.

Before taking the AP examination, students would be advised to test themselves by recreating the major graphs, given only the titles of these graphs. The students should check their work with the text graphs. They would then know their strengths and weaknesses and the major concepts could be identified and related to the graphs.

Finally, to the extent that you have time, look at each of your answers and ask yourself, "Does this answer make sense?"

Free-Response Questions

It is much more difficult to give advice for the writing of answers to free-response or essay questions than to render assistance for answering multiple-choice questions. However subjective these questions may appear to be, there are very specific objective factors that the readers (graders) look for in the answers. Indeed, graphing earns you one point for one part of the answer (for example, P = MC for allocative efficiency) or one-half point on another part. The student should be advised to take three steps before answering the free-response questions:

1. Quickly review the questions. Often, there is a suggested allocation of time, such as, "use one-half of the time to do question number one and divide the balance of the time for the other two questions." (Usually there are 50 minutes to do three questions.) Make a time schedule for yourself and remember to have a watch with you. *No buzzers or alarms are allowed!*

2. Make short "sketch" notes on the questions on points that you may well forget later in the rush to complete your answers on time. You can do this during the 10-minute "reading period" that precedes the free-response section of the exam. Think of evidence you can provide that demonstrates the correctness of your answer. A graph often fills this requirement.

3. Draw appropriate graphs. Often, graphs are not supplied. Even when graphs *are* supplied, the graders will accept a different or similar graph from the student for, at least, a partial answer. Use graphs! The readers (economists) love graphs when appropriate.

Additionally, you must remember to label each axis, curve, point of tangency, and intersection that is relevant. The readers want to see the directions of changes on the graph. You need to direct and refer your written responses clearly to the symbols and labels on the graph.

As an example of this, consider the case of two markets, one for coffee and one for tea. If coffee is discovered to have an antidepressant effect, what would be the effect on the equilibrium price and quantity of coffee? (The rest of the question would deal with further shifts in supply and demand in one market with subsequent effects on the other market; we will explore this labeling and identification of directions of change when we provide answers and explanations for the model examinations.) For the answer to this question, the students should provide the appropriate graph followed by an explanation. The graph is provided below (Figure 1.1).

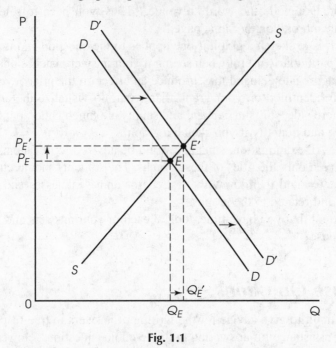

Fig. 1.1

This graph shows the shift in demand (increase) from DD to D′D′ as the result of the health news. Thus, the student would draw D′D′ and show, with arrows, the movement of DD to the new demand curve, D′D′. Also, as depicted in the graph, the student would show with arrows and symbols the increases in equilibrium price and equilibrium quantity.

Further, you need to provide explanations and analysis for your answers. Avoid lengthy and excessive explanations, as you need to conserve time. However, simply stating the answers or results will not suffice; you need to explain how you arrived at the answers. Always, direct your answer to the question asked. This sounds obvious but the advice is often ignored.

1. It is strongly suggested that you review the major graphs that are in both the micro and macro section of this book. As suggested in the section on multiple-choice questions, you should consider listing these graphs by title, such as Aggregate Demand and Aggregate Supply, The Regulated Monopolist, etc. Then see if you can draw the related graph. You will be able to determine which graphs you know well and which ones will require some additional review. By comparing these graphs with those in this book, you will be able to continue to narrow the field until you have all the graphs under your command.
2. Next, you should identify the important points on the graph, for example, the natural rate of unemployment, profit-maximizing level of output. You may wish to review summaries and lists of important things to know in the text to determine which concepts to emphasize in your study.
3. Then, you should take the model examinations that we have supplied on a timed basis. Compare the answers to the answer key; you will be able to see which areas you know well and which areas will require additional review. For your weak areas, return to the questions in the text and at the ends of the chapters for review questions.

If you establish a schedule of these steps well in advance of the AP exam, you will need only a brief review before the exam date. You should be well rested and confident by the time that you take the examination! Best of luck!

TABLE 1.1
CHECKLIST OF ITEMS TO BRING TO THE EXAM

- No. 2 pencils (for multiple-choice answers)
- Black or dark-blue ballpoint pens (for free-response answers)
- Your secondary school code number
- Your Social Security number (optional)
- Watch (turn off the alarm and beeper)

ITEMS THAT ARE STRICTLY FORBIDDEN

- Calculators
- Scratch paper
- Rulers, correction fluid, compasses, dictionaries, etc.
- Pagers or cellular phones
- Food or drinks

2 The Discipline of Economics

Economics Defined

Economics is a social science that studies how resources are used and is often concerned with how resources can be used to their fullest potential. Is it wise to use our resources to explore outer space or should we build low-income housing instead? Should we explore for oil fields in the United States or should we use our resources for other endeavors while we import the oil we need?

Consider the case of a student who has only 24 hours to spend each day. Some of this precious resource (time) must be spent on the necessities of life such as eating and sleeping. But of the hours remaining, how many should be devoted to studying? Socializing? Relaxing? Too much socializing and relaxing will not allow the student to live her life to its fullest potential. Neither will going overboard on the study time. One problem every student faces is just how much time should be allocated to each of the various activities that make for a full life. This is an economic problem since the student must decide how the resource (time) will be used to its maximum potential.

The discipline of economics is not directly concerned with money or politics or the stock market; however, economic problems abound in each of these areas. People want to spend their money in the best way. Politicians want to make decisions to achieve the maximum benefit, and investors want the highest return from their savings. Any time someone is trying to make the most out of what he has, we are in the realm of economics.

It is only natural for families, firms, and nations to strive for the best outcomes, given their initial endowments of resources. For that reason every person and institution must grapple with economic problems every day.

MACROECONOMICS VERSUS MICROECONOMICS

The discipline of economics is broken into two fields: macroeconomics and microeconomics. Macroeconomics involves economic problems encountered by the nation as a whole. For example, do we spend too many of our resources on national defense and not enough on education of our youth? If households are required to pay fewer taxes, will national savings be affected? Will prices rise or fall because of the tax cut? Will increasing the money supply increase production levels in the economy?

Microeconomics is concerned with the economic problems faced by individual units within the overall economy. Here we will be focusing in on particular families, individuals, and firms. Some examples of microeconomic issues are: Does a particular family save enough to provide for its future needs? How will a tax break affect XYZ Corporation's output? If the Smiths win the lottery, how will their spending patterns change?

The general distinction between macroeconomics and microeconomics is that the former deals with the overall economy whereas the latter is concerned with particular individuals, firms, industries, or regions within the economy.

POSITIVE VERSUS NORMATIVE ECONOMICS

The discipline of economics can be split into two in another way—positive and normative economics. Positive economics is based on the scientific method. That means hypotheses are formulated and tested. For instance, one theory holds that if a family's income increased, their spending will increase but not by as much as the increase in income. There are several ways that this theory could be tested. One way is to observe how a group of families behave when their income is increased. Another might be to survey lottery winners to see how they disposed of their winnings.

Normative economics involves value judgments. Someone may feel that resources are better spent exploring outer space than providing free breakfasts for elementary school children. If this is the person's opinion, not based on a scientific investigation of the matter, then we are in the realm of normative economics. Normative economics is economics based on the way someone believes things *ought* to be.

It may appear as if positive economics is a superior form of the discipline since it is grounded in the scientific method and normative economics is based on opinions. However, normative economics is a crucial part of the economics discipline. Any scientific study will require an experiment, and experiments can be designed to highlight a scientist's prejudices. Even if an economist can keep his biases out of a study, why did he choose this particular question to investigate? However much economists strive to be like biologists and physicists, there will always be a large normative aspect to economics. Some economists claim that the normative side of the economics discipline is the more interesting.

Resources

Economists, like most professionals, have special words and phrases that are used to describe concepts and ideas that occur frequently in their work. In order to understand economics, one must master the jargon. Familiar words and expressions can take on new meaning as economic jargon. The term "resource" is a case in point. To the layperson, a resource is something that can be used or drawn upon in a particular situation or endeavor. Economists do not dispute this definition, and use the word "resource" to mean much the same thing. However, the economist gives the term a special, more particular definition. *A resource is anything that can be used to produce a good or service*. This definition is broad enough to cover such dissimilar things as farmland, crude oil, machinery, and even intellectual ability.

In macroeconomics every resource is classified into one of three categories: land, labor, or capital.

- Land does not only refer to the ground we walk on, but all natural resources. Therefore resources such as farmland, crude oil, timber stands, oceans, and mineral deposits are all classified under the term "land."
- Labor, the second classification, encompasses all human attributes that are productive. Humans have the ability to perform a multitude of tasks, so there are many forms of this type of resource. Labor can be the person pounding nails at a construction site or the neurosurgeon in the operating room. Any time anyone is performing a service, function, or task, it is the resource "labor" at work. The professor in the classroom is using his intellectual

capability to provide a service, just as a professional basketball player uses her athletic ability to produce points. In both cases, humans are using their attributes to produce things society finds valuable.

- Capital, in the economic sense of the term, is productive equipment or machinery. Again, many disparate items can fit into this classification: factory buildings, forklifts, computers, and paper clips are a few examples.

Not all resources fit neatly into this classification scheme. Resources such as time, health, money, adventurousness, and the willingness to take risks would all be difficult to categorize. Some economists have added categories to the classification system so that hard-to-classify resources have a place of their own, but most economists stick with the jargon and maintain that the productive assets of an economy are land, labor, and capital.

Opportunity Cost

Opportunity cost is what must be sacrificed to obtain something. The concept of opportunity cost is quite general and ubiquitous in everyday life. When someone decides to spend two hours studying—obtaining wisdom or better grades—something must be sacrificed. For some individuals this might be two hours of watching TV; for others the opportunity cost of two hours of study time may be two hours of lost quality time with the family.

When someone decides to attend college, costs are always a consideration. Even if the money cost of tuition and books is not an issue for the student, the opportunity costs are. The opportunity costs of attending college will be different for each student, since each student sacrifices something different to attend. For most students the opportunity cost of college is the work experience or leisure activities that must be foregone in order to be in college.

In the macroeconomic sphere, opportunity cost takes on a more specific meaning. If a nation decides to produce one more unit of product A, how many units of product B will have to be sacrificed? Producing another unit of product A will use up resources. Exactly how many units of product B could have been produced with those resources?

Table 2.1 shows various combinations of guns and butter that an economy can produce using all of its resources fully and efficiently. Using resources efficiently means that they are not used foolishly or wasted in the production process. Efficiency implies using resources to their maximum potential.

TABLE 2.1
HYPOTHETICAL PRODUCTION POSSIBILITIES

POINT	GUNS	BUTTER
A	0	30
B	3	25
C	6	20
D	9	15
E	12	10
F	15	5
G	18	0

It may seem peculiar that this society produces only guns and butter. Guns can be thought of as all types of national defense, while butter represents wholesome consumer goods. The number of products in our example could be increased, but that would complicate the analysis unnecessarily.

Notice that each time the country portrayed in Table 2.1 produces 3 more guns, it must give up 5 pounds of butter. If it were decided to produce 1 more gun, then 1.67 pounds of butter would have to be sacrificed. Therefore, the opportunity cost of guns is 1.67 pounds of butter for this nation.

Conversely, if 1 more pound of butter were produced, society would have to forego the production of 0.6 guns. The opportunity cost of butter is 0.6 guns.

To calculate the opportunity cost of guns, divide the change in butter production by the change in gun production as you move from one line of Table 2.1 to the next.

$$opportunity\ cost\ of\ guns = \frac{change\ in\ butter\ production}{change\ in\ gun\ production} = \frac{5}{3} = 1.67\ pounds\ butter$$

The opportunity cost of butter is the reciprocal of the opportunity cost of guns.

$$opportunity\ cost\ of\ butter = \frac{change\ in\ gun\ production}{change\ in\ butter\ production} = \frac{3}{5} = 0.6\ guns$$

The concept of opportunity cost illustrates the simple fact that some amount of one product must be given up when more of another product is desired.

Production Possibilities Frontier

The production possibilities frontier is the graphical portrayal of the information contained in Table 2.1. It shows the combinations of two goods that can be produced if the economy uses all of its resources fully and efficiently. Figure 2.1 is the production possibilities frontier that corresponds to Table 2.1. Points A through G are plotted with gun production measured on the vertical axis and butter production along the horizontal axis.

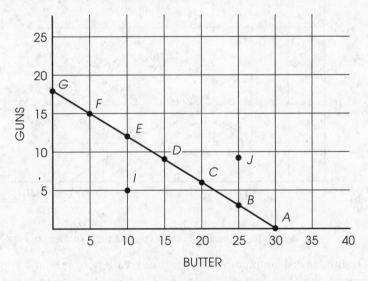

Fig. 2.1 Production Possibilities Frontier

The economy has the option of producing any combination of guns and butter along the frontier. At Point B most of the economy's resources are devoted to butter production. Only 3 guns are produced. At Point F gun production is predominant. Still, the economy is using its resources fully and efficiently at both points. A normative analysis is required to determine which point is preferred. On efficiency grounds all the points along the frontier are equal.

Points inside the frontier (Point I) are possible also. However, if the economy is operating at a point inside the frontier, resources are not being used fully or efficiently. Consider Point I, where 10 pounds of butter and 6 guns are being produced per year. By the definition of the production possibilities frontier we know that when the economy produces 10 pounds of butter, 12 guns could be produced if resources were used fully and efficiently (Point E). Point I represents a combination of guns and butter that does not require full or efficient resource utilization. The economy could do better by producing some combination of the two goods that lies on the frontier.

Points outside the production possibilities frontier (Point J) are unobtainable. Point J represents a combination of 25 pounds of butter and 9 guns per year. By the definition of the production possibilities frontier we know that if 25 pounds of butter are produced, only 3 guns can be produced (Point B) if resources are used fully and efficiently. Therefore, points outside the frontier cannot be attained at this time.

Points outside the production possibilities frontier may be attained at some future date because the frontier may shift so that points like J lie along the new frontier. The frontier can also shift inward representing a change for the worse. Two factors cause the production possibilities frontier to shift:

1. changes in the amount of resources in the economy, and
2. changes in technology and productivity.

It stands to reason that if the economy obtains more resources, larger combinations of guns and butter could be produced. This would shift the frontier to the right as in Figure 2.2. Similarly, a technological advance that made a given amount of resources more productive would also shift the frontier to the right.

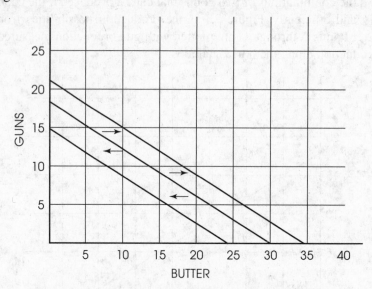

Fig. 2.2 Shifts in the Production Possibilities Frontier

The amount of resources in a country can increase for a variety of reasons. The amount of labor could increase through population growth. New territories could be acquired or existing land could be opened up for oil exploration or mining. The amount of capital could be increased by producing and putting in place more equipment and machinery.

The production possibilities frontier would shift to the left if the amount of resources were decreased or technology took a step backward. It is easy to imagine the amount of resources in an economy decreasing due to devastating weather, war, or a decline in population. But why take a technological step backward? However, economies sometimes do use less efficient production techniques because of government regulation or tradition.

Government regulations to ensure worker safety or protect the environment often force firms to use less efficient production techniques. Hopefully, the benefits of increased worker safety and a less polluted environment are worth the cost of lower output. By tradition, Amish farmers still use horses to plow their fields. When less efficient production techniques are adopted, the production possibilities frontier shifts to the left. Again, the costs of maintaining this tradition (less output) might be worth the benefits (a more wholesome life).

Law of Increasing Costs

The production possibilities frontier is not typically a straight line as in Figures 2.1 and 2.2. You may have noticed that each time gun production increases by 3 in Table 2.1, butter production decreases by 5. The opportunity cost of gun production is $5/_3 = 1.67$ pounds of butter between all points. In other words, opportunity cost is constant throughout Table 2.1. This gives rise to the straight-line production possibilities frontier.

However, there is a good reason why opportunity cost will not be constant in the real world. The law of increasing costs states that as more of a product is produced, the opportunity cost increases. Table 2.1 presents data that comply with the law of increasing costs. The opportunity cost of guns is $2/_3 = 0.67$ pounds of butter between Points A and B, and rises to $3/_3 = 1$ pound of butter between Points B and C. A quick check will show that the further down Table 2.2 we go, the higher the opportunity cost of guns. The more guns we are initially producing, the more expensive it will be to produce one more gun in terms of butter production lost.

TABLE 2.2
HYPOTHETICAL PRODUCTION POSSIBILITIES WITH INCREASING COSTS

POINT	GUNS	BUTTER
A	0	25
B	3	23
C	6	20
D	9	15
E	12	8
F	15	0

This holds true for butter production also. In this case we move up Table 2.2 since more butter is produced as we go toward the top of the table. Between Points D and C the opportunity cost of butter is $3/_5 = 0.6$ guns, whereas the opportunity cost is $2/_3 = 0.67$ between Points B and A. These numbers are in line with the law of increasing costs, which states that the more of a product that is initially being produced, the higher the opportunity cost will be to produce still more.

When the numbers in Table 2.2 are graphed to form the production possibilities frontier the result is a line that is curved concave to the origin. This is shown in Figure 2.3. Concave-to-the-origin production possibilities frontiers are due to the law of increasing costs.

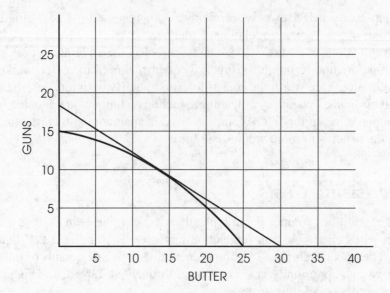

Fig. 2.3 Concave to the Origin Production Possibilities Frontier

But what is the cause of the law of increasing costs? Why does it cost more (in terms of butter) to produce another gun when a lot of guns are already being produced? To see the answer to these questions you must imagine the situation in an economy that is already producing a lot of guns. Most of the resources in the economy will be devoted to gun production, while only a few resources, such as farmers, cows, milking machines, and so forth, are engaged in butter production. Now, if society wants to produce more guns, resources will have to be taken from butter production and used to produce guns. This means some farmers and cows will be employed in gun manufacture. (The cows could be used to turn mills that polish gun bores.) But farmers and cows are good at making butter and not used in gun production, so when the resources are shifted from butter to gun production, not many more guns are produced, but a lot of butter must be sacrificed. In short, the opportunity cost of producing guns is high when gun production is already at a high level.

When gun production is low, the opportunity cost of increasing gun production is low. That is because most of society's resources are employed making butter. Imagine gunsmiths and gun-making equipment being used to make butter since they are not needed to make the small number of guns being produced. Now, when gun production is increased, the resources that are adept at making guns can be shifted off the farm and into gun production—not much butter will be lost, but many more guns are produced. The opportunity cost of guns is low when a low level of guns is being produced.

The law of increasing costs is due to the fact that some resources are more adept at the production of one good than another. When resources are forced to work in an industry where they are not proficient, they are less productive. Thus, the opportunity cost of producing a good becomes greater as more resources are forced into industries where they are not as productive. This causes the production possibilities frontier to be concave to the origin.

Comparative Advantage

A survey of economists undertaken in the early 1990s indicates that 93 percent of them believe that restrictions to free trade, such as tariffs and quotas, reduce economic welfare. The basis for this widespread support of free trade is the law of comparative advantage.

The law of comparative advantage was delineated convincingly by David Ricardo in the early 1800s. The law is an important element in introductory micro- and macroeconomics courses. It is also an application of the concept of opportunity cost.

The law of comparative advantage advocates specialization for increased output. The idea that specialization can improve productivity impressed Adam Smith when he visited a pin factory in the 1700s. In his famous tome *The Wealth of Nations* he wrote about his observations:

> One man draws out the wire, another straights it, a third cuts it, a fourth points it, a fifth grinds it at the top for receiving the head; to make the head requires two or three distinct operations; to put it on is a peculiar business; to whiten the pins is another; it is even a trade by itself to put them into the paper; and the important business of pin making is, in this manner, divided into about eighteen distinct operations, . . .

Smith showed how the division of labor into specialized tasks could increase productivity and output. The law of comparative advantage shows that the notion of specialization for increased productivity and output applies to nations as well.

When David Ricardo wrote about the benefits of free trade it was in opposition to the Corn Laws of England. The Corn Laws prohibited the importation of grains from outside England in order to protect domestic farmers. Ricardo, like 93 percent of today's economists, felt that the economic well-being of England suffered because of this restriction of trade.

To prove his point, Ricardo set up a scenario very similar to the one depicted in Table 2.3.

TABLE 2.3
A HYPOTHETICAL EXAMPLE OF PRODUCTION COSTS

	Labor Hours Needed to Produce a Unit of:	
Country	Wheat	Cloth
Portugal	10	20
England	20	60

The table shows how many hours of labor are required to produce one unit of wheat or cloth in England and Portugal. According to Table 2.3, Portugal can produce both products more efficiently than England. In Portugal, a unit of wheat can be produced with 10 hours of labor, while it requires 20 hours in England. One unit of cloth can be produced in Portugal with 20 hours of labor, while the corresponding number in England is 60.

Portugal is said to have the absolute advantage in the production of both wheat and cloth. Absolute advantage implies that the product can be produced more efficiently, that is, with fewer inputs. You might wonder why Portugal would want to trade with England at all, as England is an inefficient producer of both products. That was the genius of Ricardo's exposition—trade can be mutually advantageous to both countries even if one country has the absolute advantage in all products, because mutually advantageous trade is based on comparative advantage, not absolute advantage.

Comparative advantage means that a nation can produce the good with a lower opportunity cost. Consider the opportunity cost of wheat in Portugal. It takes 10 hours to produce a unit of wheat. If it was decided to produce another unit of wheat in Portugal, then half a unit of cloth would have to be given up since the labor would be pulled off cloth production and it takes 20 hours to produce a unit of cloth.

Opportunity cost, you will recall, is how much of one thing must be sacrificed in order to obtain a unit of something else. Here half a unit of cloth must be given up in order to obtain an extra unit of wheat. By similar reasoning, the opportunity cost of cloth in Portugal is 2 units of wheat. Table 2.4 outlines the calculations required to determine the opportunity costs of wheat and cloth in Portugal and England.

TABLE 2.4
CALCULATIONS OF OPPORTUNITY COSTS FROM TABLE 2.3

Portugal
Opportunity cost of wheat = 10/20 = 1/2 cloth
Opportunity cost of cloth = 20/10 = 2 wheat

England
Opportunity cost of wheat = 20/60 = 1/3 cloth
Opportunity cost of cloth = 60/20 = 3 wheat

Portugal has the lower opportunity cost in cloth production (2 units of wheat), and England has the lower opportunity cost in wheat production ($^1/_3$ unit of cloth). Portugal has the comparative advantage in cloth, and England in wheat. Ricardo showed that if each country produced only the good in which it held a comparative advantage and traded for the other product, then both countries could consume more of both goods.

You might convince yourself of this by assuming that each nation has 120 hours of labor to divide between the production of both goods. For instance, England could use 120 hours to produce a unit of cloth and 3 units of wheat; Portugal could produce 5 units of cloth and 2 units of wheat. Total cloth production by both countries would be 6 units, and total wheat production would be 5 units.

However, if Portugal devoted its entire 120 hours to cloth production, there would be 6 units produced and England could use 120 hours to make 6 units of wheat. This is specialization according to comparative advantage. Notice that total cloth production is 6 units as it was before specialization, but total wheat production is now 6 units, not 5. The extra unit of wheat could be shared by the citizens of each country through specialization of production and trade.

The idea that trade is beneficial to all parties involved even when one party has an absolute advantage in everything has an analogy in microeconomics. Consider a lawyer who happens to be a very fast and accurate typist. It would still pay for the lawyer to hire a secretary to do the typing, even though the secretary is probably not as efficient. The lawyer is better at writing law briefs and typing, yet the lawyer benefits by hiring a secretary to do the typing. That is because the secretary has the comparative advantage (lower opportunity cost) in typing. If the lawyer does her own typing, the opportunity cost is the income that could have been earned writing law briefs. The secretary presumably has a lower opportunity cost.

Summary

- Economics is about using resources wisely. When we focus in on one individual or one household or one firm and analyze its use of resources we are practicing *microeconomics*. When we study whether a nation is allocating its resources in an efficient manner, we are practicing *macroeconomics*.
- Both macro- and microeconomics will require some normative analysis. That is, value judgments will have to be made at some point to answer most economic questions, but there is a tendency to be as positive as possible. Being positive means sticking to the scientific method of reaching conclusions and avoiding personal biases and opinions.
- Even if you have never studied economics before, you are well acquainted with it because everyone is striving to make the most out of what they've got. Many people associate businesspersons or stocks and bonds with economics. That is correct because businesspersons are trying to make the most out of their company's resources, while stock and bond traders are trying to maximize their returns—but economics is so much more than that. Whenever

a person, a firm, or a nation is trying to make the most out of its resources, it is practicing economics.

- Remember that the next time you have to decide between studying and watching TV. Economists don't think it's wrong to watch TV; they just want you to realize that there is a cost to watching TV that goes beyond the cost of the electricity and the cable hookup. The opportunity cost of watching TV is the study time you sacrificed. If you think it's worth it, then go for the TV, especially if you have a headache and wouldn't get much out of studying anyway. It's not just businesspersons and Wall Street players that make economic decisions.

- The idea that something must be sacrificed in order to pursue an alternative is captured in the concepts of opportunity cost and the productions possibilities frontier. The law of increasing costs suggests that the production possibilities frontier will be bowed and concave to the origin as opposed to a straight line.

Terms

Absolute Advantage   the ability to produce something more efficiently

Capital   productive equipment or machinery

Comparative Advantage   the ability to produce something with a lower opportunity cost

Economics   a social science that studies how resources are used and is often concerned with how resources can be used to their fullest potential

Efficiency   using resources to their maximum potential

Labor   all human activity that is productive

Land   all natural resources

Law of Increasing Costs   law that states that when more of a product is initially being produced, the higher the opportunity cost will be to produce still more

Macroeconomics   economic problems encountered by the nation as a whole

Microeconomics   economic problems faced by individual units within the overall economy

Opportunity Cost   the amount of one good that must be sacrificed to obtain an alternative good

$$\text{Opportunity cost of Good X} = \frac{\text{Change in Good Y production}}{\text{Change in Good X production}}$$

Positive Economics   economic analysis that draws conclusions based on logical deduction or induction. Value judgements are avoided

Production Possibilities Frontier   the combinations of two goods that can be produced if the economy uses all of its resources fully and efficiently

Normative Economics   economics involving value judgments

Resource   anything that can be used to produce a good or service

Multiple-Choice Review Questions

1. Economics is a social science that

   A. is primarily concerned with money.
   B. is primarily concerned with how resources are used.
   C. relies solely on the scientific method for analysis.
   D. is primarily concerned with maximizing spiritual well-being.
   E. is purely normative.

2. Macroeconomics focuses on

   A. government and its laws that affect commerce.
   B. individuals and their resource use.
   C. corporations and their production levels.
   D. the resource use of the entire nation.
   E. money.

3. Given the table below what is the opportunity cost of wheat in France?

   | | Labor hours needed to produce a unit cf: | |
Country	Wheat	Cloth
France	5	10
England	20	60

   A. $\frac{1}{2}$ cloth.
   B. $\frac{1}{2}$ wheat.
   C. 2 cloth.
   D. 2 wheat.
   E. $\frac{1}{4}$ cloth.

4. Given the table below, which statement is true?

   | | Labor hours needed to produce a unit of: | |
Country	Wheat	Cloth
France	5	10
England	20	20

   A. England has the absolute advantage in both products.
   B. France should specialize in and export wheat while England should specialize in and export cloth.
   C. France has the comparative advantage in cloth.
   D. England has the comparative advantage in wheat.
   E. France has the absolute advantage in wheat while England has the absolute advantage in cloth.

5. Which of the following statements is positive?

   A. An economy that produces more butter than guns is better off than an economy that produces more guns than butter.
   B. Nations should concentrate their resources on producing wholesome consumer goods as opposed to the weapons of war.
   C. The production possibilities frontier is concave to the origin because of the law of increasing costs.
   D. Nations ought to devote at least some of their resources to national defense.
   E. Nations would do better by producing toward the middle of their production possibilities frontiers as opposed to the extreme points near the axes.

6. The primary focus of microeconomics is

   A. families and how they make money.
   B. firms and how they make profits.
   C. individual units within the overall economy.
   D. government.
   E. small countries.

7. Economists use the term "capital" to mean

   A. money.
   B. plant and equipment.
   C. where the central government is located.
   D. the center of the economy.
   E. a major idea.

8. Land refers to

  A. all productive resources.
  B. all natural resources.
  C. farmland only.
  D. real estate.
  E. chattels.

9. What you give up to pursue another alternative is known as

  A. capital.
  B. land.
  C. money cost.
  D. the price of the product.
  E. opportunity cost.

10. Given the following table

(combinations that can be produced using resources fully and efficiently)

Apples	Oranges
0	20
7	10
14	0

the opportunity cost of apples is

  A. $^{10}/_7$ oranges.
  B. $^{7}/_{10}$ oranges.
  C. $^{10}/_7$ apples.
  D. $^{7}/_{10}$ apples.
  E. 70 percent.

11. Given the following table

(combinations that can be produced using resources fully and efficiently)

Soup	Nuts
0	15
1	10
2	5

the opportunity cost of soup is

  A. 5 nuts.
  B. 5 soup.
  C. 20 percent.
  D. 500 percent.
  E. constant.

12. Production possibilities frontiers are concave to the origin because

  A. of inefficiencies in the economy.
  B. of opportunity cost.
  C. of the law of increasing costs.
  D. of constant opportunity costs.
  E. the extreme points are not as well established.

13. When opportunity cost is constant across all production levels, the productions possibilities frontier is

  A. concave to the origin.
  B. convex to the origin.
  C. undefined.
  D. shifted.
  E. a straight diagonal line sloping downward from left to right.

14. When an economy produces a combination of goods that lies on the production possibilities frontier,

  A. resources are being used fully and efficiently.
  B. prices are constant.
  C. opportunity cost is constant.
  D. resources will never be depleted.
  E. prices will rise.

15. The law of increasing costs

  A. does not apply to guns and butter.
  B. is the result of resources not being perfectly adaptable between the production of two goods.
  C. implies that prices will rise when the costs of making a good rise.
  D. causes the production possibilities frontier to be a straight line.
  E. implies that opportunity costs will rise as production levels fall.

MULTIPLE-CHOICE REVIEW ANSWERS

1. **B**	4. **B**	7. **B**	10. **A**	13. **E**
2. **D**	5. **C**	8. **B**	11. **A**	14. **A**
3. **A**	6. **C**	9. **E**	12. **C**	15. **B**

Free-Response Review Questions

I. The law of increasing costs states that the opportunity cost of producing a good will rise as more of the good is initially being produced. Explain why this is so.

II. Select two goods for which the law of increasing costs might not apply. Explain why the law would not apply in this case.

III. Select two goods for which it is clear the law of increasing costs would definitely apply. Explain why the law is definitely applicable in this case.

FREE-RESPONSE REVIEW ANSWERS

I. The law of increasing costs indicates that the opportunity cost of producing a good will be higher when more of the good is being produced. This is because when the economy is devoting a significant amount of its resources toward the production of a particular product, all the resources that are proficient in the production of the good are already being used to produce it. If more of the good is to be produced, resources that are not as proficient will have to be drawn into the production process. You won't get much more production of this good but production of other goods will fall significantly. This means the opportunity cost of producing more of the good is high. The situation is reversed when production levels of the good are low to begin with.

II. The law of increasing costs would not apply to refrigerators and freezers because the resources required for the production of these two goods are essentially the same. Since the resources are perfectly adaptable between the two goods, we always have to give up the same amount of refrigerators to produce one more freezer, regardless of how many freezers we are producing to begin with.

III. The law of increasing costs would most likely apply to milk and computers. Most of the resources required to produce milk are not very useful in computer production. Therefore, when most of the economy's resources are already being used to produce computers, only cows, farmland, tractors, and farmers are left producing milk. In order to produce still more computers you will have to take these resources off the farm and use them to make computers. You will have to give up quite a bit of milk just to produce one more computer.

CHAPTER

3 Economic Systems

The Fundamental Economic Questions

In every nation there are a variety of issues that demand attention: What can be done about poverty and unemployment? Pollution? The national debt? Inflation? And so on. Yet before these questions can be addressed, indeed, before these problems even crop up, there are some fundamental economic questions that each and every country will have to contend with.

Even Robinson Crusoe had to deal with economic issues on his deserted island. What resources were on hand to provide food and shelter? Was clothing necessary? Crusoe had to decide how to best deploy his meager resources to ensure his survival. In the same manner, each nation must decide what is the best way to use the resources at its disposal.

Would it be wise for Crusoe to spend all his time keeping a signal fire burning and searching the horizon for a rescue ship? Or should the same wood that might be used in the signal fire be used to build a shelter? Should the United States use its resources to explore Mars or to build low-income housing? One of the most fundamental questions any economy will have to address, whether it is one man trapped on an island or a highly industrialized nation, is what should be produced given its resources.

In Cuba it is virtually impossible to get cosmetic surgery, while the United States devotes a significant amount of its resources to this. Part of the reason why this is so has to do with the fact that the United States has so many resources compared to Cuba, but another reason why Cuba spends hardly any resources on plastic surgery is because of the way the decision is made about what will be produced in Cuba.

OPPORTUNITY COSTS

Before exploring further the differences in the way economic decisions are undertaken in Cuba versus in the United States, let us consider some other fundamental economic questions. Once it is decided to produce a certain set of goods and services, how much of each item should be produced? The concept of opportunity cost comes into play here. If it is decided to produce more than one item, then some amount of another item must be sacrificed.

Not only that, but many goods and services are related to one another. For instance, if it is decided to produce more wheat, this will require an increase in the production of tractors, seed, fertilizer, and other products needed to produce wheat. Considering opportunity costs and the fact that many products are related, the decision of how much to produce of each good and service becomes an extremely complex issue.

Who Gets What?

After having decided what and how much of each item is to be produced, there is still another basic question: Who is going to get how much of each good and service? In the United States, a medical doctor can obtain more and higher-quality goods and services than a schoolteacher. In Cuba doctors and teachers have roughly equal living standards. Certainly a person's income is important in determining how many goods and services can be obtained. But why do doctors receive so much more income than teachers in the United States and not in Cuba? The answer to that question involves how each economy responds to the basic economic issue of who gets what?

So there are two fundamental economic questions that any society will have to address:

1. How much, if any, of each good and service should be produced?
2. Who will get how much of each good and service?

In order to appreciate the complexity of these questions, imagine yourself shipwrecked on a desert island with 12 other people. It is possible to produce only a limited number of items with the resources on hand. The necessities of life will have to be produced: food, clothing, and shelter.

Should you attempt to build a boat large enough to take 12 people back to civilization? Or is a signal fire more logical? It would be possible to provide haircuts, and makeup could be manufactured, however crude. Exactly what should be produced?

If the production of cosmetics and haircuts is eschewed in order to produce more food, it will be necessary to produce more tools for working the land and harvesting the crops.

Who will get how much of each item produced? Should the doctor get more than the food production manager? Should the sick people get more or less than the others?

Now try and imagine coping with these questions when there are 275 million people and the array of goods and service encompasses everything from rubber bands to space shuttles. The organization of large economies is a mind-boggling task. How is it accomplished?

Strategies for Dealing with the Fundamental Economic Questions

There are three basic ways to address the economic questions that are imposed upon a society: (1) government commands, (2) capitalism, and (3) a blend of government commands and capitalism.

THE COMMAND ECONOMY

A command economy is one in which the central government dictates what will or will not be produced. The government also stipulates how much of each item is to be produced and finally, who is to get how many of the final products. Cuba and North Korea are examples of nations that rely heavily on the command system. The terms *communism* and *socialism* are sometimes used to describe economies that use central commands to address the fundamental economic questions.

Cosmetic surgery is not available in Cuba because the central government does not allow resources to be used on this service. Through the use of quotas and production plans, the Cuban government dictates how much of each good and service will be available. This is no simple task since thousands of items are produced.

Moreover, the production levels of the various goods and services must be coordinated so that if more sugar is to be produced, then more arable land, fertilizer, farm labor, and so on must be provided.

Finally, by setting the prices on almost all goods and services, and by setting the wage rates for almost all citizens, the Cuban government can dictate who gets what share of these products.

Setting prices and wages and stipulating how much of each item is to be produced for the whole economy are Herculean tasks. It is done with the help of computers by a large bureaucracy. Often, mistakes are made. The quota of sugar cannot be met because not enough tractors are available. Without sugar, the rum quota cannot be met.

On the other hand, the command system has some commendable features. Wages can be set so that there is no lower class. However, if everyone makes about the same income, incentives to work hard and develop new lines of business are discouraged. Still, the price of alcohol can be set high to curtail alcoholism, while the price of textbooks can be established artificially low to encourage education.

The Cuban economy is not a pure command economy. There is some experimentation with households and firms being allowed to sell their excess production in markets where prices are not fixed by the government. And there are many transactions between households that the government cannot control. Some products and a variety of services are provided on the "black market."

CAPITALISM

Capitalism has been defined by different writers in remarkably different ways. Some point to the importance of private property in capitalist economies, while others note the emphasis on risk taking and entrepreneurial skills. The best definition of capitalism, however, is in regard to how the basic economic questions are addressed. Capitalism is an economic system where supply and demand determine prices. These prices coordinate the economy by resolving what and how much will be produced. Supply and demand will also determine a person's income and therefore how much of the production the person can obtain for his or her own use.

In this type of system, the government does not run the economy but, instead, attempts to create an environment where prices can be determined in free markets. Amazingly, these prices coordinate the economy.

In a capitalist economy, prices determine how much of each item will be produced. If consumers want more baggy, pleated pants instead of blue jeans, then the price of baggy, pleated pants increases and the price of jeans falls. Producers, with an eye on profit possibilities, then manufacture more baggy, pleated pants and fewer jeans. In fact, textile manufacturers who do not respond to the price changes could go out of business.

Consumers, not the government, determine how much of each item will be produced. They do this by purchasing the products they like. When consumers demand and purchase products, they are voting for those products. The prices of consumers' favorite products rise and this sends a signal to suppliers to provide more of that product.

An individual's income determines how much of the production he can obtain and enjoy, but income is largely determined by the wages an individual receives. And the wage rate is just another price in the economy: the price of labor.

Notice that the government does not have to get involved in setting prices and wages in capitalist economies. Prices and wages are determined in free markets and these prices serve to coordinate the economy and answer the basic economic questions. Prices govern the behavior of consumers and producers who seek to make the most out of their respective resources. Just the right goods and services are produced in just the right amounts. This is known as "allocative efficiency" in economic jargon.

PRICE DETERMINATION

Prices in capitalist economies are determined by supply and demand. The Law of Demand states that when the price of a product increases the quantity demanded decreases, *ceteris paribus*. *Ceteris paribus* (pronounced KET-er-us PAR-i-bus) is Latin for "all other things remaining unchanged." The Law of Demand can also be stated conversely: When the price of a product falls, the quantity demanded will increase, *ceteris paribus*.

It is common sense that higher prices will result in fewer units being demanded by consumers but we may observe prices rising and consumers buying even more units of the product if something else changes simultaneously. For instance, the income of consumers may have increased along with the prices and this explains why more units of the product are demanded. The Law of Demand stipulates the relationship between the price of the product and the quantity demanded when all other factors remain constant.

If we were to graph the demand for a product, say corn, then a high price of corn would be associated with a rather low demand. When the price of corn fell, the quantity demanded would rise. This results in a demand curve that slopes downward from left to right.

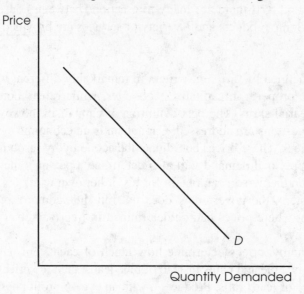

Fig. 3.1 A Demand Curve

Notice that by tradition the price of the product is measured on the vertical axis and the quantity demanded on the horizontal axis. Demand curves can be steeply sloped or more flat, but they will always slope downward in order to conform with the Law of Demand. A demand curve that sloped upward would imply that when the price of the product increased, the quantity demanded would increase. That could happen only if the *ceteris paribus* assumption of the Law of Demand was violated.

The price of any given product is determined by the demand for it relative to the supply. The Law of Supply states that when the price of a product increases the quantity supplied increases, *ceteris paribus*. This law may also be stated conversely: when the price of a product falls the quantity supplied falls, *ceteris paribus*.

The graph of the supply of corn slopes upward from left to right in order to conform with the Law of Supply.

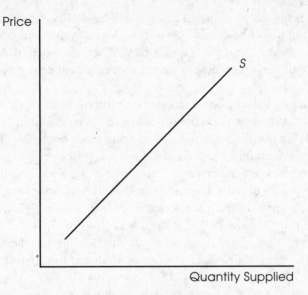

Fig. 3.2 A Supply Curve

Notice that the graph of the supply curve has the same axes as that of the demand curve. We can put both curves on the same graph.

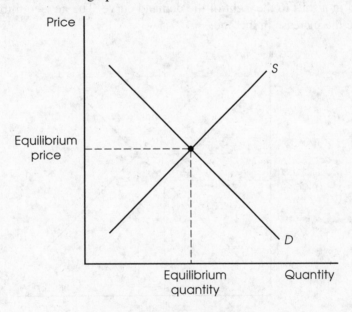

Fig. 3.3 Supply and Demand

Equilibrium Price

The intersection of the supply and demand curves is known as the *equilibrium point*. A line drawn from the equilibrium point to the vertical axis determines the equilibrium price. The equilibrium price is the price that will prevail in a free market. A line drawn from the equilibrium point to the horizontal axis determines the equilibrium quantity, which is the amount of the product that will be bought and sold in a free market.

If the price of corn is not the equilibrium price, it will be shortly, because when the price of corn is above its equilibrium, it will be driven down. It will be driven down because a surplus of corn will emerge when the price is *above* its equilibrium. When the price of corn is *below* its equilibrium value, it will be driven up because a shortage of corn will emerge when the price is below its equilibrium.

Equilibrium is a state of balance between opposing forces. In this case the opposing forces are surpluses and shortages. When the price of corn is above the equilibrium price, consumers will cut back on their demand, but suppliers are induced to bring more to market. This results in a surplus of corn. The surplus of corn induces suppliers to lower the price.

Just the opposite occurs when the price of corn is below the equilibrium price. Consumers will have a brisk demand for corn because the price is relatively low. Suppliers, however, are not motivated to provide much corn when the price is relatively low. The result is a shortage and the shortage of corn drives the price higher.

Only at the equilibrium price will there be no shortage or surplus. This is how allocative efficiency is achieved: Just the right amount of corn is produced to satisfy the demand; there is no shortage or surplus.

The preceding analysis of how prices are determined makes it seem that the price of corn will stabilize at its equilibrium value. This is true, but the equilibrium value is constantly changing because the demand and supply curves are constantly shifting left and right.

For instance, an increase in consumers' incomes would increase the demand for corn. This would be reflected in a shift to the right of the demand curve. The new equilibrium price will be greater than before the increase in income.

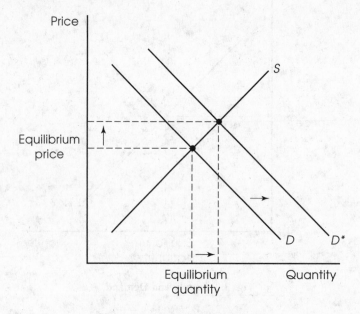

Fig. 3.4 An Increase in Demand

Demand Curve
A variety of things could cause the demand curve to shift:

1. Consumers' tastes could change and they may prefer some other vegetable to corn. This would cause the demand for corn to decrease and the demand curve to shift to the left.
2. If the prices of substitute products change, this will change the demand for corn. For example, an increase in the price of carrots would increase the demand for corn, shifting the demand curve to the right.

3. If the prices of complimentary products change, this will change the demand for corn. The example is the price of butter rising to exorbitant levels. Few people want to eat corn without butter, so the demand for corn decreases.

4. Finally, the expected future price of corn can affect the current demand for corn. If consumers expect the price of corn to be higher in the future, they will demand more right now. It is best to buy it before the price goes up. Table 3.1 lists the major determinants of demand.

TABLE 3.1
DETERMINANTS OF DEMAND

Price of the product
Income
Consumer tastes
Prices of substitute products
Prices of complementary products
Expected future price of the product

The primary determinant of the demand for a given product is its own price. If the price of a product changes we would move from one point on its demand curve to another, but the demand curve would not shift. The demand curve shifts only when one of the other determinants of demand changes. Economists distinguish between these two situations by using, or not using, the word *quantity*.

When the price of a product decreases and we move from point A to point B on the demand curve, this is referred to as an "increase in the *quantity* demanded."

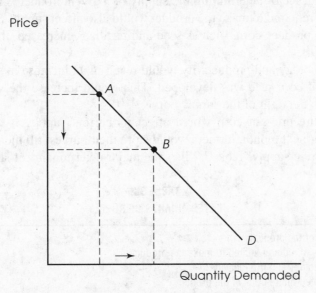

Fig. 3.5 An Increase in the Quantity Demanded

An increase in income would shift the demand curve to the right because more of the product is demanded at any price now that income has risen. This is referred to as an "increase in demand," dropping the word "quantity."

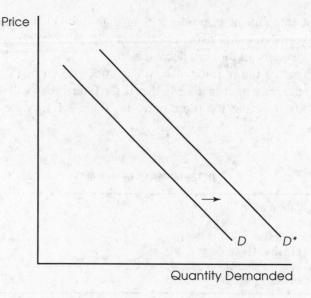

Fig. 3.6 An Increase in Demand

Supply Curve

The same principle applies to the supply curve. If the price of the product were to change, we would move from one point to another along a stable supply curve. This would be called a "change in the *quantity* supplied." However, if the supply curve shifted, this would be called a "change in supply."

The most important factor determining the supply of a given product is its price, but a change in the costs of inputs required to make the product would also affect supply. Specifically, if the cost of inputs required to produce corn, such as seed and fertilizer, increased, then the supply of corn would decrease.

Advances in technology and productivity would result in an increase in supply. Imagine that a new drought-resistant corn seed was developed. This would increase the supply of corn and be reflected by a shift to the right of the supply curve.

The expected future price of corn would affect its current supply. If the price of corn was expected to be higher next month, farmers would store their harvest till then. This would result in a decrease in the current supply. Table 3.2 lists the major determinants of supply.

TABLE 3.2
DETERMINANTS OF SUPPLY

Price of the product
Prices of inputs required to make the product
Technology and productivity
Expected future price of the product

End Result

Let us use what we have learned about supply and demand to determine how prices would react to different events in a capitalist economy. Suppose there was an increase in income and consumers demanded more corn. The demand curve for corn would shift to the right. The equilibrium price of corn would rise. The higher price of corn would induce farmers to supply more. The end result is a higher price for corn while more is bought and sold.

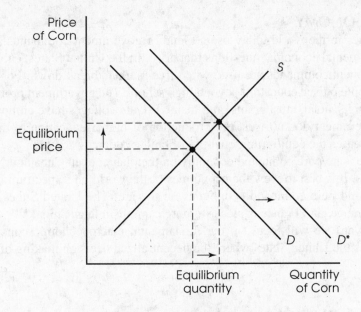

Fig. 3.7 An Increase in the Demand for Corn

Suppose the cost of corn seeds rises. This would shift the supply curve to the left. The equilibrium price is now higher. The higher price of corn causes consumers to lower their quantity demanded. The new equilibrium point reflects a higher price and less corn being bought and sold.

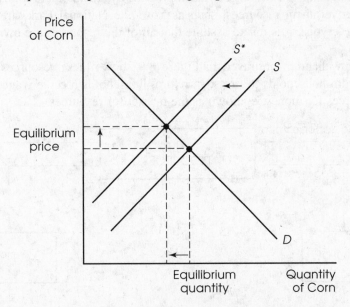

Fig. 3.8 A Decrease in the Supply of Corn

When the price system works it is truly an elegant system. Just the right items are provided in just the right proportions to satisfy society's wants. The economy is almost automatically coordinated. This stands in contrast to the command economy where a huge effort and bureaucracy are required to coordinate an economy that is usually far from being allocatively efficient. But the command economy can easily ensure that goods and services are distributed fairly or equally, while an unequal distribution is the norm in economies that rely on free markets.

THE MIXED ECONOMY

All of the countries in the world today use a blend of government commands and capitalism to address the fundamental economic questions that arise. In the United States, capitalism is emphasized, but government commands are used when free markets break down. For instance, society benefits when people pursue education beyond high school. The government promotes higher education by providing scholarships, grants, and loans. Private colleges have competition from state schools. Our government doesn't trust the production of higher education to the market. It gets involved and increases the equilibrium quantity of college degrees granted.

Similarly, there is no pure command economy on the planet; even Cuba and North Korea have some free markets. It is best to view the economies of the world on a spectrum with pure capitalism on the right and pure command economies on the left. The United States is closer to pure capitalism than France, and France is closer to pure capitalism than China.

As we go forward we will focus on the fundamental macroeconomic concepts of capitalist economies such as the United States where the decentralized decision making of the price system predominates.

The Circular Flow Diagram

In capitalist economies, most of the resources are owned by individuals and households. The government and business enterprises will own some resources in such a system, but not the lion's share. Moreover, since most of the large firms are owned by stockholders (individuals and households) and most government resources, such as Yosemite National Park, are considered to be jointly owned by everyone, it is fair to assume that all of the resources are owned by individuals and households.

The circular flow diagram portrayed in Figure 3.9 shows these resources (land, labor, and capital) flowing from households to firms. In return, households receive wages and profits. This exchange of resources for money is known as the market for resources.

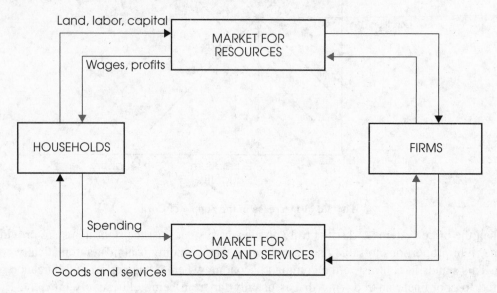

Fig. 3.9 The Circular Flow Diagram

Households spend their money income to purchase the goods and services supplied by firms. This exchange of income for products is known as the *market for goods and services.*

The circular flow diagram shows how resources are used to produce goods and services and how these goods and services are distributed. Essentially, individuals and households sell their resources to firms that use the resources to produce goods and services. Individuals and households use the proceeds from the sale of their resources to purchase the output of the firms.

The circular flow diagram can be expanded to include the government and banks. There would be more boxes and more lines representing flows of money and products, but no matter how complicated or simple, the circular flow diagram shows how institutions in capitalist economies are tied together.

Summary

Even if you drop out of society and go to live as a hermit on an isolated mountaintop, you will have to cope with the fundamental economic questions: What should be produced with the resources on hand and how much of each item should be produced? Hermits, however, do not have to deal with the other fundamental economic question: How much of the production should each member of society get?

- Government commands and capitalism are two general ways to address the fundamental economic questions. Each approach has its strengths and weaknesses. Basically, an economy organized by government commands can be more equitable while a market economy is more efficient.
- When supply and demand are allowed to determine prices, we argued that just the right amount of goods and services would be produced to satisfy society's wants. This is known as *allocative efficiency.* Resources are deployed in the production of the things society desires.
- No country in the world is purely capitalistic. Even in the United States the government does not allow free markets to determine all prices. Similarly, no nation is a pure command economy. Even Cuba has some free markets.

Terms

Allocative Efficiency   term for resources being deployed to produce just the right amount of each product to satisfy society's wants

Capitalism   an economic system where supply and demand determine prices

Circular Flow Diagram   diagram that shows how households and firms are related by the exchange of resources and products

Command Economy   economy in which the central government dictates what will or will not be produced and who gets what

The Law of Demand   law that states that when the price of a product increases, the quantity demanded decreases, *ceteris paribus*

Law of Supply   law that states that when the price of a product increases, the quantity supplied increases, *ceteris paribus*

Mixed Economy   a blend of government commands and capitalism

Multiple-Choice Review Questions

1. Which of the following is a fundamental economic question?

   A. Who will get how much of each good and service?
   B. Who should pay taxes?
   C. Who will work?
   D. Who will make the economic decisions?
   E. Who will be allowed into the economy?

2. In a command economy

   A. the market dictates the answers to the fundamental economic questions.
   B. competition helps answer the fundamental economic questions.
   C. state and local governments respond to the fundamental economic questions.
   D. the central government dictates the answers to the fundamental economic questions.
   E. laws are set up to answer the fundamental economic questions.

3. Market economies

   A. rely on markets to coordinate economic activity.
   B. rely on the government to address the fundamental economic questions.
   C. rely on elected officials to make the most important economic decisions.
   D. rely on courts to ensure people and firms get what they deserve.
   E. are more equitable than command economies.

4. Prices in capitalist economies are

   A. unfair.
   B. determined by supply and demand.
   C. determined, in most cases, by the federal government.
   D. a reflection of our basic values.
   E. a means to achieve equality.

5. If people expect the price of a particular product to increase in the near future,

   A. this will not affect the demand for the product right now.
   B. this will decrease the demand for the product.
   C. this will not affect the demand for the product now or later.
   D. this will cause firms to expect the same thing.
   E. this will increase the demand for the product.

6. A decrease in the price of a particular product will result in

   A. an increase in demand.
   B. a decrease in demand.
   C. an increase in the quantity demanded.
   D. a decrease in the quantity demanded.
   E. a change in the expected future price.

7. If firms that make a particular product expect its price will be lower in the future,

   A. this will cause the supply of the product to increase right now.
   B. this will cause the supply of the product to decrease right now.
   C. this will have no effect on the amount of the product supplied right now.
   D. this will have no effect on the supply of the product now or later.
   E. this will cause consumers to expect the price to be higher in the near future also.

8. What will happen to the equilibrium price and the equilibrium quantity of good Z when the price of good X, which is a close substitute for Z, rises?

   A. The equilibrium price will rise and the equilibrium quantity will fall.
   B. The equilibrium price will fall and the equilibrium quantity will rise.
   C. The equilibrium price and the equilibrium quantity will both rise.
   D. The equilibrium price and the equilibrium quantity will both fall.
   E. There is not enough information to answer definitely.

9. What will happen to the equilibrium price and the equilibrium quantity of good A when producers of good A expect the price to be higher in the near future?

   A. The equilibrium price will rise and the equilibrium quantity will fall.
   B. The equilibrium price will fall and the equilibrium quantity will rise.
   C. The equilibrium price and the equilibrium quantity will rise.
   D. The equilibrium price and the equilibrium quantity will fall.
   E. There is not enough information to answer definitely.

10. What will happen to the equilibrium price and the equilibrium quantity of corn when the prices of corn seed and fertilizer fall?

    A. The equilibrium price will rise and the equilibrium quantity will fall.
    B. The equilibrium price will fall and the equilibrium quantity will rise.
    C. The equilibrium price and the equilibrium quantity will rise.
    D. The equilibrium price and the equilibrium quantity will fall.
    E. There is not enough information to answer definitely.

11. Suppose the demand for a particular product falls while the supply simultaneously increases. What will happen to the equilibrium price and the equilibrium quantity?

    A. The equilibrium price will rise while the equilibrium quantity is indeterminate.
    B. The equilibrium price will fall while the equilibrium quantity is indeterminate.
    C. The equilibrium price is indeterminate while the equilibrium quantity will rise.
    D. The equilibrium price is indeterminate while the equilibrium quantity will fall.
    E. There is not enough information to answer definitely.

12. Suppose consumers expect the price of corn to be lower in the near future while the price of seed corn and fertilizer fall. What will happen to the equilibrium price and the equilibrium quantity?

    A. The equilibrium price will rise while the equilibrium quantity is indeterminate.
    B. The equilibrium price will fall while the equilibrium quantity is indeterminate.
    C. The equilibrium price is indeterminate while the equilibrium quantity will rise.
    D. The equilibrium price is indeterminate while the equilibrium quantity will fall.
    E. There is not enough information to answer definitely.

13. Allocative efficiency

    A. means that no inferior products will be produced.
    B. implies that the economy's output is distributed evenly.

C. means that those who work hardest will get more.

D. implies that resources are used to produce the goods and services society desires in just the right amounts.

E. can only occur in command economies.

14. The Law of Demand states that

A. the quantity demanded of a product will fall when the price of the product falls.

B. the quantity demanded of a product will fall when the price of the product rises.

C. when the demand for a product falls, so will its price.

D. when the demand for a product falls, its price will rise.

E. a product's price and the quantity demanded of that product are positively related.

15. *Ceteris paribus*

A. is Greek for "never changing."

B. means anything can change at any time.

C. is Latin for "everything else remains constant."

D. means "when in equilibrium."

E. is Latin for "holds true."

MULTIPLE-CHOICE REVIEW ANSWERS

1. **A**	4. **B**	7. **A**	10. **B**	13. **D**
2. **D**	5. **E**	8. **C**	11. **B**	14. **B**
3. **B**	6. **C**	9. **A**	12. **B**	15. **C**

Free-Response Review Questions

I. What are the fundamental economic questions?
II. Contrast how the fundamental economic questions are addressed in command versus capitalist economies.
III. Cite the advantages and disadvantages of command economies.

FREE-RESPONSE REVIEW ANSWERS

I. There are two fundamental economic questions that any society will have to address: (1) How much, if any, of each good and service should be produced? and (2) Who will get how much of each good and service?
II. In command economies the central government stipulates what and how much of most products will be produced. By setting prices and wages the central government can also dictate how much of the production is allotted to each household. In short, the central government controls production and income in command economies.

In capitalist economies free markets coordinate output and income. Supply and demand, which depend upon the decentralized decision making of all consumers and producers, determine what and how much will be produced. Supply and demand also determine incomes and, therefore, who gets how much of each good and service.

III. One disadvantage of command economies is that there can be a lack of incentive to work hard to get ahead. Since the government decides one's income level, it may not pay to put one's nose to the grindstone—the government may reward you all the same, anyway. One advantage of command economies is that prices can be set to achieve social goals. For example, the price of textbooks could be set low to promote education. Another advantage of command economies is they can be set more equitably than capitalist economies.

Capitalist economies are typically more allocatively efficient than command economies; also, they do not require the large bureaucracy of command economies.

MICROECONOMICS

4 Demand and Supply: The Basics

Introduction

This chapter is fundamental to the study of economics, in general, and to the study of microeconomics, in particular. Indeed, the trend in most colleges and universities is to place microeconomics first in the sequence of micro- and macroeconomics. Many contemporary issues involve applications of supply and demand which are often at the base of more complex economic concepts. Microeconomics is sometimes called the economics of the firm or price theory. We are interested in the role of prices in decision making and in the allocation of scarce resources. How are markets and their price mechanisms designed to produce efficient outcomes? In order to address this question, we need to explore prices in terms of the basics of supply and demand.

BASIC CONCEPTS

Based on the most frequently asked questions on previous advanced placement exams, the following are the most important concepts. In the balance of the chapter, we will expand on these and other concepts and examples.

1. Changes in demand (supply) vs. changes in quantity demanded (supplied). Changes in demand (supply) show how non-price variables cause a shift (change in) of demand (supply) to a new demand (supply) function or curve. Changes in quantity demanded (supplied) depend only on a change in the price of the particular good being analyzed.
2. The role of competitive markets. This setting allows us to see how prices could function according to the design of the system. Firms or sellers are *price-takers*.
3. Market Equilibrium. This is the level of output and price at which the quantity demanded equals the quantity supplied. This provides a reference point for discussion of shortages and surpluses as well as a base of government policies.
4. Non-price determinants of supply and demand. Examples follow in this chapter on what factors influence increases or decreases in demand (supply).
5. Simultaneous changes in demand and supply. Examples and a table will follow to illustrate this situation.
6. Government induced changes in the form of price ceilings and price floors. Examples and graphs will follow in this chapter.

Competitive Markets

With a competitive market, the sellers or firms are price-takers; in other words, any one firm or groups of firms cannot significantly alter the terms of exchange or transaction terms—the price. Put another way, there are too many sellers for any effective price conspiracy to take place. The seller or firm must sell at the market price, the price established by the interaction of all buyers and sellers in a market setting. Later, we will review what happens in the real world of imperfect competition. For now we will concentrate on the function of prices: disciplinarians (competitive pressures to keep prices down to the market norm efficiency), signals (the what, when, how much, where, and for whom goods and services should be produced), and rationers (high prices encourage economizing of relatively scarce resources and goods; low prices encourage more use of relatively abundant resources and goods).

Market Equilibrium—Demand and Supply

TRIAL AND ERROR
The establishment of prices in competitive settings comes about by trial and error—sellers initiating a price only to discover that a surplus or glut occurs; a lowering of this initial price reduces the surplus until it disappears at equilibrium. The converse holds with too low a price resulting in shortages; therefore, a distinction between relative and absolute prices is important. An absolute price is the price of a good as stated. A price is high or low relative to other prices or to a base-year price. Increases in the price reduce the shortage (buyers or consumers "bid" against one another) until it disappears at equilibrium. This equilibrium (illustrated below) has the following characteristics:

1. There is no tendency for change; the demand function and supply function stay the same or constant.
2. The amounts demanded equal the amounts supplied (at the intersection of supply and demand).
3. There is no surplus or shortage; the equilibrium price "clears" the market.

EQUILIBRIUM—THE ILLUSTRATION

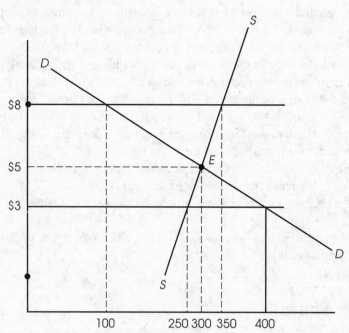

Fig. 4.1 Market Equilibrium

Equilibrium occurs at E (Price—$5; quantities exchanged = 300), the intersection of SS and DD (supply and demand), where the quantities demanded = quantities supplied. The characteristics of equilibrium (above) apply.

DISEQUILIBRIUM

If the price is $8, then there is disequilibrium since the quantities demanded at $8 would equal 100 and the quantities supplied would equal 400; therefore, there would be a surplus of 300. As the market (suppliers) react to the surplus, the price will drop until it equals $5 (equilibrium price) at which the market is "cleared" of the surplus. The converse holds, when the price is *below* the equilibrium, such as $3, when a shortage of 100 would develop. At $3, the quantities demanded exceed the quantities supplied (350 > 250) and the consumers (buyers) would bid the price up until it reaches $5 (equilibrium price) and the market is cleared of any shortage.

DEMAND AND AMOUNTS DEMANDED

There are important distinctions between these two terms; these distinctions are bound to be included in any AP test in economics. Amounts demanded refer to the amounts consumers are willing to buy of a particular good or service at varying prices of that good or service. Changes in amounts demanded refer to changes along a demand curve or function as a result *only* of a change in the price of that good, *ceteris paribus*. Changes in demand occur when these *ceteris paribus* conditions or determinants change.

CETERIS PARIBUS CONDITIONS OR DETERMINANTS OF DEMAND

- the number of consumers
- tastes and preferences of consumers
- prices of related goods—substitutes and complements
- consumers' income
- price expectations

We will consider the market for SUVs (Sports Utility Vehicles). For each of the above determinants (except for complements under "prices of related goods"), a positive change will cause an increase in demand that is a change (shift) to a new demand schedule for which there will be higher amounts demanded for each price. Thus, an increase in the population or in the number of consumers would mean more buyers of SUVs at the same prices. Similarly, if consumers' incomes increase, they can afford to buy more SUVs at the same price. Recently, consumers have indicated an increase in preferences for sports utility vehicles over other vehicles, leading to an increase in demand for SUVs. If the prices of luxury sedans, a substitute for SUVs increases, then there will be an increase in demand for SUVs. If consumers expect that there will be a sharp increase in prices for SUVs in the near future, they may increase their demand now for SUVs to "beat the price increase." In each of these situations, one of the determinants of demand had a positive change leading to a shift (increase in demand) as illustrated on page 44:

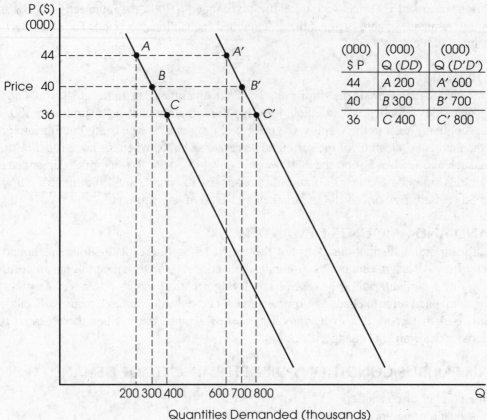

(000) $P	(000) Q (DD)	(000) Q (D'D')
44	A 200	A' 600
40	B 300	B' 700
36	C 400	C' 800

Fig. 4.2 SUVs: Shift in Demand

The shift in demand is illustrated as the changes from A to A', B to B', and C to C'; in each case the quantities demanded at each price (44, 40, 36) increased with the event (for example, consumers' incomes increasing). Each of these changes is an increase in demand, a shift to a new demand function.

The converse holds for each of these same determinants if a negative event were to occur—if the prices of SUVs were expected to decrease in the near future or if the prices of luxury sedans, substitute good, decreased. We would have, for these changes in determinants, a decrease in demand to a new function or curve such as D"D" (see Figure 4.2). However, if the prices of complement goods, such as 17-inch tires for the large SUVs *increase*, there would be a decrease in demand for SUVs.

However, a change from A to B on demand curve DD is a change in amounts demanded as a result of the price of SUVs *decreasing* from $44,000 to $40,000 with amounts demanded *increasing* from 200,000 to 300,000 SUVs. This is an example of an inverse relationship between the price of SUVs and the quantities demanded, or, as the price of SUVs decrease, the quantities demanded increase, ceteris paribus (the non-price determinants of demand remaining constant).

SUPPLY AND AMOUNTS SUPPLIED

Similar distinctions apply here as they did with demand. Amounts supplied refer to the amounts suppliers or sellers (providers) are willing to provide of a particular good at varying prices of that good. This is a direct relationship (curve): As the price of the good *increases*, the amounts willing to be supplied increases (the converse holds). Changes in amounts supplied refer to changes along a supply curve or function as a result only of a change in the price of that good, *ceteris paribus*.

Changes *in supply* occur when these *ceteris paribus* conditions or non-price determinants of supply change:

1. the number of sellers (providers, suppliers)
2. costs of resources or production
3. prices of substitute goods (goods that are also produced or could be using similar resources)
4. price expectations
5. technology
6. taxes/subsidies

Of the above determinants, increases in costs of production (2), prices of substitute goods (3), expectation of a price increase for this good in the near future (4), and increases in taxes on this good (6, taxes) would all cause a decrease in supply—a shift to the left of the original supply curve, as in the shift to S′S′, illustrated below:

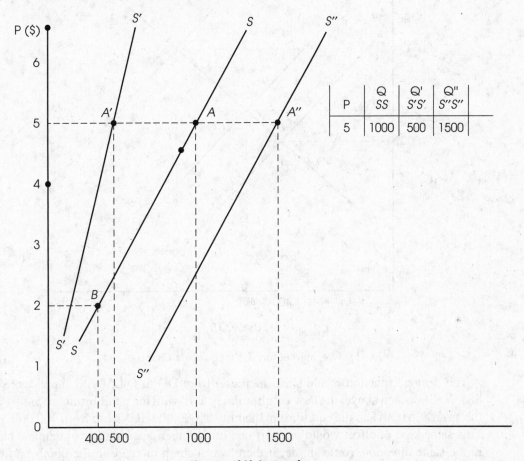

P	Q SS	Q′ S′S′	Q″ S″S″
5	1000	500	1500

Fig. 4.3 Shift in Supply

This would be lower than the amounts supplied of the good at each of the prices as compared with SS supply curve. For example, the change from A to A′ is a change in supply (decrease) or a shift in supply as a result of a non-price determinant. For the determinants listed above, increases in the number of sellers (1), technology (improvement), and government subsidies would cause the supply function (SS) to shift (increase) to S″S″, thus, the change from A to A″ (500Q to 1,500Q) at price $5. However, the change from A to B, is a change along a supply function (a decrease in amounts supplied from 1,000 to 400) as a result only of a price change for this good from $5 a unit to $2 a unit.

CHANGES IN EQUILIBRIA

1. Demand and/or supply shifts will cause new equilibrium positions (new intersections of supply and demand). With supply given (constant), changes in the demand determinants (as explained above) would cause shifts in the demand function. These shifts would cause new equilibrium price and equilibrium quantity positions. For example, if there is an increased preference for SUVs, then the demand for SUVs would increase in the form of a shift in the demand function or curve (as illustrated):

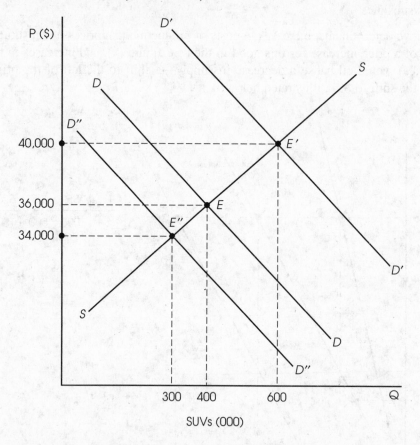

Fig. 4.4 Market for SUVs: Equilibria Changes

The demand function would shift (increase) from DD to D'D' (with supply constant at SS). As illustrated above, the new equilibrium is at E' with the equilibrium price of $40,000 (up from $36,000) and the equilibrium quantity at 600,000 SUVs (up from 400,000 SUVs). This same kind of effect would occur if one of the other determinants of demand changed in the same direction, for example, if there was a sharp increase in the number of buyers with very high incomes.

2. With supply again given at SS, and with the expectation that the prices of SUVs will decrease very soon since the market is becoming saturated with new models from competitors, demand for SUVs will now decrease as potential buyers wait for a better deal. This is illustrated (above) with a shift of DD to D"D" and a new equilibrium at E" (equilibrium price at $34,000, down from $36,000, and equilibrium quantity at 300,000, down from 400,000 SUVs).

Useful Hint: With supply given or constant, an increase in demand will cause an increase in equilibrium price and equilibrium quantity. The converse holds: A decrease in demand leads to a decrease in equilibrium price and quantity.

3. In brief, we will now analyze shifts (increases or decreases) in supply with demand as given or constant.

   Useful Hint: With demand constant or given, an increase in supply will lead to a decrease in equilibrium price and an increase in equilibrium quantity; conversely, a decrease in supply will lead to an increase in equilibrium price and a decrease in equilibrium quantity; the change in supply is followed in the same direction (increase or decrease) by equilibrium quantity and in the opposite direction (increase or decrease) by equilibrium quantity.

   Thus, if a producer of a particular form of steel faces increasing costs of coking coal (input in steel production), *ceteris paribus*, he will decrease his supply of steel. This is illustrated below.

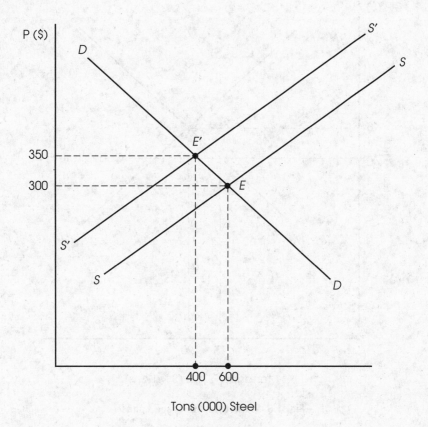

Fig. 4.5 Steel Market

As a result of a supply shift (decrease) from SS to S'S', the equilibrium price increases to $350 a ton (from $300) and the equilibrium quantity decreases to 400 tons (from 600).

4. What happens if there are changes in demand and, simultaneously, in supply? Below is a schedule of which effects on price and quantities are determinable.

TABLE 4.1
EFFECTS ON PRICE AND QUANTITIES

Change In Demand	Change In Supply	Effect on Equilibrium Price	Effect on Equilibrium Quantity
Increase	Increase	Not Determinable	Increase
Decrease	Decrease	Not Determinable	Decrease
Increase	Decrease	Increase	Not Determinable
Decrease	Increase	Decrease	Not Determinable

GOVERNMENT-INDUCED CHANGES—PRICE CEILINGS AND PRICE FLOORS

For varying reasons, a government may wish to establish a price ceiling, which prohibits prices to rise above a certain level as in rent (city-controlled prices or rents for apartments), or as in the establishment of a ceiling or interest rates for mortgage loans. In other situations, a government may wish to establish a price floor making it illegal, for example, to hire workers at a wage lower than the minimum wage. Thus, as illustrated below, if the state government sets 6 percent as the maximum rate that can be charged on mortgage loans, and if the market equilibrium price would be 8 percent, the amount of mortgage loan funds actually exchanged would decrease to $15 million from $20 million.

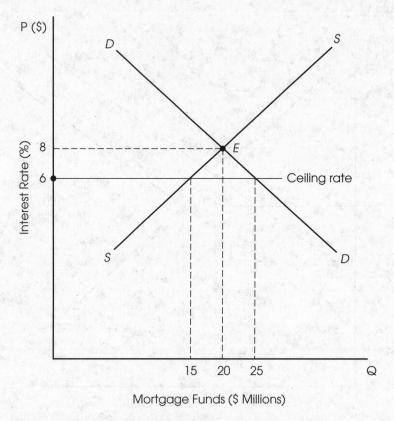

Fig. 4.6 Market for Mortgage Loans

The above is an example of a price ceiling with the effect that suppliers—financial institutions, for the most part—of mortgage funds will be willing to supply only $15 million of loans instead of the 20 million that would have been exchanged at 8 percent, the market equilibrium, for instance, a shortage of funds relative to the amounts desired by borrowers.

Price Floor

A price floor might be instituted by the federal government for agricultural prices in order to support farmers who take losses under market prices and to maintain an adequate supply of agricultural products to the population. The floor would be established above the equilibrium or market price while a price ceiling would be established under the equilibrium or market price. A price floor is illustrated on page 49:

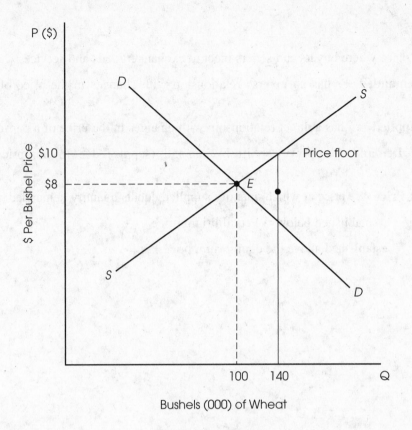

Fig. 4.7 Wheat Market

With the equilibrium price of $8, 100 bushels of wheat are exchanged (the amounts demanded are equal to amounts supplied). At the price floor, by government, of $10, supplies are willing to provide 140 bushels. Thus a surplus develops.

Summary

- The distinction between changes in quantity demanded (supplied) and changes in demand (supply) is significant in that the former refers only to a price change in a particular product in terms of movement along a demand (supply) curve and the latter refers to non-price factors that cause a shift (change) to a new demand (supply) curve.
- Equilibrium occurs in a market when:
  a. quantity demanded equals quantity supplied.
  b. no tendency for change given supply and demand.
  c. the equilibrium price "clears" the market of any surplus or shortage.
- Determinants of demand include the number of consumers, tastes and preferences, prices of related goods (substitutes and complements), consumer income and price expectations.
- Determinants of supply include the number of sellers, costs of production, technology, prices of substitutes, price expectations, taxes, and subsidies.
- Price ceilings are established under the equilibrium price when the equilibrium price is considered too high.
- Price floors are established over the equilibrium when the equilibrium price is considered too low.

Terms

Market   place where buyers and sellers meet to exchange goods and services

Quantity Demanded   has an inverse relationship with changes in the price of a particular good

Quantity Supplied   has a direct relationship with changes in the price of a particular good

Changes in Demand (Supply)   shift in demand (supply) due to non-price factors or determinants

Equilibrium Price   price at which quantity supplied equals quantity demanded

Price Ceiling   established below the equilibrium price

Price Floor   established above the equilibrium price

Multiple-Choice Review Questions

1. A price ceiling is characterized by

   A. a price set below the current (or equilibrium) market price of the good.
   B. a price set above the current (or equilibrium) market price of the good.
   C. a shift of the demand curve (function).
   D. a shift of the supply curve.

2. For which of the following statements are both the price change and quantity change determinable (for a particular good)?

   A. Both the supply of and the demand for the good decrease.
   B. Both the supply of and the demand for the good increase.
   C. The supply increases and the demand for the good decreases.
   D. The supply decreases and the demand increases.
   E. None of the above.

3. If the government subsidizes the production of halogen headlights,

   A. the demand curve will shift to the left.
   B. the demand curve will shift to the right.
   C. the supply curve will shift to the left.
   D. the supply curve will shift to the right.
   E. the amounts demanded will increase along the demand curve.

4. If consumers are advised that multi-grained bread will substantially lessen the risk of cancer, which of the following will happen in the market for multi-grained bread?

   A. The demand curve will shift to the left, decreasing the price of multi-grained bread.
   B. The supply curve will shift to the left, increasing the price of multi-grained bread.
   C. The demand curve will shift to the right, increasing the price of multi-grained bread.
   D. The supply curve will shift to the right, decreasing the price of multi-grained bread.
   E. None of the above.

MULTIPLE-CHOICE REVIEW ANSWERS

1. **A**   2. **E**   3. **D**   4. **C**

Free-Response Review Question

1. For each of the following simultaneous changes in demand and in supply for Product A, indicate the effect on equilibrium price *and* equilibrium quantity.

1) increase in demand and an increase in supply
2) decrease in demand and a decrease in supply
3) increase in demand and a decrease in supply.

How might a government establish a price ceiling or price floor to offset any *one* of the changes (1,2,3) above? Explain.

FREE-RESPONSE REVIEW ANSWER

1. A. 1) an increase in demand and an increase in supply would result in an increase in equilibrium quantity; the effect on equilibrium price is not determinable.

   2) a decrease in demand and a decrease in supply will result in a decrease in equilibrium quantity and the effect on equilibrium price is not determinable.

   3) an increase in demand and a decrease in supply would result in an increase in equilibrium price and the effect on equilibrium quantity is not determinable.

   B. If the government wants to offset the increase in equilibrium price in (3) above, it could establish a price ceiling below the new equilibrium price and/or subsidize the supplier to increase supply.

CHAPTER
5 Applications of Demand and Supply—Elasticity

Introduction

The application of elasticity to the basics of demand and supply lends itself well to the solution or resolution of many buyer and seller decision-making dilemmas in personal consumption, business finance, corporate finance, and societal or public finance settings. Elasticity, in the broad sense, relates to responsiveness to price changes. Normally we expect that as the price of a particular good increases, suppliers or producers will wish to increase the amounts they provide to the markets, *ceteris paribus*. On the other hand, consumers will reduce the amounts they wish to buy of the same product with its price increase, *ceteris paribus*. There are, of course, exceptions to this normality as we reviewed Giffen goods and inferior goods in Chapter 4. The *ceteris paribus* clause refers to no changes in the conditions underlying the demand and supply curves; they do not shift.

How sensitive are consumers to a price change in terms of the quantities they are willing to consume? Should they be expected to stop buying pizza when its price increases from $8 to $10 for a whole pizza? Should they be expected to continue buying pizza but less of it? If so, how much less? This appears as a consumer decision but it is also a producer's question. As a producer of pizza, what effect will the $2 increase have on your sales and total revenue? To answer the latter question, the producer has to estimate the degree of sensitivity to price changes from the consumers. On the one hand, the producer will realize $2 more from each pizza sold. However, the expected decrease in the number of pizzas sold could result in a greater decrease in quantity demanded than the increase in the per unit price of the pizza; therefore, the total revenue will decrease. Whether or not the total revenue depends on the degree of sensitivity to the consumer to the price change.

BASIC CONCEPTS

Based on the most frequently asked questions on previous advanced placement exams, the following are the most important concepts. The balance of this chapter will include other concepts and examples.

Consider the following as a guide:

1. $P \times Q = TR$
    *   Thus, if price (P) increases by 20 percent and quantity demanded (Q) decreases by 20 percent, total revenue (TR) will stay the same. This is called a *unit elastic* or *proportional change*.
    *   If P increases by 20 percent and Q decreases by 25 percent, then TR will decrease. This is called an *elastic* or *greater than proportional change*.

- If P increases by 20 percent and Q decreases by 10 percent, then TR will increase. This is called an *inelastic* or *less than proportional change*.

2. Price Elasticity of Demand $= \dfrac{\% \, \Delta \, \text{Quantity Demanded}}{\% \, \Delta \, \text{Price}}$

(The percentage change in the quantity demanded of a particular good divided by the price of the same good, *ceteris paribus*.) Using the three examples above (number 1), in the first case, the value of the ratio = 1 since the percentage change (Δ) in quantities demanded equals the percentage change in price. This is called *unit elastic*. In the second case, the value of the ratio = 1.25 25/20 = 5/4. Since the change in Q is more than proportional to the change in P, the response is *elastic* or greater than 1. In the third case, the value of the ratio = 10/20 or .5. Since the change in Q is less than proportional to the change in P, the response is inelastic or a ratio value of less than 1.

3. If we want to measure the numerical coefficient of elasticity (E), we would rewrite the ratio in number 2 above to read as follows. (**Note**: This uses the average price and the average quantity or *ARC* elasticity to avoid biases when using beginning or ending prices.)

$$E = \frac{(Q_1 + Q_2)/2}{\Delta P} \div \frac{(P_1 + P_2)/2}{\Delta Q}$$

$$\text{or} \quad \frac{\Delta Q \left(\dfrac{P_1 + P_2}{2} \right)}{\Delta P \left(\dfrac{Q_1 + Q_2}{2} \right)}$$

$$= \frac{(P_1 + P_2)/2}{\Delta P} \times \frac{\Delta Q}{(Q_1 + Q_2)/2}$$

4. Price elasticity of supply uses essentially the same formula except that as P increases, Q supplied also increases, rendering the total revenue check useless in the supply case. For Elasticity of Supply:

$$P \times Q = TR$$

$$\frac{\Delta Q \left(\dfrac{P_1 + P_2}{2} \right)}{\Delta P \left(\dfrac{Q_1 + Q_2}{2} \right)}$$

In brief, the relationship of price changes, elasticity, quantities demanded, and total revenue can be summarized as follows:

Price	Q Demanded	TR	Price Elasticity of Demand
increases	decreases	decreases	>1, elastic
increases	decreases	increases	<1, inelastic
increases	decreases	stays the same	=1, unit elastic
decreases	increases	increases	>1, elastic
decreases	increases	decreases	<1, inelastic
decreases	increases	stays the same	=1, unit elastic

Note: The negative sign is ignored so that the nature of the response—elastic, inelastic—will not be confused with a negative slope or inverse relationship.

PROBLEM TO SOLVE (FREE-RESPONSE QUESTION)

An out-of-state tourist uses a laundromat in Langley, Washington. A large, handwritten sign advises the users of this service that the owner was experiencing some economic difficulties including rising costs of water and propane gas. The monthly charge to the owner for water use was $2,225 and the cost for propane gas was $542 a month. Thus, the owner felt justified in increasing the price for the use of a washer from $1.50 to $1.75. The owner advised the users that her service represented a monopoly since it was the only laundromat on the southern end of the island. She claimed that she was not taking undue advantage of the customers but she wanted to be able to continue serving them while "making a living." Please answer the following:

1. What percentage of decrease in quantities demanded of the owner's services would allow her to maintain the same level of total revenue (given the increase in the price of use of a washer)?
2. What percentage of decrease in quantities demanded would realize an increase in total revenue?
3. What percentage of decrease in quantities demanded would result in a decrease in total revenue?
4. For numbers 1, 2, and 3 above, indicate whether the price elasticity of demand is elastic, inelastic, or unit elastic.
5. What are the connections between her increase in costs of providing the service and the price elasticity of supply? What are the connections between her increase in cost and the supply of her service?

Answers:
1. The increase in price is 16.67 percent (.25 on a basis of $1.50). Thus, the owner could experience the same (16.67 percent) decrease in quantities demanded to maintain the same level of total revenue $P \times Q = TR$ and

$$\text{Price elasticity of demand} = \frac{\% \, \Delta \, \text{Quantity Demanded}}{\% \, \Delta \, \text{Price}}$$

2. Less than 16.67 percent
3. More than 16.67 percent
4. For number 1, unit elastic; for number 2 inelastic; for number 3 elastic.
5. She must cover her costs; in other words, the higher the price/cost ratio, the more willing she is to supply more. Also, the closer she is to a monopolist, the more she can determine the price.

Limits and Degrees of Elasticity

Perfectly elastic, coefficient of elasticity is infinity. This means that the buyer is so sensitive to price changes that if one seller raises his price, the buyer will switch to another seller. This situation implicitly assumes that there are many sellers so that no one seller or group of sellers can exercise any significant control over the terms of exchange: prices, quantities, market share, etc. Nowhere is this better exemplified than in the norm for competition in product markets, that is perfect competition (more on this later in Chapter 10). The seller is a "price taker," that is, the market of all buyers and sellers for a particular product determines the price that the seller must charge or lose business to other competitors who produce the identical product that becomes a perfect substitute. It is illustrated on page 56.

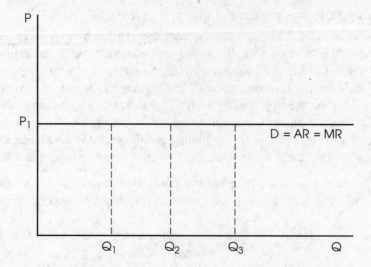

Fig. 5.1 Perfectly Competitive Firm (Perfectly or Infinitely Elastic)

This is the only curve that can be called elastic, since it is *perfectly* elastic. As demand curves approach this horizontal function, they become relatively more elastic until they reach the horizontal shape. As demand curves approach the perfectly vertical function (*perfectly inelastic*), they become relatively more inelastic. Hence, the perfectly elastic and imperfectly elastic curves (functions) set the mathematical or graphical limits on elasticity. The perfectly inelastic demand function would be illustrated as follows:

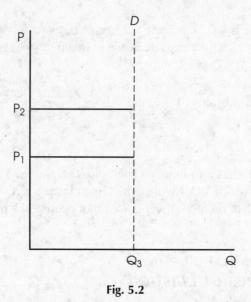

Fig. 5.2

Price elasticity of demand can vary along a demand function or curve. The slope does not change along a linear function or curve but elasticity does change along a linear function. This is illustrated by the following:

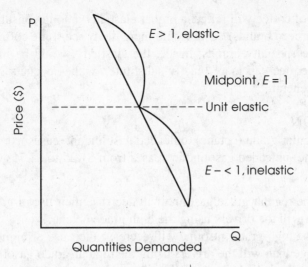

Fig. 5.3

Also, price elasticity of demand will vary between the short run and the long run. In the short run, buyers have more limited choices because of the relative scarcity of products and resources. Over the long run (when supply fully adjusts to changes in demand), the choice of products and resources becomes greater and hence, buyers are more resistant to price increases for any given product or resource.

Therefore, the long run demand function for any given product will be relatively more elastic than the demand function in the short run.

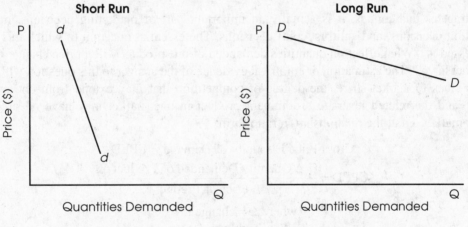

Fig. 5.4

> **Hint**: Remember, that as a demand curve approaches the perfectly horizontal shape (perfectly elastic), it becomes relatively more elastic.

The degree of elasticity also depends on the competitive structure of the market as we have already noted for perfect competition and will observe in the chapters on market structures (Chapters 9–12).

Degrees of elasticity also depend upon the nature of the product. Goods that are considered luxuries will be relatively more sensitive to price increases than will goods that are considered necessities. For example, suppose that a blight on coffee plants causes the price in the market to increase. Which kind of coffee will reflect a higher elasticity among consumers: regular brands or the specialty (higher-priced brands)? One would more likely see some coffee drinkers substituting regular brands for the specialty brands; hence, the elasticity would be higher for the specialty brands since regular coffee can more readily substitute for the specialty kind than tea can substitute for coffee, in general.

SAMPLE QUESTION

As the price for regular grade (octane), unleaded gasoline increases from \$1.00 to \$1.25, and higher grade (octane) unleaded gasoline increases from \$1.25 to \$1.75, which is most likely to occur?

A. Drivers using the regular grade gasoline will decrease their use of gasoline by a higher percentage than will the drivers using the high grade octane.

B. Drivers using the high-grade gasoline will decrease their use of high-grade gasoline by a higher percentage than will the drivers using the regular-grade gasoline.

C. Both the drivers using the high-grade gasoline and the drivers using the regular-grade gasoline will continue to use the same amount of gasoline.

D. The drivers using the regular-grade gasoline will switch to the high-grade gasoline and the drivers using the high-grade gasoline will switch to the regular-grade gasoline.

(Answer: **B.**)

Cross-Elasticity of Demand

As abstract as this sounds, it is actually an important part of marketing decisions, merger or acquisition decisions, and antitrust court decisions. The essential question to which this concept is addressed is, "What effect on quantities demanded of one product will a price change in another product have?" The estimation or empirical evidence of the answer to this question will, in turn, give us clues to market share, the degree of competition that may extend from one market to another, and the related leverage a dominant product in one market may have on products in another market. First, the relationship in ratio form:

$$\text{Cross Price Elasticity of Demand} = \text{CPED}$$

$$\text{CPED} = \frac{\% \, \Delta \, \text{Quantity Demanded of Product Y}}{\% \, \Delta \, \text{Price of Product X}}$$

$$(\text{where } \Delta = \text{change in})$$

Suppose that the price of plastic wrap increases by 20 percent, and the quantities demanded of waxed paper increased by 50 percent. What would that tell us about the ability to substitute waxed paper for plastic wrap? Are the two goods, plastic wrap and waxed paper, good substitutes or are they complements? They would be good substitutes because of the positive sign on the ratio that indicates substitutes: If the quantities demanded of waxed paper increase as the price of plastic wrap increases, *ceteris paribus*, substitution of waxed paper for plastic wrap is occurring. If instead, as the price of plastic wrap increases, the quantities of waxed paper decreases with the resultant negative sign on the ratio, the two goods are complements: both used for wrapping or storing different goods.

In summary form, the following are the determinants of price elasticity of demand:

DETERMINANTS OF PRICE ELASTICITY OF DEMAND

1. The period of adjustment, or the long run versus the short run. The short run is the time over which supply cannot fully adjust to changes in demand so that there is a relative scarcity of goods compared to the change in demand for the goods. Therefore, in the short run, prices act as rationers of the relatively scarce goods; in other words, the prices are "bid up" by the excess demand; there are more buyers willing to purchase these goods than there are goods available, the result being that the goods go to the highest bidders. In the 1970s fuel-efficient automobiles, produced mostly by the Japanese, were in high demand, particularly during the oil shortage crisis. Since the supply of these automobiles was limited relative to the demand, retail automobile dealers were able to charge prices well above the suggested list ("sticker") price rather than to charge prices at some typical discount. Over the long run, when more choices are available (supply having adjusted to the increase in demand), consumers have more choices and are more sensitive (higher price elasticity of demand) to price changes. We illustrated this earlier with the long-run demand curve being more elastic (less steep) than the short-run demand curve.

2. The ratio of the cost of a particular product to the total budget of the consumer:

$$\frac{\$ \text{ Cost of Product A}}{\$ \text{ Total Budget}}$$

   In general, the higher the value of this ratio, for a particular product, the more sensitive (more price elastic) the consumer will be to any price increases. Thus, a relatively small price increase for a home and/or its financing charge (mortgage loan interest rate) could cause a delay in the purchase of a house or cause a decision to move in with relatives or purchase a smaller house, rent an apartment, or postpone the purchase of a house. However, a small percentage increase in the price for many staples will have virtually no effect on the purchases of these products since their costs are low and constitute only a small portion of the consumer's budget.

3. Competitive structure of the market and consumer choices. The outcome of this determinant is similar to that of number 1. That is, the consumer will have more choices of products and substitutes the more competitive the product market. Thus, we can see that more competition among producers will develop over the long run (as in number 1), making the consumers more sensitive (more price elastic) to price changes. As in the fuel-efficient automobile example, more competitors in Japan and elsewhere will produce more automobiles (more choices) as time allows producers to adopt fuel-efficient technology.

Income Elasticity of Demand

In addition to consumers being constrained by prices in their purchasing decisions, they are also constrained by their budgets or incomes. Thus, we consider consumers' sensitivity in terms of their responses to changes in both prices and incomes. Income elasticity of demand is defined as:

$$\frac{\text{Percentage (\%) Change } (\Delta) \text{ in Quantities (Q) Demanded}}{\text{Percentage (\%) Change } (\Delta) \text{ in Consumer Income (I)}}$$

or

$$\frac{\% \, \Delta \, Q \text{ demanded}}{\% \, \Delta \, I}$$

This ratio for normal goods will have a positive sign, that is, as consumer income (I) increases, we expect that quantities (Q) demanded of a normal good will also increase. If the increase in quantities demanded is more than proportional to increase in income,* then the value of the ratio is greater than one (>1) and the response is more than proportional to the change in income, making the response elastic (>1). If the change in Q demanded is less than proportional to the change in income (ratio is <1), then the response is inelastic but still with a positive sign. If the change in Q demanded is exactly proportional to change in consumer income, then the value of the ratio is one and the response is unit elasticity (=1).

Income elasticity can explain some market phenomena that could not be explained entirely, if at all, by changes in prices. For example, the sale of automobiles continued to increase through the fifties, sixties, and seventies and at least until the increase in imports of foreign automobiles introduced some price competition into an oligopolistic industry. The earlier increases in sales seemed to contradict the downward sloping demand curve and any sensitivity to increases in prices.

Price Elasticity of Supply

The basic relationship of the degree of the response of quantities supplied to changes in prices is the same as that for quantities demanded. For supply, however, the normal reaction of suppliers to changes in the prices of their goods in the market is to increase amounts willing to be supplied as prices increase, a direct relationship as opposed to the inverse relationship with price elasticity of demand. In both cases we ignore whether the slope is positive or negative. We deal only with the degree of the response, such as >1, <1, or =1.

As prices increase for computers, suppliers are more willing to produce and sell more computers. The ratio for the determination of the coefficient for price elasticity of supply is:

$$\text{Price Elasticity of Supply} = \frac{\% \, \Delta \, \text{Quantities Supplied}}{\% \, \Delta \, \text{Price}}$$

Incidence of Tax on Suppliers and Consumers

If a government imposes a tax on a supplier, part of the burden can be in the form of an increase in the price that the consumer pays for the product and/or a burden on the supplier who can produce less (cost in the form of the tax) can result in less production. The degree to which the burden falls more on the consumer or the supplier is determined by the relative price elasticity of demand; the consumer may have a highly elastic response to any tax passed on to him or her by the supplier. This is illustrated as follows:

---

* (See Chapter 4.) A normal good increases in consumption with an increase in income.

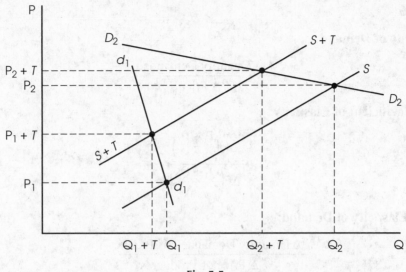

Fig. 5.5

Thus, the consumer facing relatively inelastic demand function D_1D_1 will take more of the incidence of the tax in the form of paying a higher price than will the supplier who has a relatively small reduction in quantities supplied ($P_1 + T$ compared to P_1; $Q_1 + T$ compared to Q_1). With a relatively more elastic demand function, D_2D_2, the supplier takes on the higher burden ($Q_2 + T$ compared to Q_2) than the consumers ($P_2 + T$ compared to P_2).

Summary

- Price elasticity of demand or the percentage of change in the quantity demanded of a particular good divided by the price of the same good demonstrates the sensitivity of consumers to price changes. $P \times Q = TR$ allows a revenue test, i.e., whether a price change will increase or decrease total revenue.
- Price elasticity of supply shows the sensitivity of producers or firms to price changes for their products.
- Price elasticity of demand or supply which has a numerical coefficient >1 is elastic, =1 is unit elastic or <1 is inelastic.
- Cross price elasticity of demand is the percentage change in the quantity demanded of one product in response to the percentage change in the price of a second product. If this ratio produces a positive sign, the two products are good substitutes. If this ratio produces a negative sign, then the two products are complements.
- The determinants of the price elasticity of demand are the period of adjustment, the ratio of the cost of a particular product to the total budget of the consumer and the competitive structure of the market.
- Income elasticity of demand measures the responsiveness of consumers to changes in their income.
- The incidence of a tax imposed on suppliers will have an impact on consumers in the form of price increases depending on the price elasticity of demand, i.e., the greater the elasticity, the smaller the impact on prices.

Formulas

Price Elasticity of Demand:

$$\frac{\%\ \Delta\ \text{Quantity Demanded}}{\%\ \Delta\ \text{Price}}$$

Numerical Coefficient of Elasticity:

$$\frac{\Delta Q\left(\dfrac{P_1 + P_2}{2}\right)}{\Delta P\left(\dfrac{Q_1 + Q_2}{2}\right)}$$

Cross Price Elasticity of Demand:

$$\frac{\%\ \Delta\ \text{Quantity Demanded of Product Y}}{\%\ \Delta\ \text{Price of Product X}}$$

Income Elasticity of Demand:

$$\frac{\%\ \Delta\ \text{Quantity Demanded}}{\%\ \Delta\ \text{Consumer Income}}$$

Price Elasticity of Supply:

$$\frac{\%\ \Delta\ \text{Quantity Supplied}}{\%\ \Delta\ \text{Price}}$$

Multiple-Choice Review Questions

1. When price elasticity of demand is greater than 1, demand is

   A. perfectly inelastic.
   B. elastic.
   C. inelastic.
   D. unit elastic.
   E. not measurable.

2. Price times quantity measures

   A. the international trade gap.
   B. the budget deficit.
   C. total revenue.
   D. price elasticity of demand.
   E. price elasticity of supply.

3. A positive sign on cross price elasticity of demand indicates that the two products are

   A. luxuries.
   B. necessities.
   C. substitutes.
   D. complements.
   E. independent.

4. The price elasticity of demand for a product is greater if

   A. the proportion of the good of the consumer's budget is high.
   B. the period of time to respond to a price change is short.
   C. the number of substitute products is limited.
   D. the product is a necessity.
   E. imports decrease.

5. A tax imposed on a supplier will more likely be passed on to the consumer in the form of price increase if

   A. price elasticity of demand is highly elastic.
   B. price elasticity of demand is highly inelastic.
   C. price elasticity of demand is unit elastic.
   D. wage elasticity of demand is highly elastic.
   E. wage elasticity of demand is highly inelastic.

MULTIPLE-CHOICE REVIEW ANSWERS

1. **B**   2. **C**   3. **C**   4. **A**   5. **B**

Free-Response Review Question

The Free-Response Question for this chapter appears on page 55.

FREE-RESPONSE REVIEW ANSWERS

NOTE: answer to sample question on page 55 is "B".

CHAPTER

6 Theory of Consumer Choice or Behavior

Introduction

Economics is the study of choices involving decisions set in the context of scarcity limited by constraints. We buy a basket of goods knowing that we cannot buy as large a selection as we might want, given the constraints of prices and income. How do we make these choices? How does a consumer allocate a limited income among the many choices of goods and services?

BASIC CONCEPTS

Based on the most frequently asked questions on previous advanced placement exams, the following are the most important concepts. For this chapter, there are only a few concepts that have appeared in question form on the exams. We identify these below and in the balance of this chapter, we will expand on these and other important concepts.

1. The basic tenets of the theory of **consumer choice**. This involves many subconcepts including **law of diminishing marginal utility**. The student needs to identify this law as being associated with **consumer choice** as opposed to the law of diminishing marginal productivity which is associated with procedures or suppliers.
2. **Consumer Surplus.** Students can count on one or two questions on consumer surplus. This concept is revisited in the chapter on monopoly; students can expect a related question on "dead-weight loss" which we deal with in the chapter on monopoly. With consumer surplus, the price in the market would favor consumers who placed a higher value on a product than the market price paid by all consumers. Often, there is a question on this concept.

The Basic Tenets of the Theory of Consumer Choice

1. **The consumer is rational.** The consumer wants to get the most satisfaction (utility) for the money expended on the products and services in the basket.
2. **The consumer can rank goods** in order of preference: "I prefer a new cell phone to a pair of running shoes."
3. **The consumer understands diminishing marginal utility.** As a consumer buys a hot dog, her utility (satisfaction) increases (from zero); as she consumes a second hot dog, her total utility (satisfaction) from the second hot dog is likely to be less than the satisfaction she derived from the first. That is, satisfaction derived from a continuing consumption of hot

dogs is going to increase at a decreasing rate, or each additional hot dog is going to add less to total satisfaction than that of the previous hot dog. The *marginal utility* (the addition to total satisfaction) is decreasing, while the total satisfaction continues to increase up to the level of disutility when too many hot dogs lead to a point at which one more hot dog actually *decreases* total utility or satisfaction, that is, the marginal utility of the "one more hot dog" is negative. Diminishing marginal utility becomes a factor in a consumer's choice when comparing goods and their prices with a limited income. Diminishing marginal utility is also a factor in the determination of a pricing strategy for firms.

4. **The consumer faces constraints of prices and incomes.** The factors of rationality, preferences, and diminishing marginal utility are not sufficient in order for the consumer to make final decisions about what to buy and how much to buy. The consumer is constrained from buying every good or service that meets the first three tenets of consumer choice listed above. She can be effectively prevented from purchasing every item on the "list" by a limited income and the prices of the goods and services.

5. **The utility-maximizing rule.** Using the above four tenets of consumer choice, the consumer wants to make choices from a variety of goods and services that will maximize her total utility or satisfaction relative to the constraints of prices and income. To do that, the consumer will want to obtain as much extra satisfaction for one good per its price as will be obtained from any other good per its price, given the amount of income available for "N" number of goods. Thus,

$$\frac{MU_A}{P_A} = \frac{MU_B}{P_B} = \frac{MU_C}{P_C} \ ..... \ \frac{MU_U}{P_U}$$

with as much income as is available being spent, given a discrete number of goods. In other words, whatever combination of two goods (for instance, four of good A and three of good B) that meets this condition with the available income will maximize the consumer's total utility. The consumer would be in equilibrium with this combination. There would be no tendency to change this combination of the two goods. There would be no other combination of units of good A and good B that would produce a greater total utility given the same prices of goods A and B and the same income for the consumer. Different consumers are going to have different tastes and preferences and therefore, different utility maximizing combinations of the same two goods with the same prices and the same income. This holds for a particular period time only. A sample question follows:

TABLE 6.1
MARGINAL UTILITY AND UTILITY MAXIMIZING COMBINATION

Units of J	MU_j	Units of k	MU_k
1	56	1	32
2	48	2	28
3	32	3	24
4	24	4	20
5	20	5	12
6	16	6	10
7	12	7	8

Given:

Consumer income = $52
Price of J   8
Price of K   4

8J + 4K = 52

J + K = 6

The consumer will maximize her utility by purchasing

A. 3 units of J and 6 units of K
B. 6 units of J and 3 units of K
C. 4 units of J and 5 units of K
D. 5 Units of J and 5 units of K
E. 2 units of J and 7 units of K

(Answer: **C**.)
Based on Table 6.1: answer is C. 4 units of J and 5 units of K 45@ 8 = $32 + 5K @ 4 = $20 = $52.

Consumer Surplus

Even with diminishing marginal utility, the consumer may enjoy the situation in which the marginal utility is greater than the price charged for the good. Later (Chapter 11) we will review price-discriminating (*not* racial- or gender-discriminating) firms that would like to charge each buyer the maximum price each buyer would be willing to pay, for instance, each buyer would pay a different price based on each consumer's price elasticity of demand (perfect price discrimination) or at least, charge different groups of buyers different prices. However, in competitive markets, such as we are assuming here, sellers are often pricing their products at the going market price. Therefore, in competitive markets, and even in imperfectly competitive markets with less than full information, sellers face downward sloping demand curves in which sellers price at the last unit purchased with the effect that previous units were sold at prices *below* the values received, at the margin, by the consumers. To illustrate:

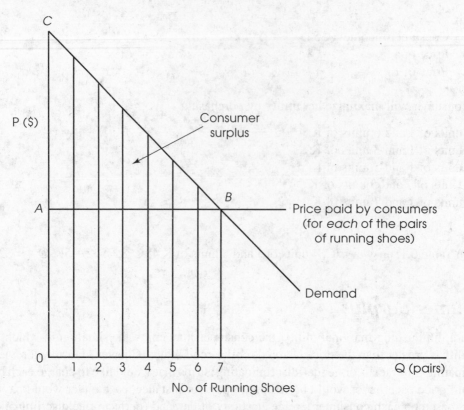

Fig. 6.1 Running Shoes

The consumer surplus is the area, ABC, that represents the amount of total utility the consumer receives (summation of MU for each unit, 0 through 5, or total utility under the demand curve up to the last unit, 5, consumed) minus the price paid by the consumer (OA) times the number of units or the area, OEBA. This surplus reveals the difference between what the consumer is willing to pay (based on marginal utility) for each good and the price actually paid (OA). Therefore, if a consumer is willing to pay $100 for a pair of running shoes, but the market price charged is $60 (price OA), the consumer has a bonus on consumer surplus of $40.

Since the firm selling the running shoes has imperfect information about consumers and faces a downward sloping demand curve, the market price could favor consumers who place a higher value on the shoes than is charged by the market; these consumers would realize a bonus or *consumer surplus*.

Example
A farmer has such a surplus of apples that he drops the price from $10 a bushel to $4 a bushel. A consumer surplus would be evident in which of the following?

A. A consumer buys the apples at $4 a bushel on the basis that at higher prices, she would not be willing to make a purchase.
B. A consumer would have purchased the apples at $10 and buys them at the $4 price.
C. The farmer's cost of production of the apples is $3 a bushel.
D. A consumer prefers pears to apples but buys the apples at $4 a bushel.

(Answer: B.)

Income and Substitution Effects

A brief discussion of income and substitution effects relative to the downward sloping demand curve is placed here in order to more fully explain the theory of consumer choice. In the discourse on the utility-maximizing rule (page 66), we referred to the combination of two goods that would maximize total utility. Diminishing marginal utility (DMU) helps explain the downward sloping demand curve, for example, as marginal utility decreases, the consumer may compare the MU of good A and its price with the MU of good B and its price. Thus, the income effect and the substitution effect also help explain the downward sloping demand curve. If we consider the market for apples, we assume that the price of oranges as a substitute good would remain constant. If the price of apples increases, *ceteris paribus*, the price ratio of apples to oranges would change so that oranges may be an attractive substitution for at least some of the purchases of apples. This would reinforce the notion that as the price of apples increases, *ceteris paribus*, the amounts demanded of apples would decrease. This is known as the *substitution effect*. Also, as the price of apples increases, *ceteris paribus*, the consumer can afford less of both apples and oranges, and thus will purchase fewer apples (the ratio of change between apples and oranges is dependent on other factors). This is known as *the income effect* and further reinforces the notion of a downward sloping demand curve.

Summary

- The basic tenets of the theory of consumer choice include consumers being rational, ranking goods in order of tastes and preferences, understanding diminishing marginal utility, facing constraints of prices and income and making choices of goods on the basis of the utility-maximizing rule.
- Consumer Surplus. This surplus of utility over cost (price paid) for the consumer is exemplified by consumers who place a higher value on the product than is charged by the market.
- Income and Substitution Effects. The income effect allows consumers to buy more products as the price of one product decreases. The substitution effect allows consumers to buy more of a product as its price decreases with the price of a substitute good remaining constant.

Terms

Total Utility   the total satisfaction a consumer receives from the consumption of a good or service

Diminishing Marginal Utility   at some point in the consumption pattern of a good, each additional unit consumed yields less additional satisfaction (utility)

Income Effect   as the price of a particular good decreases, a consumer can afford more of it and other goods

Substitution Effect   as the price of a particular good decreases, a consumer may buy more of this good relative to the price of a substitute good

Consumer Surplus   the difference between the utility gained and the price paid by the consumer. The utility gained would measure the value of the product to the consumer. The price paid by the consumer would be the market price

Multiple-Choice Review Questions

1. If the price of a product decreases with the price of a substitute product remaining constant such that the consumer buys more of this product, this is called the

   A. income effect.
   B. substitution effect.
   C. marginal effect.
   D. supply effect.
   E. CPI effect.

2. If the price of a product decreases so that the consumer can buy more of it and other products, this is called the

   A. income effect.
   B. substitution effect.
   C. marginal effect.
   D. supply effect.
   E. CPI effect.

3. Consumer surplus is

   A. the price of a good divided by its marginal utility.
   B. the marginal utility of the good divided by its price.
   C. the total utility of the good.
   D. the difference between the consumer's value and the market price.
   E. consumers' annual savings.

4. The utility maximizing rule is to choose the basket of goods that

   A. has the highest marginal utility of each good in the basket.
   B. has the lowest prices for the goods.
   C. has the highest value of marginal utility to price for each good.
   D. the marginal utility to price ratio equal for all goods in the basket.
   E. the marginal utility to price ratio equal for all goods in the basket subject to the income constraint.

5. According to the principle of diminishing marginal utility,

   A. marginal utility stays the same.
   B. total utility stays the same.
   C. marginal utility decreases with each additional unit of a good that is consumed.
   D. marginal utility and total utility both decrease.
   E. total utility declines.

MULTIPLE-CHOICE REVIEW ANSWERS

1. B   2. A   3. D   4. E   5. C

Free-Response Review Question

See question and answer inside the chapter.

M

7 Government and Public Sector: Market Failure, Rents, Externalities, Public Goods, and Efficiency

Introduction

This chapter flows from the knowledge of the function of the market system and its ability, at least in its design, to allocate resources efficiently. Indeed, most of the definitions of economic efficiency manifest themselves best, if not only, in competitive markets. However, not all people are satisfied, in normative judgments, with the outcomes of a market system. These outcomes include some differences among groups with respect to income and wealth distribution. Also, there is market failure when buyers and sellers do not come to terms, when the sale is not consummated, for instance. In other words, the market cannot determine the terms of exchange—price, quantity, location, service, financing, etc.—and/or one party is not willing or able to pay the price. The market fails. In both of these situations, we have possible functions for the government. Also, the presence of externalities, negative and positive, can be the basis of government taxation or subsidies to move the market to a more efficient or equitable position. With respect to the efficient position, remember the market role of efficiency, but if the market fails or there are externalities, the market will not be the vehicle for efficiency. The government may then intervene to promote a desirable social outcome.

Important Concepts

Based on the most frequently asked questions on previous Advanced Placement exams, the following are the most important concepts. In the balance of this chapter, we will expand on these and other concepts and examples.

1. *Externalities*. In an externality, either the buyer or the seller does not "capture" all of the benefits or costs of a transaction, that is, some of the benefits or costs accrue to the public as social costs or benefits. Often there will be questions asking how the government might react to a positive or to a negative externality.

   The right answer in terms of *positive externality* would be the granting of a *subsidy* to private producers in order to continue production for this positive externality.

   Conversely, there is a *negative externality*—the government might impose a tax to improve economic efficiency. This situation of a negative externality is often used in the context of a pollution by a firm. The purpose of the tax is to promote efficiency in the controlling of pollution. Often, the tax will vary directly as the pollution by the firm varies. Thus, the more the pollution and the subsequent tax rises, the greater the incentive by the firm to control pollution.

   Also, with respect to negative externalities, the private markets will determine a price that is relatively low; the relatively low price encourages more sales, more production, and more negative externalities. Here, a tax on the producer might be considered a factor or determinant of a shift to the left of supply (a decrease in supply), which would cause a higher price and reduce output or production of the good. Conversely, with respect to positive externalities, the price of the product would be relatively high. A government subsidy would cause an increase in supply (shift to the right of the supply curve), which would cause a lower price and increase output (see Figures 7.1 and 7.2 in this chapter).

2. *Social costs, private costs, and externalities*. Since externalities are, by definition, those costs *not* incurred by the buyer or the seller of a market transaction (the costs are incurred by the public, such as polluted waterways), then social costs are equal to private costs and the value of the externalities. Thus, we can distinguish marginal private costs (MPC or MC) from marginal social costs, knowing that MSC > MC (private) since marginal social costs incorporate marginal private costs. These distinctions will serve us well when we discuss the government, the market, and optional amounts of pollution. These definitions and distinctions support the knowledge of externalities, taxes, and subsidies identified above. For example, social costs will equal private costs when government either taxes negative externalities or subsidizes positive externalities by the amounts of the externalities. In this way, the government hopes to move the markets to some level of efficiency to compensate for market failure.

3. *Definitions and nature of efficiency*. Efficiency and its several implications take up much of advanced microeconomic analysis. For purposes of this review text, we will discuss only three definitions: *technological*, *allocative*, and *Pareto optimality* (sometimes used as a general definition of efficiency). A condition in society where any further improvement in well-being for some people will come at the expense of others is a point of efficiency or optimality. Details will follow later in this chapter.

4. *Public goods and private goods*. The two major distinctions between public goods and private goods are that private goods are exclusive and distributive and public goods are nonexclusive and nondistributive. These distinctions refer to pure public goods and pure private goods. One can be excluded from the benefits of private goods by not being willing or able to pay the price. Also, one more good for me means one less good for you. For public goods, I cannot be excluded from their benefits by refusing to pay for them, and the cost of

one more unit of a public good does not result in one less unit available to someone else. A question sometimes asked on the Advanced Placement exam is on the marginal cost of one more unit of a pure public good. The answer is that the marginal cost in such a situation is equal to zero. In this chapter we will discuss other public goods, including congestible and price-excludable public goods. The reader might expect a question in the form of congestible public goods. For example, a bridge or tunnel leading to a city may be a public good (nonexclusive and nondistributive) until rush or commuting hours. At commuting time, the highway crowding takes the form of an externality, since one more car on the congested bridge means that much less space or slower traffic for other cars. (Correct answer for AP test.)

5. *Other roles of government.* You should be able to identify these on exam questions, for instance, antitrust for monopolies, provision of information, redistribution of income, etc.

Private Goods and Public Goods

To extend the discussion above, the following are the definitions, uses, and examples of private and public goods. A *private good* is a good that has exclusion and distributive characteristics. That is, one who is unwilling or unable to purchase a good is denied its benefits. Thus, if I am unwilling to pay $20 to purchase a ticket to a major league baseball game, I am denied the fun of watching the game in person (the *exclusion* characteristics). Also, if there are 40,000 seats available, one more ticket for me means one less for someone else (the *distributive* characteristic). Private goods are divisible into discrete units such as the example of 40,000 baseball tickets. If private goods have externalities, then there is a less efficient or inefficient outcome. We will discuss externalities and the government use of taxes and subsidies later in this chapter.

Measures of Efficiency

As stated earlier, Pareto efficiency is the general measure of efficiency. First, we will define and explain two specific measures of efficiency. We will see how they are related and how they are subsumed under Pareto or general efficiency.

TECHNOLOGICAL EFFICIENCY
The study of microeconomics or the economics of the firm is focused on the efficient allocation of resources. Technological efficiency is the identification of those inputs that have the greatest impact on outputs per dollar of input expenditure. In a simple engineering sense, output ÷ input. We discuss this in the chapter on costs, production, and supply, Chapter 8, in terms of economies of scale. Economists want to know which production process gets the most output per dollar cost of inputs. We could look at this as a given amount of output and which input or combination of inputs (resources) could produce the output at the least cost. The firm has an incentive to find the most cost-effective method of production since it can expand profit margins. Technological efficiency allows us a standard to achieve in terms of obtaining increasing returns to our technology. Any improvement in the value of the ratio of output to input will allow us to increase our productivity, or to make more efficient use of resources.

ALLOCATIVE EFFICIENCY
Ideally, every society would like to channel its resources (land, labor, capital, entrepreneurial ability) to their most productive and desired uses. Thus, the industries and firms that have the highest productivity are rewarded with higher profits; their profits are the motivation to continue

to produce. If consumers are voting with their dollars, the firms will produce the products that consumers are willing and able to purchase.

PARETO EFFICIENCY

Pareto efficiency has been identified earlier in this chapter. The general notion here is that there is an improvement for society as long as some people are gaining without others losing ground or benefits. Society reaches its optimal point or efficiency when any further improvement for some comes at the expense of others.

As indicated earlier, the competitive market economy, with its price mechanisms, is the best vehicle for efficiency. However, market failure, externalities, and other societal needs give rise to public goods and other forms of government intervention to recreate efficiency lost by market failure and externalities. Also, the government may attempt to create perceived need for equity by transferring payments for a redistribution of income.

PUBLIC GOODS

Public goods lack the exclusion and distributive characteristics of private goods, and become public goods by default. Public goods have nonexclusion and nondistributive characteristics. A pure public good would be available for all regardless of any inability or unwillingness to pay. If a person does not approve of taxes being used for national defense and withholds the appropriate percentage of taxes used for that purpose (we would advise *against* this action to avoid problems with the law), that person would *not* be denied any of the benefits of national defense. Pure public goods are not marketable since benefits cannot be denied and because the units of a pure public good are not divisible. Thus, one more citizen that is qualified for a public good comes at zero marginal cost. One more unit of a public good does not come at the cost of one less for me. We cannot divide national defense into discrete units and even if we could, who would be willing to buy shares of military defense in the marketplace?

QUASI-PUBLIC GOODS

However, there are many public goods that have some private good characteristics that make them *quasi-public* goods. Sometimes, these goods are classified as public goods with some private goods attributes, such as *contestable public goods* and *price-excludable public goods*. (Contestable public goods occur when a public highway, bridge, or tunnel becomes acutely crowded at certain times, such as commuter rush hours. This might mean that at non-rush hours, one more car on the George Washington Bridge at say, 11:00 A.M. would not tie up traffic or in any way interfere with the normal speed of other vehicles on the bridge (one more car space for me does not mean, in this situation, one less car space for another person—the nondistributive, nondivisible principle). However, at around 4:30 to 5:00 P.M., the traffic begins to build so that, at least, until 7:00 to 7:30 P.M. there can be considerable delays in getting on the bridge (one-half hour to one hour) and once on the bridge, effective speed is lowered because of the very heavy traffic. This is a *negative externality*. Some economists have suggested that variable tolls be instituted at different times during the day, so that up to 6:30 or 7:00 A.M. and before 4:30 or 5:00 P.M., lower bridge fares would be in effect (this assumes tolls going both ways on the George Washington Bridge, for example). During the rush hours a higher toll would be in effect. These varying rates would more efficiently allocate scarce resources (time, space). Drivers, to a certain extent, would decide whether their time or their money is more important. Thus, the public bridge takes on the distributive characteristic of a private good as it becomes a contestable public good and therefore, officials can "bribe" enough drivers to travel at alternate times with a market mechanism, varying prices. Therefore, the city would effect a more efficient solution than that of a private good with externalities. Also, we can have public goods with a price-exclusion feature. For example, the government may make provision for medical insurance for the elderly, but the deductibles and co-payments may exclude some lower-income elderly from some or all of the benefits of medical insurance and the related medical care.

Bases for Public Goods or Government Interference with Market Outcomes

The general case for some government action is a case for efficiency in the event of market failure rents, or externalities, or the case for equity in the event of an unequal distribution of income or wealth (normative judgment that unequal = inequitable).

MARKET FAILURE

In the most extreme form, market failure means that the buyer and seller are not able or willing to agree on the terms of the transaction—price, quantity, financing, etc. In the broad social sense, a desired social outcome does not occur. For example, individuals who have the HIV virus or AIDS may be unable to pay for health care or pay the health insurance premium; therefore, the market fails to "clear the market of any surplus or shortage" and there continues to be a demand greater than any willing suppliers of health care or health insurance. Market failure also refers to failure of the market mechanisms to achieve optimal or efficient outcomes. An efficient social outcome would be when marginal social benefits (MSB) equals marginal social costs (MSC). Therefore, market failure to produce efficient outcomes becomes a general basis for government intervention. A complete market failure to find MSB = MSC for certain goods is the case for a *public good* as discussed earlier in this chapter.

EXTERNALITIES

Another form of market failure is the presence of externalities. Externalities are costs or benefits that are not "captured" by the price mechanisms. For example, a college student does not capture all of the benefits of a college education; some of the benefits would accrue to others in society who might benefit from a lab discovery or a work of art. Conversely, the producer of a product that causes pollution does not incur all of these costs; most of the costs are external to the producer.

The connection between externalities and social costs/benefits is through the relationship with private costs and benefits. The private market mechanisms have an equilibrium price, which is where private marginal benefits (MB_P) equal marginal social costs (MSC). However, in Figure 7.1, there is the presence of a positive externality associated with prenatal visits.

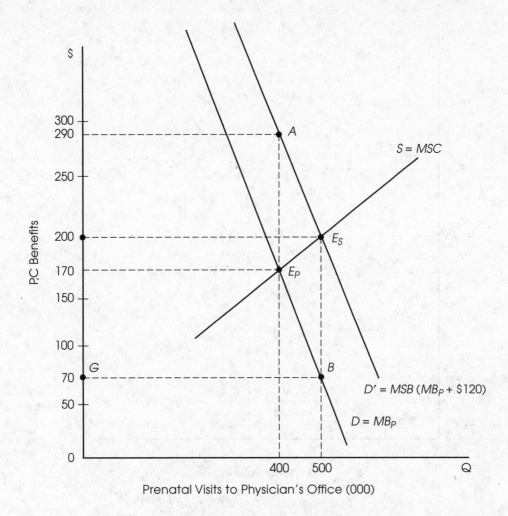

Marginal Social Benefits = Marginal Benefit (Private) + Externality
Positive Externalities Subsidy

Fig. 7.1 Positive Externalities and Related Subsidy

A positive externality means that benefits accrue to others as in the case of prenatal visits by women to a physician. In France, the government has allowed women these prenatal visits at zero cost. In addition, the women are paid a nominal sum when they do visit the physician. There is a social benefit of assuring the health of the mother and the fetus that is not captured in the market equilibrium price of $170. There is an externality of $120 (the difference between the marginal social benefits of $290—point A on the graph, and the equilibrium price of $170, the value of private marginal benefits). Therefore, the values of the externality are internalized in the price mechanisms as a subsidy. To sum up, marginal social benefits (MSB) equal private marginal benefits (MB$_p$) plus the externality. In this case, the subsidy is paid to the consumers in order to effectively lower the price. In a positive externality, the price is too high and the output is too low (too few prenatal visits at the market equilibrium of 400,000 visits). With the subsidy, the number of prenatal visits increases to 500,000 at which level, MSC = MSB or optimal (efficient output). Government interference is justified so that this efficient level of output will be obtained. Otherwise, the level of 400,000 prenatal visits is below the optimal level.

With negative externality (as illustrated in Figure 7.2) the market equilibrium price is too low and the market equilibrium quantity is too high (P$_p$, X$_2$).

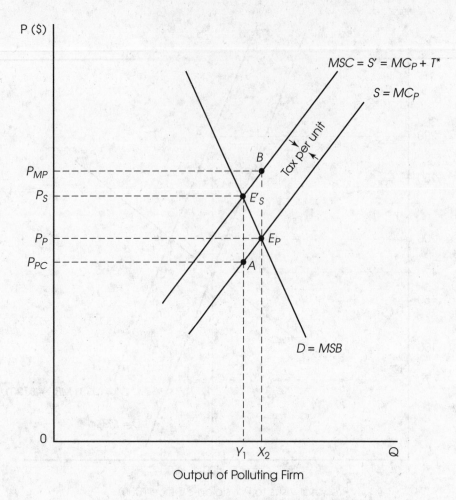

T^* Tax per unit = Externality per unit
$P_S E'_S A P_{PC}$ = Total taxes = Total externality $(E'_S - A) \times X_1$ units output
Social costs = Private costs + Externality value
Negative externality = Tax

Fig. 7.2 Negative Externalities and Related Tax

The use of a tax to correct for this situation reflects this negative externality. Further, the tax equals the value of the negative externality and thus corrects or internalizes this externality. With the tax correction, the optimal (efficient) outcome is achieved (P_s, X_1) at the level of output of the polluting firm, MSB = MSC. Thus, the price that was too low is now higher ($P_s > P_p$) and the output that was too high is now lower ($X_1 < X_2$). Remember, marginal social cost (MSC) = marginal cost private (MC_p) + tax (T). The tax (T) = value of negative externality.

This negative externality of pollution can also be illustrated in terms of a *tolerable level of pollution* or that level of water pollution at which MSB = MSC. This is illustrated in Figure 7.3, entitled, Pollution, Optimal Output, Social Costs.

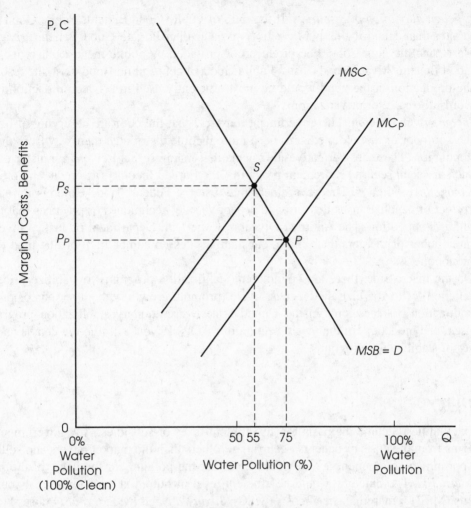

Fig. 7.3 Pollution, Optimal Output, Social Costs

The tolerable level of pollution would be 55 percent (MSB = MSC); however, the private market equilibrium level of pollution would be 75 percent pollution (where private marginal cost, MC_p, equals MSB). If the government wants to internalize this negative externality, it would tax this externality ($MSC - MC_p + tax$, where the tax = negative externality). This tax will not end pollution but it would pass the external costs to the firm with the likely outcome of a lower level of pollution (55 percent versus 75 percent) and a decrease in supply (MC_p shifts to the left).

OTHER BASES FOR GOVERNMENT INTERFERENCE

1. *Information*. Information might be considered a public good. Since the provision of full information about a good by its manufacturer would come at a cost to the manufacturer without a corresponding benefit at the margin of providing this information, we might expect that this full information will not be forthcoming. Since this information (nutritional content, fat content, additives, price per unit, etc.) is of social benefit, the government might require appropriate labeling, weights and measure control, price per unit information, warnings, etc. As you know, this information is now mandatory.

2. *Meritorious nature*. Richard Musgrave coined this phrase. Some goods and services may be of such a meritorious nature as to transcend any economic criteria in the determination of public goods. The United Kingdom (UK) has determined that health care services are public goods even though these services possess, to some degree, the private good characteristics of exclusion and distribution.

3. *Efficient allocation of resources*. If the ratio of Public Good Benefits/Public Good Costs is greater than 1 and if this public ratio is greater than Private Good Benefit/Private Good Cost, then the good should be produced or provided by public means; otherwise, Private Good Benefit/Private Good Cost > Public Good Benefit/Public Good Cost, the resources in the production of the good would be most efficiently used in private production, in other words, the case for privatization.

4. *Income redistribution*. The government may feel that the poor are deserving of help from the non-poor or that older citizens need more income distributed their way from the young population. These are normative judgments that manifest themselves in transfer payments such as social security retirement programs, the Earned Income Tax credit, and others.

5. *Competitive markets*. The government may use the Federal Trade Commission (FTC) to correct or penalize firms that provide deceptive sales techniques or practices that promote unfair competition. The Antitrust Division of the U.S. Department of Justice investigates monopolies or mergers that tend to substantially lessen competition or that tend to create monopolies.

6. On the macro side, there are government stabilization programs to stabilize prices (curb inflation) or to stabilize the business cycle (promote growth without serious or prolonged contraction or recession). In the United States, discretionary stabilization programs are fiscal and monetary. In the macro section of this book, you will find the details and analyses of stabilization programs.

Summary

- Externalities become the basis for government taxes or subsidies. Any government action stems from the costs or benefits occurring to others than the market buyers and sellers.
- Appropriate government action would be to *tax* the polluter for the value of the *negative externality*. The outcome would be efficient level of output at which marginal social benefits (MSB) = marginal social costs (MSC). *Taxing a Negative Externality* raises "too low" market price and reduces "too high" market output.
- The government *subsidies* the amount of a *positive externality* such that the subsidy = value of the positive externality. The outcome would be an efficient level of output at which MSB = MSC and that the market price which was "too high" will be reduced and the market output which was "too low" will be increased.
- The study of microeconomics or the economics of the firm is focused on the efficient allocation of resources. Measures of efficiency include technological, allocative and pareto efficiency.
- Private goods have exclusion and distributive characteristics which, in competitive market settings, promote efficiency. Public goods lack these characteristics such that the marginal *cost* of one more unit of a *pure* public good is equal to *zero*. There are examples of price exclusive and congestible public (quasi) goods.
- With the presence of market failures, rents, externalities, inequity, non-optimal social outcomes and need for information, price stability, cyclical stability and competitive markets, there are bases for government interference in the market.

Terms

Externalities either the buyer or the seller does not "capture" all of the benefits of a transaction

Social Costs   those costs which are incurred by the public, i.e., polluted waterways; these are costs not captured by the market

Social Benefits   Those benefits which are realized by the public or outside the buyer/seller exchange

Pure Private Good   a good that has exclusion and distributive characteristics

Technological Efficiency   the identification of those inputs that have the greatest effect on output per $ of input expenditure

Allocative Efficiency   the channeling of resources to their most productive and desired uses

Pareto Efficiency   the optimal point (efficient point) for society when any *further* improvement for some comes at the expense of others

Pure Public Goods   goods which have non-exclusion and non-distributive characteristics

Quasi-Public Goods   goods which have some limited private good characteristics such as contestable public goods and price-excludable public goods

Formulas

Marginal Social Cost (MSC) = Private marginal cost (MC_p) + Negative Externality

$MSC = MC_p +$ Tax where tax = the value of the Negative Externality

Marginal Social Benefits (MSB) = Private Marginal Benefits (MB_p) + positive externality

Multiple-Choice Review Questions

1. Which of the following is true about the pure public good?

   A. The marginal cost of providing an additional unit of the good to additional citizens is greater than zero.
   B. Consumers can be excluded from its benefits by not paying for it.
   C. One more unit of a public good for some consumers means one less unit for other consumers.
   D. The good cannot be divided into discrete units.
   E. It has a pure moral nature.

2. If there is a negative externality associated with the production of a private good, which of the following is an action by government that would most likely move the market to an efficient outcome?

   A. Close the firm producing the good.
   B. Subsidize the firm or its customers.
   C. Tax the firm.
   D. Appoint a commission.
   E. Relocate the firm.

3. If there is a positive externality associated with the production of a private good, which of the following is an action of government that would most likely move the market to an efficient outcome?

   A. Close the firm producing the good.
   B. Subsidize the firm or its customers.
   C. Tax the firm.
   D. Appoint a commission.
   E. Relocate the firm.

4. For a polluting steel company, a government action to most likely achieve an optimal or efficient outcome would produce what effect on the market equilibrium price and output?

   A. Output would increase; no change in price.
   B. Output would increase; price would decrease.
   C. Output would increase; price would increase.
   D. Output would decrease; price would decrease.
   E. Output would decrease, price would increase.

5. Which of the following is true?

   A. Marginal Social Costs = Private Marginal Costs + Negative Externality.
   B. Marginal Social Costs = Private Marginal Costs + Subsidy.
   C. Marginal Social Benefits = Private Marginal Benefits + Tax.
   D. Tax = Positive Externality.
   E. Subsidy = Negative Externality.

MULTIPLE-CHOICE REVIEW ANSWERS

1. D   2. C   3. B   4. E   5. A

Free-Response Review Question

1. With the use of a graph, illustrate and explain the following:

   A. How a government might take action to correct a negative externality, i.e., either through the imposition of a tax or through the granting of a subsidy.

   B. Explain what your answer in "a" above indicates about the equilibrium price (too low, too high) and about the equilibrium quantity.

   C. Explain how the government action in "a" could result in a socially optimal outcome.

FREE-RESPONSE REVIEW ANSWER

The government would impose a tax to correct a negative externality. This would produce the optimal (efficient) outcome. The price that was too low to produce the optimal outcome is now higher. The output that was too high is now lower. Marginal Social Cost (MSC) = Marginal Private Cost (MPC) + tax. The tax (T) = *value* of the negative externality.

CHAPTER
8 Costs, Production, Supply

Introduction

All of the basic concepts of costs and production and their interrelationships upon which price and output decisions are made are the subject matter of this chapter. We are not able to fully analyze decisions on prices and outputs without the appropriate revenue data and the related market structure (perfect competition, monopoly, monopolistic competition, oligopoly). The following chapters on product markets will allow us to complete the analysis.

Production data alone provide us with the "engineering" information but fall short of what is necessary to determine cost-effectiveness or to identify the least cost combination of resources for a given level of output. For profit maximization, we will need price and revenue data as well.

THINGS TO KNOW

Based on the most frequently asked questions on previous Advanced Placement exams, the following are the most important concepts. In the balance of this chapter, we will expand on these and other concepts and examples.

1. *Law of diminishing marginal productivity or returns.* In the short run, as variable inputs are applied to fixed inputs, production first increases at an increasing rate; then, production increases at a decreasing rate (diminishing marginal returns or additions to total production become less and less at the margin). Later, there is actually a decrease in total production or output as successively equal increments of variable inputs are added. Examples, graphs, and explanations will follow in this chapter.

2. *Relationships among average and marginal cost and product curves.* Basically, marginal cost (MC) intersects both the average variable cost (AVC) and the average total cost (ATC) curves at their minimum points. This means that if MC > AVC, AVC must be rising (see Figure 8.2); if MC < AVC, AVC must be declining. Similarly, the marginal physical product curve (MPP) intersects the average physical product curve (APP) at the maximum point of the APP curve (see Figure 8.1(a)).

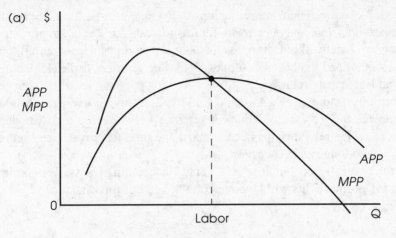

Fig. 8.1(a) Average Product, Marginal Product

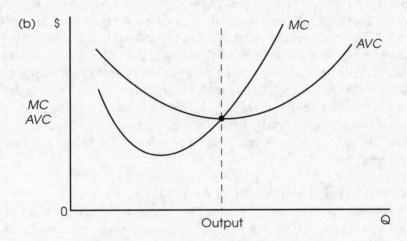

Fig. 8.1(b) Average Cost, Marginal Cost

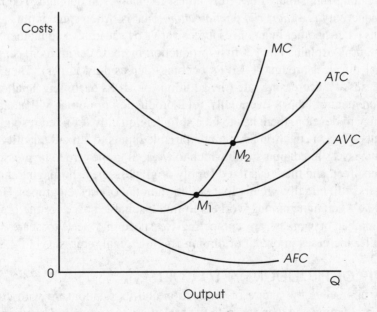

Fig. 8.2 Average Variable Cost, Average Fixed Cost, Average Total Cost, and Marginal Cost

3. *Economies of scale*. There are reductions in average cost per unit as production increases. *Constant*, *increasing*, and *decreasing* returns to scale (concepts, graphs, etc., will follow in this chapter). Briefly, if a firm triples its labor input and triples its output (constant returns); triples its labor and doubles its output (decreasing returns); triples its labor and quadruples its output (increasing returns).

4. Relationships among AFC, AVC, ATC, MC, and among average costs and *total costs*; *between MC and total costs*. You will progressively develop a cost table. Also, you will need to know the relationships between cost and product curves (see Figures 8.1, a and b).

5. Short run and long run cost curves.

6. Opportunity costs, economic costs versus accounting costs, economic profits versus accounting profits. (This will be covered at the end of this chapter.)

Production

In the theory and practice of the firm, we start with the basic facts of the need of the firm to combine its resources into a product or a service. The resources are land, labor, and capital, and entrepreneurial ability. The latter suggests this task of combining resources with some "taking" or assuming of risks. The firm or entrepreneur needs to be innovative and able to adjust to changing technology, labor supply, and new sources of funding capital projects including venture capital. Microeconomics is really the economics of the firm, the theory of the firm, or price theory. Before a firm can engage resources in any effective manner, it needs to know basic production concepts such as the relationship between resources (also known as inputs, factors of production, or agents of production) and output. This is the basic production function or $X = F(a, b, c \ldots n)$ where X is output, F is function, and a, b, c, ... n are factors of production. So, output is a function of inputs a, b, c up to n inputs.

DISTINCTION BETWEEN SHORT RUN AND LONG RUN

The distinction between the short run and the long run is significant in economics. It is *not* the difference declared by a student; the student posited that a long run was any run over one mile in distance. In economics, the distinction is that in the short run, supply cannot fully adjust to changes in demand. In the long run, supply does fully adjust to changes in demand. The law of diminishing marginal productivity is a *short run phenomenon*. That is, when some inputs are fixed in number, what happens when another input or resources varies by successive equal increments? The law of diminishing returns explains how, at first, production increases at an increasing rate (the additions or marginal physical products—MPPs become increasingly larger). Then, at some point, production increases at a decreasing rate (the additions or MPPs becoming smaller with each successive equal increment of labor). Eventually, total production or output will actually decrease. In order for efficiency to develop, there has to be a sufficient quantity of fixed resources or inputs for the variable inputs. Thus, as the firm adds more variable inputs to a fixed quantity of other inputs, each added input has less fixed inputs with which to work. If grapes are to be pressed for juice with the use of workers' feet, and there is a fixed supply of grapes, one can imagine that increasing the number of workers will, initially, greatly increase the amount of pressed grapes. However, at some point, there will be a scramble among workers to find a suitable space for the pressing of grapes. An increasing number of workers are competing for space and need to share space leading to smaller and smaller increases in output or diminishing marginal returns.

RELATIONSHIP OF PRODUCTION TO COSTS

In order to fully appreciate the nature of production and its relationship with costs, we need to define terms for production and then set forth the transition or connection between production and costs.

The relationship between average physical product (APP) and marginal physical product (MPP) is illustrated in Figure 8.2. You will note that when MPP is at its peak, APP intersects MPP. Also, when MPP is negative total physical product, TPP has just peaked. Any further additions of variable inputs will be associated only with decreasing total product or output. Therefore, there can be no economic rationale for hiring any additional units of labor since these units will have some cost. See Table 8.1.

TABLE 8.1
PRODUCT CURVES AND SCHEDULES

No. of Grape Pressers	Total Output (Grape Juice)	Average Product	Marginal Product
1	60	60	60
2	160	80	100
3	250	83.3	90
4	330	82.5	80
5	400	80	70
6	460	76.67	60
7	510	72.86	50
8	550	68.75	40
9	580	64.44	30
10	600	60	20
11	610	55.45	10
12	610	50.83	0
13	600	46.15	−10

On this table you will see that if the firm hires a twelfth grape presser, output remains at 610. If the firm hires at thirteenth presser, there is an associated decrease in output to 600 costs. Average physical product (APP) is defined as the total product or output divided by the number of units of variable input, e.g., labor, and

$$APP* = \frac{\text{total output}}{\text{variable input}}$$

$$MPP* = \frac{\text{change in output}}{\text{change in input}}$$

where MPP = marginal physical product. Marginal physical product is the more significant measure of these two. We need to know the impact of adding one more unit of input, such as labor, on output. As we identify costs and revenues later, we will be able to ascertain whether the additional cost of an additional unit of input relative to its marginal contribution to revenue is justified. We will reserve that analysis until the chapter on resource markets (Chapter 13). In this current chapter, and the chapters to follow on product markets, we will emphasize the various cost curves related to increases in product and their connection to prices and revenues.

Costs

Relationship of MPP and APP to AVC and MC:

In Figure 8.1(a) and (b), there is an illustration of this relationship. It is as if we are in a maximum/minimum symmetry. That is, the relationship of marginal physical product (MPP) to aver-

* We use marginal and average *physical* product in this chapter to distinguish these terms from average and marginal *revenue* product, which we use later.

age physical product (APP) is the converse of the relationship of marginal cost (MC) to average variable costs (AVC). In both cases, as the marginal (MPP, MC) is less than the average (APP, AVC), the average is declining. As the marginal (MPP, MC) is greater than the average (APP, AVC), the average is increasing. However, the MPP curve intersects the APP at the *maximum* point on APP, but the MC curve intersects the AVC curve at the minimum point on AVC. Thus, as MPP declines, each additional unit of labor adds less and less to total product (think of MPP as the addition to total product or the difference in total product as one more unit of labor is added). Regardless of the loss of an additional unit of labor, if each successive equal increment of labor adds less and less to total product, then MC will tend to rise as MPC decreases.

A Word of Caution

Simply because MPP is declining (diminishing marginal productivity) and MC is rising does *not* necessarily mean that the firm should discontinue production. We need to have the comparison of marginal revenue (MR) with marginal cost (we will look at this in the unit on product markets (Chapter 9)). If MR > MC, then the firm will want to continue since it is adding more to revenue than to cost at the margin of producing an additional unit of output.

This relationship of cost to production will be extended to economies of scale later in this chapter. The different measures, AFC, AVC, ATC, MC, TFC, TVC, TC:

1. *Fixed costs*: Total fixed costs are those that, in total, do not vary with changes in output. At zero output, total costs = total fixed costs. Examples would be depreciation costs, capital costs or building and equipment, property taxes, mortgage interest, administrative salaries, and sometimes employee salaries or wages (all or a portion of, such as, tenured faculty, high percent of nurses' salaries, etc.). Average fixed costs (AFC) are total fixed costs divided by output or TFC ± Q. As you might expect, since total fixed costs are constant over varying output, then average fixed costs are going to decline as output increases. So, if TFC are constant or

    $$\frac{\text{TFC}}{\text{Q}}$$

    then as output increases, AFC decline.

    $$\frac{(\text{TFC})}{\text{Q}\uparrow} => \text{AFC} \downarrow$$

    where Q = output. This AFC along with the other marginal and average cost curves are depicted in Figure 8.1.
2. *Variable costs*. Total variable costs are costs that, in total, vary as output changes. As we will see in the next section on economies of scale, these costs tend to decline initially, then reach a minimum, and then increase. Variable costs include the changes in number of employees, energy costs related to production changes, travel expenses, materials related to production, etc. Average Variable Costs (AVC) equal Total Variable Costs (TVC) divided by Q where Q equals the output level. AVC is illustrated in Figure 8.2.
3. *Total costs*. Total Costs = Total Fixed Costs + Total Variable Costs or TC = TFC + TVC. This relationship and the others identified in this section will become important as the readers will progressively complete a table of cost data; different columns will be blank in total or part on different tables. The correct or final table will appear in the chapter on perfect competition, Chapter 10; indeed, this final table will become the basis for a problem on best or optimal output in that chapter. Also, the total of the average costs is significant and necessary to know to complete the cost tables. Thus, ATC = AFC + AVC. As with TC = TFC + TVC, the above identity can be completed if one knows two of the three numbers or has progressively developed the necessary numbers. Thus, if one knows TC and TVC, one can determine TFC and

so on. Before we expand the discussion to the long run, Figure 8.2 illustrates these cost curves (average and marginal) including their relationships. The reader will note that MC intersects both the average variable cost curve (AVC) and the average total cost curve (ATC) at their respective minimum points (M_1, M_2). *This is important to know*. Also, as in our previous discussion, the AFC curve declines rapidly approaching zero level as Quantity (Q) of output increases with total fixed costs constant. The location or level of average variable costs (AVC) and average total costs (ATC) are significant as you will need to know the shut-down position (minimum AVC) and the relationship of price to ATC at best output (P > ATC, profits; P < ATC, losses) under perfect competition (Chapter 10).

COSTS: A TABULAR EXERCISE

In order to visualize these costs and their interrelationships, complete the table started below in two steps. The first step is to complete Table 8.2(a)—complete the TC, ATC columns and the balance of the MC column (the first entry at output level 1 is given as $100). Next, place this completed table out of sight and begin anew with Table 8.2(b) and complete the AFC column. You may wish to check your results with the same table used in the chapter on Perfect Competition, Chapter 10. You may experience some rounding differences.

TABLE 8.2(a)

Output	TC	AFC	AVC	ATC	MC
1		$400	$100		$100
2		200	75		
3		133	70		
4		100	73		
5		80	80		
6		67	90		
7		57	103		
8		50	119		
9		44	138		
10		40	160		

TABLE 8.2(b)

Output	TC	AFC	AVC	ATC	MC
1	$500		$100	$500	$100
2	550		75	275	50
3	610		70	203	60
4	690		73	173	80
5	800		80	160	110
6	940		90	157	140
7	1,120		103	160	180
8	1,350		119	169	230
9	1,640		138	182	290
10	2,000		160	200	360

COSTS: THE LONG RUN AND ECONOMIES OF SCALE (AND THE ASSOCIATED ADJUSTMENT FROM THE SHORT RUN)

First, we might need a refresher on the differences between the long run and the short run. When we looked at diminishing marginal productivity, we were considering the short run since we held some input (resources) constant, such as land or capital, to see the effect of adding successive equal increments of a variable input, such as labor (grape pressers) on the output (grape juice). In the short run, not all of the inputs have sufficient time to adjust to the changes in demand. In this section, we will consider the variability of all inputs and therefore, the long run.

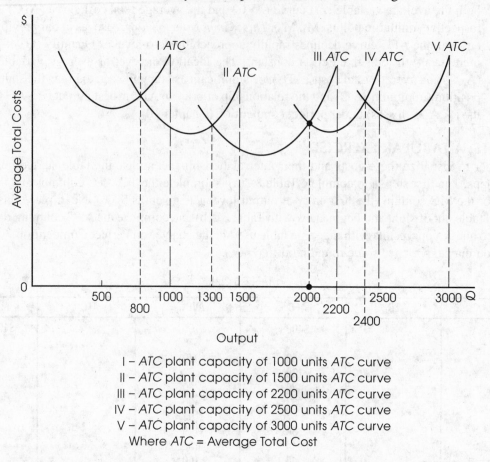

I – ATC plant capacity of 1000 units ATC curve
II – ATC plant capacity of 1500 units ATC curve
III – ATC plant capacity of 2200 units ATC curve
IV – ATC plant capacity of 2500 units ATC curve
V – ATC plant capacity of 3000 units ATC curve
Where ATC = Average Total Cost

Fig. 8.3 Adjustment In Plant Size (capacity) From Short Run to Long Run Cost Curves

Economies of scale are those savings in average cost of production per unit that are realized as the firm increases production of its goods. In Figure 8.3, we have illustrated hypothetical plant size (capacity) for different "runs" of production. That is, the firm has an average total cost (ATC) curve I for production up to 1,000 units, ATC curve II for up to 1,500 units, and so on. The decision comes at production of 800 units whether to stay with plant size I and its related ATC curve or to expand capacity to plant size II. The advantage of expanding the plant size at this juncture would be to enjoy the economies of scale evident in II ATC. That is, at 800 units the firm could produce more efficiently on curve II ATC since it is downward sloping—lower per unit average costs, while curve I ATC is upper sloping at 800 units to its limit of 1,000 units. Thus, the firm could produce 800 to 1,000 units more cheaply with plant size II than with plant size I. However, the caveat is that demand for the firm's production will be sufficient to justify the move to a plant size (capacity) of 1,500. Much of this decision will rest on the ability to know the market, use forecasting tools, and to have some confidence in the general economy, including but not limited to the expected level of consumer income and the expected actions of the government (regulation, antitrust, and so on) and the monetary authorities. A firm may conclude that the demand increase is only temporary and might be better supplied by outsourcing. For example, when the Great Atlantic and Pacific Tea Company (the A&P) owned its brand name (Ann Page Foods) factory in Big Flats, New York, it took orders from other name brand companies to produce their products with their names according to the brand name companies' own specifications. On a visit to the factory in New York State, one might have encountered the production of a name brand pasta complete with the brand name packages. Since the pasta company had excess orders from industries that were one-time-only orders, it figured that it would be foolish to expand its plant capacity and, instead, to have Ann Page Foods produce their order.

Similarly, when Ford Motor Company and General Motors faced an increase in demand for diesel engines for passenger cars, they took different paths in their decision making. Ford hired the services of experienced diesel engine manufacturers in Germany in order to meet its demand, while at the same time to determine whether this was simply a temporary situation. General Motors undertook a major investment in changing piston engines to diesel engines and had to adjust and expand its production capacity.

Thus, if the demand increase seems long term and sufficient to justify increased plant capacity, and the related utilization of that capacity, the firm would move to the next-larger plant size when the ATC curve of one size intersected the ATC curve of the next-larger size (e.g., when ATC I intersects ATC II at 800 units of production rather than waiting until production reaches 1,000). The extent to which this becomes an on-going process, the long run average total cost curve becomes the envelope curve that touches base with these decision points—800, 1,300, 2,000, and 2,400 units.

Thus far, we have explained the nature of economies of scale, which implies that as output or production increases, there are some savings in per unit average cost of production. The sources of these savings or economies are of two types: external economies of scale and internal economies of scale. With respect to internal economies, there are those economies that derive from specialization and those that derive from efficiency gains with large size.

Value of a Large-Size Firm

The value of having a large-size firm is that it can hire specialists in finance, marketing, distribution, public relations, corporate communications, information technology, and even economics! The sole proprietorship or "Mom and Pop" operation has to be "Jack and Jill of everything"—all those specialized areas listed above—and "master of none." Thus, the larger firm can become more efficient than the small firm simply on the basis of being able to hire more expertise. The other general internal efficiency is the gain that comes from the increase in volume that allows fixed costs to be spread over a larger output of goods and services lending to a decrease in average per unit costs (ATC). In the chapter on imperfect competition, Chapter 12, we cite the case of too many gasoline stations at a busy intersection. The volume of sales, gallons of gasoline, is too low in total to provide any basis for economies of scale for any of the four gasoline stations. It is a classic example of underutilization or excess capacity as the major source of inefficiency in the long run under monopolistic competition. This situation could be illustrated with the graph in Figure 8.4(c). You will see the economies of scale (ATC declining) being very quickly exhausted and then a long range of diseconomies of scale (the longer, upward sloping portion of the ATC curve). Each station simply cannot pump enough gallons of gasoline over which to spread its fixed costs. Figure 8.4(c) illustrates a relatively small firm. Conversely, a very large firm such as an automobile manufacturing company can enjoy an ATC curve as illustrated in Figure 8.4(b) since it can cover its fixed costs over a very large number (millions) of its output or automobiles. This ATC curve has a long downward declining shape with economies of scale. Also, the company can use the most modern technology that would be, in many cases, too expensive for smaller firms or the smaller firms would have to purchase smaller technology. This smaller technology would be more expensive per unit produced. For example, a machine with 1,000 horsepower would not cost twice as much as one with 500 horsepower.

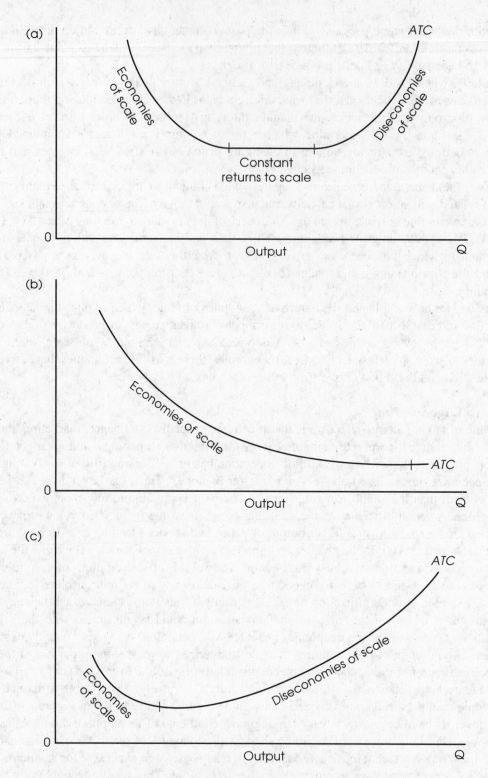

Fig. 8.4 Economies of Scale—The effect of varying cost curves (a, b, c)

External economies of scale do not depend upon the efficient operation of a firm but rather derive from the large-scale advanced industrial economy. It is going to be much more efficient (less costly) to build a steel company in Germany or the United States than it is to build one in Afghanistan, which lacks the infrastructure of the more advanced industrial countries. Infrastructure would include a highly trained, educated, and experienced labor force; a well-developed telecommunications system; an advanced computer technology, a ready-made source of supplies, and retail/wholesale buyers of products. Given an advanced industrial economy like the German economy, there will be many companies that rely on steel products for part or all of their production. These are external economies of scale.

ECONOMIC COSTS

There is a particular definition of economic costs that is at variance with the definition of business or accounting costs. Further, this particular definition will help explain the distinction between economic profits and accounting or business profits. Economic profits involve opportunity or implicit costs as well as the explicit costs of accounting.

In economics we reason that the cost of producing one good or service or engaging in a particular activity is measured in terms of what other goods or services could have been produced or what other activity could have been undertaken using the same resources, including time. For example, if an F-16 fighter plane costs $16 million (hypothetically), how many automobiles, air conditioners, or computers could have been produced with the same amount of resources for $16 million? So, the production of what a fighter plane *costs* us (consumers) is what we could have had available in the form of these other products. Also, we could say that that economic cost is what must be paid, at minimum, to maintain or attract production of the goods and services that we are demanding.

Economic costs include the implicit cost of what could have been earned elsewhere with the same resources that are employed in the current business. For example, if Mom and Pop spend $100,000 on a building and equipment to open a restaurant, what might be included as implicit costs? If the $100,000 were invested in a similar risk mutual fund and the return on the investment was 9 percent compared to a 6 percent return on one capital investment in the restaurant, the *implicit* cost would be 3 percent or $3,000, or the amount that could be earned elsewhere compared to the investment in the restaurant. Similarly, if Mom and Pop paid themselves $40,000 each as salary and, with the same number of hours they could have earned $50,000 each working for some other restaurant, their implicit cost would be $20,000 ($100,000 − $80,000). We add these implicit costs to the explicit costs in order to determine the economic feasibility of going into the restaurant business. To illustrate this, review the hypothetical data below: (assume no other implicit costs):

Sales (Income) for restaurant	$900,000
− explicit (accounting) costs	−600,000
accounting business profit	300,000
− implicit (economic) costs*	−23,000*
economic profit	$277,000

* opportunity cost ($23,000) of operating their own business versus "hiring out" their resources result from subtracting explicit *and* implicit (opportunity costs of resources in alternative uses) costs from income or revenue.

Summary

- Law of Diminishing Marginal Productivity. This is the range of output over which production increases at a decreasing rate, i.e., the additional units of production become smaller and smaller.

- Relationships Among Average Cost (AC, AVC, ATC), Marginal Cost (MC), Average Product (AP) and marginal Product (MP) Curves. The MP curve *always* intersects the AP curve at the maximum point of the AP curve. The MC curve *always* intersects the Average Cost Curve (AVC, ATC) at their minimum points.
- Economies of Scale. These reductions in average cost per unit of output as production increases may be in the form of constant, increasing or decreasing returns to scale.
- Economic Profits vs. Accounting Profits. Accounting profits result from subtracting explicit costs from income or revenue. Economic profits produce a return which is less than a return of an alternative activity using the same resources (implicit costs).
- Economic Profits. Income or revenue minus explicit *and* implicit costs.
- Accounting Profits. Income or revenue minus explicit costs.

Terms

Law of Diminishing Marginal Productivity   the range of output over which smaller and smaller additional units of output are produced as successive equal increments of a variable input are added to fixed quantities of other inputs in the short run.

Economies of Scale   savings in per unit costs of production as output increases

Short Run   period of time over which supply cannot fully adjust to changes in demand

Long Run   period of time over which supply can fully adjust to changes in demand

Opportunity Costs   the cost incurred when resources are engaged in one activity are not as productive as they would have been in a forgone activity

Formulas

Total Costs (TC) = Total Variable Costs (TVC) + Total Fixed Costs (TFC)

Average Total Costs (ATC) = Average Variable Costs + Average Fixed Costs (AFC)

Marginal Costs = the change is total costs with one additional unit of output

$$\frac{TFC}{Q} = AFC; \quad \frac{TVC}{Q} = AVC; \quad \frac{TC}{Q} = ATC$$

Multiple-Choice Review Questions

1. Which of the following is true?

   A. TC = (AVC + AFC) Q.
   B. TFC = TC at all levels of output.
   C. AVC + AFC = TC.
   D. MC = TC − TFC.
   E. ATC = AVC + MC.

2. Opportunity costs or implicit costs of a "Mom & Pop" owned business are:

   A. equal to accounting costs.
   B. equal to accounting profits.
   C. equal to earnings or profits that could have occurred using resources elsewhere.
   D. equal to earnings or profits that occurred for Mom & Pop's business.
   E. equal to earnings or profits of other Mom & Pop businesses.

3. With capital fixed at one unit with 1, 2, 3 units of labor added in equal successive units, production of the output increases from 300 (1 unit of labor), to 350 (2 units of labor) to 375 (3 units of labor). Which of the following is a correct interpretation?

   A. This is long run increasing returns to scale.
   B. This is long run decreasing returns to scale.
   C. This is long run constant returns to scale.
   D. This is short run diminishing marginal productivity.
   E. This is short run increasing marginal productivity.

4. Which of the following is *not correct* about economies of scale?

   A. Economies of scale are associated with increases in production of output.
   B. Economies of scale are associated with the rising or increasing portion of an average total cost (ATC) curve.
   C. Economies of scale are associated with the declining or decreasing portions of the ATC curve.
   D. Economies of scale result in decreases in per unit average cost.
   E. Economies of scale may be associated with the ability to use more specialists in business.

5. Marginal cost (MC) is equal to average variable cost (AVC) and average total cost (ATC) when:

   A. marginal cost (MC) intersects AVC and ATC at their maximum points.
   B. AVC and ATC intersect MC at its maximum point.
   C. MC intersects AVC and ATC at their minimum points.
   D. AVC and ATC intersect MC at its minimum point.
   E. the economy is in the recovery phase of the business cycle.

MULTIPLE-CHOICE REVIEW ANSWERS

1. **A.** Completed tables appear at the end of Chapter 10 under Free-Response Review Question 1 (see page 115)
   B. at zero output: TC = $400
2. **A**   3. **C**   4. **D**   5. **B**

Free-Response Review Question

1. A. Be sure to complete Table 8.2(a) and (b) shown on page 89 as requested in this chapter.

    B. Determine what TC would be for zero output. HINT: TFC are constant; they do *not* vary with output. Also, remember that AFC × Q = TFC and again, TFC is the same at every level of output, including zero output.

9 Product Markets: Types, Characteristics, Pricing Strategies

Introduction

This section on product markets, and this introductory chapter relate to the production of goods and services and their costs and prices in differently structured markets ranging from the theoretical model of perfect competition through the imperfectly competitive real-world models of monopolistic competition and oligopoly to monopoly. For each of these product markets, there is a set of characteristics that provides guidance in explaining different costs, efficiencies and pricing strategies.

Things to Know

Based on the most frequently asked questions on previous Advanced Placement exams, the following table of the characteristics of the different market structures provides the best overall reference guide.

Product Markets: Definitions

PERFECT COMPETITION

Perfect competition is characterized by a large number of sellers so that no one seller or group of sellers can have a significant effect on the terms of exchange (or transaction terms). These terms include prices, quantity, share of market, type of product, distribution, innovation, service/warranty/guarantee, etc. Prices for each firm in this perfectly competitive environment are determined in the market where all firms (sellers) compete for the buyers of the same (homogeneous) product. That is, the price is set in this market and each firm must charge the "going price"; to charge more would result in loss of sales to other firms that produce the identical product. As a result, these firms are price-takers; each firm sells at the price set in the market or at the intersection of demand and supply.

TABLE 9.1
PRODUCT MARKETS CHARACTERISTICS

Characteristics	Perfect Competition	Monopolistic Competition	Oligopoly	Monopoly
1. Numbers of Sellers	Many (they are price-takers from the market).	Fewer than perfect competition, more than oligopoly/ monopoly (some price-makers).	Few sellers who have some control of market share; interdependence.	One seller for whom there are no close substitutes.
2. Availability of Substitutes	One product type available (fully substitutable) available from all sellers.	Imperfect substitutions.	Fewer substitutes available = market pricing power.	No close substitutes available.
3. Degree of Elasticity	Perfectly elastic	Imperfect elasticity. Depends on degree of innovation.	Varies. Greater elasticity at high prices. Lower elasticity at lower prices.	Generally inelastic but still elastic at higher prices.
4. Similarity of Products	Homogeneous products from all sellers.	Mostly non-price competition. Some independent pricing-innovations.	Some markets— homogeneous for specialty products. Other markets heterogeneous products.	Follows from #1–3 above. Heterogeneous since there are no close substitutes.
5. Pricing Policy/ Strategy	No pricing policy or strategy. Price at market price, price-takers.	Weak barriers to entry/exit.	Much interdependence in pricing. Some evidence of monopoly pricing policy.	Monopoly pricing power. High value to ratio: $\dfrac{P-MC}{MC}$
6. Barriers to enter/exit	No barriers to entry/exit.	Less efficient than PC; excess capacity. Price = AC (not at minimum)	Formidable barriers to entry/exit.	Complete barriers to entry by definition.
7. Efficiency/* Rent-Seeking	Efficient. Each seller prices at cost. No rents. Only transfer earnings.	Inefficiency, excess capacity since P = AC (but not at minimum).	Monopoly pricing power leads to waste/inefficiency. Some economies of scale.	Dead-weight loss of monopoly (loss to society beyond monopoly profits and reduced consumer surplus).
8. Eco. Profits* P, AC	Zero economic profits. Price = Minimum AC.	P = AC; tendency for LR zero economic profits.	Tendency for existence of LR economic profits.	Empirical evidence of LR economic profits.
9. P, MC*	Ideal social pricing P = MC	P > MC	P > MC	P > MC
10. P, MR*	P = MR	P > MR	P > MR	P > MR

* Long Run Tendencies at Equilibrium.

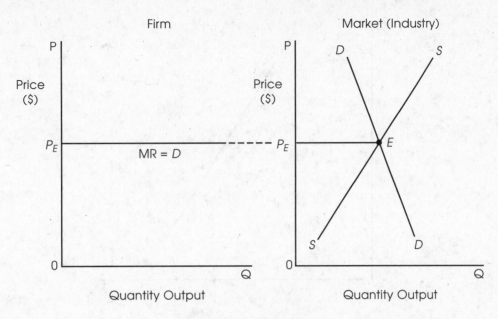

Fig. 9.1 Perfect Competition

To illustrate, under perfect competition, there are no barriers to entry for firms that want to enter the market—no technological secrets, no financial barriers, no legal or regulatory constraints, etc. Also, there are no barriers to exit, such as government subsidies, tax relief, import quotas, or high tariffs. In other words, efficiency is maintained or rewarded and inefficiency is reduced by new entrants. Perfect competition is also characterized by homogeneous (identical) product; firms must use the currently available technology and fully utilize plant and equipment to maintain the competitive norm of costs and hence, be efficient. We discovered earlier (Chapter 5) that in long run equilibrium under pure competition, Price (P) = Minimum Average Cost (AC); Price (P) = Marginal Cost (MC) and Price (P) = Marginal Revenue. Since the products produced under perfect competition are identical (homogeneous), they are perfect substitutes and have to be priced at the market (firms as price-takers). That would also mean that Price (P) = Marginal Revenue (see Figure 9.1) since each unit sells for the same price regardless of the quantity produced.

Under perfect competition, there is no pricing strategy. The price elasticity of demand for each firm (see Chapter 5) is perfectly elastic, a horizontal function indicating the products are perfect substitutes. Each firm must produce and price at minimum cost or lose sales to the other firms. Each customer buys a product at its minimum average cost. Thus, the more substitutes available, the more competitive the industry structure and the more elastic the response to price changes. The perfectly competitive model is one of price-takers with no pricing strategy or power independent of the market.

MONOPOLY

There are many forms that monopoly can take (see Chapter 11). It is important to note that we are on the opposite end of market structures than that of perfect competition. That is, monopolies are characterized as one seller of a product for which there are no close substitutes; therefore, we would expect the demand of the consumer to be less elastic in a perfectly competitive market. However, the monopoly demand curve will *not* be perfectly inelastic since the buyers can be influenced by price changes, or, as the price decreases, they may wish to buy more. This, in turn, explains why the marginal revenue function will differ from the demand function as the price is lowered; the addition to total revenue becomes less and less.

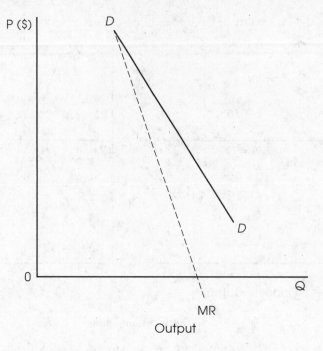

Fig. 9.2 Monopoly. Firm = Market (Industry)

Thus, under monopoly, the downward sloping demand curve implies a pricing strategy, even a pricing power. The strategy is to change prices and outputs (to have a significant effect on the terms of exchange or transaction terms) in order to maximize revenue and profits. Barriers to entry allow monopolists to increase prices and limit output; hence, no available close substitutes leads to lack of competition and the demand curve is less elastic than that of perfect competition. There are several types of monopolies and pricing strategies that we will review in later chapters.

MONOPOLISTIC COMPETITION

This market structure is the setting for many firms in the United States and other Western countries. It is characterized by many medium-sized firms that need to be innovative and differentiate their products in ways other than price. That is to say, a firm in monopolistic competition can take sales away from a rival with a variety of "price-distracting" products and services. For example, a food supermarket might develop a huge store complete with bakery, sandwich shop, restaurant, dry cleaner, specialty and take-home meals, film processing, drugstore, magazine and newspaper section, bulk foods, etc. This store could then price its regular and stable goods higher than its rival stores, thus, a strategy that is based on product differentiation and innovation that reduces competition. With few substitutes, the competition is reduced, and the demand curve becomes less elastic. The firms charge above marginal cost and above minimum average cost, in the long run. The firms are less efficient than perfect competition since they tend to have zero economic profits but price above minimum average cost. There will be a full explanation about this in Chapter 12. See the illustration which follows.

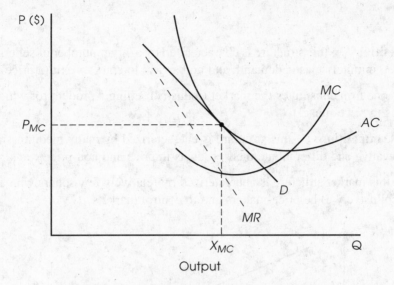

P ($)

P_{MC}

MC

AC

D

MR

X_{MC} Q

Output

* Long run *tendency* to zero economic profits

Fig. 9.3 Monopolistic Competition*

OLIGOPOLY

There are relatively few sellers (specific measurements indices in Chapter 12 who act *interdependently* and/or collusively to be price-makers in order to control markets and the terms of exchange, for example, price, quantity sold, geographic markets, specialized markets, service terms, etc. There are very strong barriers to entry (technology, financial, legal, etc.). The goods produced can be both homogeneous and heterogeneous, in other words, similar as in a product specialization such as structural steel where firms compete with each other in the *same* product market. In heterogeneous competition, firms differentiate their products to gain in revenue; for example, one firm may provide a complete line of hardware product, including some products that sell at a loss, in order to compete against firms that sell only those lines that produce profits. In the latter case, firms can increase their prices to the extent that there are fewer substitutes reflected in lower price elasticity of demand. Again, fewer substitutes, lower price elasticity of demand, and more pricing power are highly interrelated. There are more price-makers.

Oligopoly can look like Figure 9.3 as in a monopoly if the oligopoly is a collusive model. Alternately, oligopoly can be a noncollusive model as illustrated below (Figure 9.4). This is known as the *Kinked Demand Curve*, which demonstrates the interdependence of competing rivals under oligopoly (see more on oligopoly in Chapter 12).

Summary

This chapter provides an overview of the different market structures which include perfect competition, monopoly, monopolistic competition and oligopoly.

The basic reference guide to these market structures is in Table 9.1. This table compares the structures by numbers of sellers, availability of substitutes, degree of price elasticity of demand, similarity of products, pricing policy, barriers to entry/exit, efficiency/rent-seeking, economic profits, price related to marginal cost and price related to marginal revenue. One might observe that as entry is easier, products more similar, availability of substitutes is greater and the number of sellers is larger, markets are more competitive (closer to the perfect competition model) and price elasticity of demand is greater.

Terms

Perfect Competition   this structure is characterized by a larger number of sellers with a homogeneous product, infinitely elastic demand, and no barriers to entry or exit (a price-taker)

Monopoly   one firm constitutes the market (industry) selling a product for which there are no close substitutes (a price-maker)

Monopolistic Competition   this structure is characterized by many medium-sized firms who need to be innovative and differentiate their products in price and non-price ways

Oligopoly   this market structure is characterized by relatively few sellers who act interdependently and/or collusively to be price-makers and to control markets

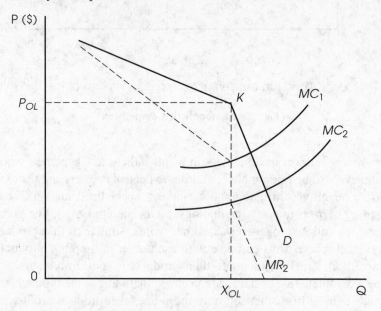

Fig. 9.4 Oligopoly-Kinked Demand Curve

Multiple-Choice Review Questions

1. For which of the following market structures are the most substitutes available for consumers?

   A. Perfect competition.
   B. Monopolistic competition.
   C. Oligopoly.
   D. Monopoly.
   E. All of the above.

2. Which of the following market structures has the greatest degree of elasticity?

   A. Perfect competition.
   B. Monopolistic competition.
   C. Oligopoly.
   D. Monopoly.
   E. All of the above.

3. Which of the following market structures has the largest number of sellers?

   A. Perfect competition.
   B. Monopolistic competition.
   C. Oligopoly.
   D. Monopoly.
   E. All of the above.

4. Which of the following market structures is *not* a price maker?

   A. Perfect competition.
   B. Monopolistic competition.
   C. Oligopoly.
   D. Monopoly.
   E. All of the above.

MULTIPLE-CHOICE REVIEW ANSWERS

1. **A**   2. **A**   3. **A**   4. **A**

CHAPTER
10 Perfect Competition

Based on the most frequently asked questions on previous Advanced Placement exams, the following are the most important concepts. In the balance of the chapter, we will expand on these and other concepts and examples.

Things to Know

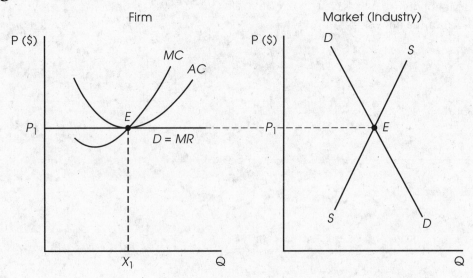

Figs. 10.1 and 10.3 Perfect Competition

Note the following:

1. Demand curve of *market* (or *industry*—all firms selling some product) is downward sloping to the right but the demand curve of the firm is *horizontal* (implies perfectly elastic demand function).
2. Since the demand curve of the individual firm is horizontal, P = MR for the firm.
3. If we take the above figure to be that of long run (LR) equilibrium, each firm will take its price from the market of industry (price-taker). Thus, regardless of the quantity produced and sold, the price for the firm remains constant with the only decision being the optimal quantity to produce given a price.
4. Also, if Figure 10.1 represents LR equilibrium, you will note that P = MR, P = MC and P = minimum average cost. P = MR implies that there is no pricing strategy (firms are price-takers); the demand function is horizontal. P = MC implies that the price of the

product (the "value" to the consumer) is equal to the extra cost incurred by the seller in producing the marginal or extra unit of production. P = Minimum Average Cost implies that firms are operating at zero economic profits (see Chapter 8 for explanation of economic versus accounting profits). This also means that efficiency has been attained, in other words, each increase in the cost of an extra unit of production equals the price that the consumer is willing to pay. We will discover later that, in contrast, monopolistic competition has a degree of inefficiency due largely to excess capacity by producing at average cost but not minimum cost.

5. If we refer to the short run (SR), price as reflected by the demand function remains horizontal but can increase or decrease in the short run; therefore, there can be profits or losses in the short run. The firm wants to maximize profits or minimize losses by producing the optimal output—the level of output at which MR = MC (with perfect competition, MR = P). Thus, if you are given a graph, a table, or a set of output and price levels, you need to find the location of the optimizing output in the short run. For example, if Price is $14, find the optimal output in the diagram below:

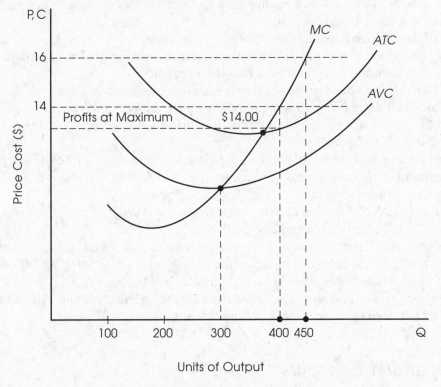

Fig. 10.2 Determination of Profits

If P = MR, then the optimal output would be at the level at which MC = MR. Follow the horizontal demand function over to where the price of $14 (MR) = MC (intersection of the MC function with Price or Demand). Drop a line perpendicular to the horizontal axis and the output of $400 would be the optimal output, the output level at which profits would be maximized or the level at which MR = MC. We will more fully develop this concept later as we look at shut-down, maximum profit, minimum loss levels of output and the criteria for best output in each of these situations.

---

*Note that MC intersects both AC curves (AVC and ATC) at their minimum levels.
**Note that, in the short run, P = MR.

As a follow-up question, what would the firm do if the price increased to $16? (Again, refer to Figure 10.2). Would the firm produce at 300, 350, 400, 450, or 525 units of output? To determine the answer, follow the general criterion of best output @ MC = MR (remember that, in the short run, P = MR). Thus, with a price (MR) of $16, MR = MC at an output level of 450. Hence, the best (optimal) output level will be 450. If there is no level at which MR = MC, select the highest level of output at which MR > MC.

6. As mentioned in the chapter on costs (see Chapter 8) and as illustrated in point 5 above, ATC = MC when ATC is at its minimum point and AVC = MC when AVC is at its minimum point. That is, MC always intersects ATC and AVC at their minimum points. When MC > ATC, ATC must be rising since the additions to total cost (marginal costs) are greater than average costs. The converse holds with MC < ATC.

7. The following are conditions that are correct about firms operating under perfect competition:

   At *long-run* equilibrium,
   a. P = MC. No pricing strategy. Firms are price-takers.
   b. P = MC. Price at which product sells (at "market") equals the extra cost incurred.
   c. P = minimum average cost.
   d. Firms realize zero economic profit or *normal* profits.
   e. Firms have no incentive to price their goods and services below the market price.
   f. The demand function for each firm is horizontal.
   g. Products are homogeneous; therefore, no purpose for advertising.

8. Profits and competition. LR equilibrium under perfect competition leads to normal profits (zero economic profits). Profits less than normal = economic losses. Economic profits > zero or normal profits.

9. The conditions (criteria) for continuing production, shut-down, profits, losses in the short run under perfect competition (expanded coverage later in this chapter). For each price (P = MR), in the short run:
   a. If P < AVC, firm should shut down and its total losses = total fixed cost (TFC). If P ≥ AVC, firm should continue production.
   b. If P > AVC, firm continues to produce as long as MR > MC up to the level of output profits are maximized or losses minimized—level at which MR = MC. (Determination of profits or losses discussed later in this chapter.)

10. Under perfect competition, price elasticity of supply is greater in the long run than in the short run since there are more opportunities for substitution of inputs.

The Expanded Concepts

1. The individual firm as a price-taker (see Figure 10.1/10.3):
   The firm is a price-taker, that is, the price for the homogeneous (same) product is determined in the market, where all buyers and sellers meet, and "dictate" to each individual firm. Since there is a sufficiently large number of firms under perfect competition, no one firm or group of firms can determine its own price. The firms must sell at the market-determined price for two basic reasons: (1) If a firm increases its price above the market price, customers will buy the identical product from another seller at the market price; and, (2) If a firm lowers its price below the market price, it will incur losses and not increase its sales significantly, if at all, since each firm has a very small share of a very large number of sellers. (For more characteristics of perfect competition, see the introductory section of Chapter 9.)

2. Criteria and output strategies for profit-maximizing (and loss-minimizing) firms in the short run under perfect competition.

    *   For the appropriate context, firms may incur some losses in the short run* as long as they are covering average variable costs (those costs that increase as output increases) with the market price. Unless a firm can cover (equal to or greater than) average variable costs with its price, it is more economical to shut down production and simply incur fixed costs (those costs that, in total, do not vary with output changes); rather than incurring the fixed costs plus the variable costs, the latter is not covered by the price. The context here is the short run only.

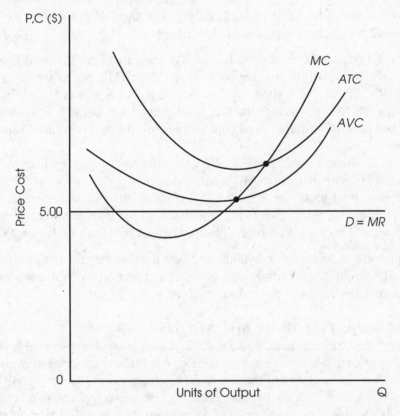

Fig. 10.4 Shut-Down Case

    *   The decision-making process to determine best (optimal) output, that is, the output level that maximizes total profits or minimizes total losses.
        a.   The firm should produce if P > Average Variable Cost (AVC). It should continue to produce as long as Marginal Revenue (MR) > Marginal Cost (MC). This means that the firm is adding more to its revenue than it is adding to its costs at the margin of producing one additional unit. Therefore, as long as MR > MC, the firm would, necessarily, be adding more to its profits or, in the situation of losses, be reducing losses. At the level of output at which MR = MR, profits would be maximized or losses minimized; hence, the optimal output would occur at MR = MC. In some cases (often used on examination questions), there will be no level of output at which MR = MC. To determine the optimal output, in such cases, select the highest level of output at which MR > MC. If the firm produced one more unit of output beyond this level, then the MC > MR, which would not lead to minimizing losses or maximizing profits.

---

*The short run is when supply cannot fully adjust to changes in demand.

b. To determine the total profits or total losses at the optimal level of output, use the following: Optimal level of output X (P – ATC) or total profits = Q(P – ATC) where Q = optimal level of output. If at the optimal output, P > ATC, then the firm would be realizing profits, in other words, P > ATC with the difference being a per unit profit. Thus, if the optimal output is 10 units with a price of $38 and average total cost of $29, total profits would be $90 (Total Profits = Q(P – ATC) or 10 (38 – 29) = 10 × $9) = or $90. If, at the best output of 10 units with a price of $38 and average total cost at $40, losses would occur (ATC > P); total losses would be = Q(ATC – P) or 10(40 – 38) = $20.

In summary, to determine best (optimal) output, use the following steps (for *each* price) Remember P = MR for the firm in perfect competition:

1. Compare the price with AVC; go down the AVC column to see if P = AVC or P > AVC. If so, the firm continues to produce as long as MR > MC up to the level of output at which MR = MC or the highest level of output at which MR > MC. This would be the optimal output. If AVC > P, then the firm would shut down and take at its losses, total fixed costs. The MR = MC criterion would not apply here—the best (optimal) output is zero units of output.
2. If the firm continues to produce (P > AVC), then the best output is where MR = MC or the highest level of output at which MR > MC.
3. To determine total profits or losses, first determine whether at best output P > ATC or ATC > P. In the former case, profits are realized. In the latter case, losses are incurred. If Q is the optimal output then for total profits, Q(P – ATC); for total losses, Q(ATC – P).

There is a problem to solve, using hypothetical cost data, at the end of this chapter. You may wish to pause with your further reading of this chapter and take on the problem now. The table of costs is taken from Chapter 8, Costs, Production, Supply.

DECISION MAKING FOR THREE SITUATIONS

1. Shut-down case (see Figure 10.4). (P < AVC, therefore, shut down; total losses = TFC) At the market price of $5, the average variable cost is higher than price at every level of output. Therefore, the firm should shut down (at least temporarily) since its cost of continuing production is greater than its revenue. It has no revenue to apply to fixed costs and cannot recover its variable costs at the price of $5 per unit. Its optimal or best output is zero and its minimal total costs are equal to its total fixed costs.
2. Profit maximization case P > AVC, which suggests that the firm should continue to produce as long as MR > MC up to the level of output at which MR = MC; this level of output will maximize profits.

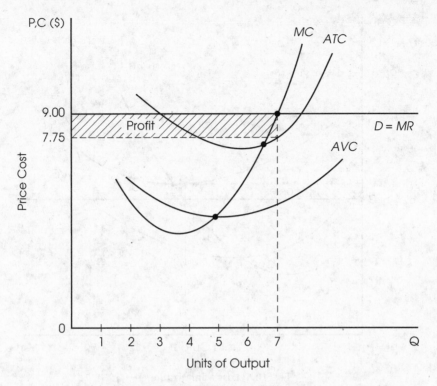

Fig. 10.5 Profit Maximization

At the market price of \$9, the firm covers its AC (P > AVC) and thus, continues to produce as long as MR > MC up to the level of output at which MR = MC (or if there is no level of output at which MR = MC, the highest level of output at which MR > MC would be the optimal output. In this case MR = MC at the \$7 units of output. The optimal (best) output is 7 at which profits are maximized. Total profits at 7 units of output would be Q*(P − ATC) = total profits. Profits are maximized when the Q* is the optimal level of output (MR = MC). So, Q*(P − ATC) becomes 7(9 − 7.75) = 8.75.

3. Loss minimization. P > AVC, which suggests that the firm, in the short run, will continue to produce as long as MR > MC up to the level of output at which MR = MC even if there are losses, then we want the level of output at which we minimize the total losses (MR = MC).

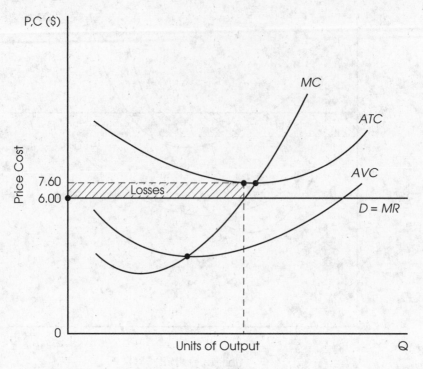

Fig. 10.6 Loss Minimization

At a market price of $6 per unit this level would be at 5 units of output (MR = MC). Total losses would be Q*(ATC − P) where Q* is the optimal or best output, that is, total losses are minimized. Thus, Q*(ATC − P) becomes 5(7.60 − 6) = 8.00. This is the rectangular area in the graph above, noted as "losses" (loss permit at best output, x number of units).

Evaluation of Perfect Competition

Some of this evaluation is reflected in our summary table in Chapter 9 and in this chapter. However, the following are areas from which questions are drawn for the Advanced Placement exams.

- In the short run, the supply curve is identified as that portion of the marginal cost (MC) curve above its intersection with the average variable cost (AVC) curve; the firm is only willing to supply its products or services if the given market price is greater than its average variable costs.
- We have efficiency with consumers buying the products and services they want at prices they pay that are equal to the minimum average cost and marginal cost of production. The producers gain (producer's surplus) from the difference between the price they are willing to supply goods and the price they receive in the market.
- With competitive market exchange and firms as price-takers, there is no "rent seeking"; firms cannot extract from the market any more than they contribute to the market at the margin of any transaction. Price = minimum average cost, which leads to zero economic profits in the long run.

The Long Run

One of the frequently asked questions on the Advanced Placement exam deals with the adjustment of firms from the short run (when supply cannot fully adjust to changes in demand) to the long run when supply fully adjusts to changes in demand. Sometimes, this question appears in the free-response (or essay) section of the exam; at other times it appears as objective, multiple-choice questions.

The following is what you have to know in order to do well on this long run adjustment process.

1. We assume that the only adjustment made, as demand changes, is that new firms enter (as demand increases leading to short run profits). The other type of adjustment is that the present firms increase production. We are not using this adjustment in order to simplify the process.
2. We also assume that the firms' average cost curves are identical and that these cost curves are unaffected by the adjustment process.
3. We assume that new firms enter with the same cost curves as the present firms and that the new firms are attracted by the short run profits in the industry. Also, we assume that firms will exit from the industry when demand decreases, leading to short run losses.

To illustrate this adjustment process, two graphs are provided below (Figure 10.7); the one on the left (a) represents the individual firms, and the one of the right (b) represents the industry or market where all buyers and sellers of the same product meet.

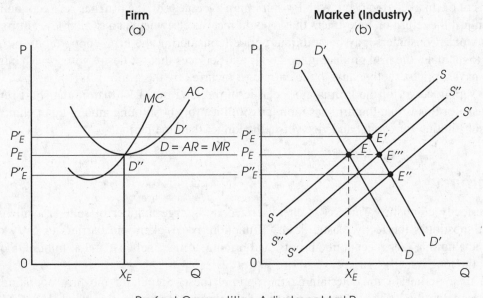

Perfect Competition Adjustment to LR

Fig. 10.7

We start at an equilibrium position with the price at P_E and quantity at X_E (think of the scale of (b) being 1/100 as compared to (a) and 10 firms in the industry). For the firm (a), note that at equilibrium, P = minimum AC, P = MR, P = MC, and that the demand curve for the individual firm is horizontal. So, at equilibrium the firm "takes" the price from the market and produces at X_E for the optimal output. There is no tendency for change from this optimal output. If the firm produces more, the average cost and MC will exceed the price; if the firm produces less, the AC > price. Now, if the demand for the industry's product increases (DD shifts to D'D') as profits appear, we might expect the adjustment process to begin, that is, demand increases (DD shifts to D'D'); then, a profit appears as a result of demand > supply leading to the demand curve for the firm increasing horizontally (from D to D'), which means the new price (P'$_E$) is greater than average costs (AC) with the consequent profits. In the short run, supply cannot immediately or fully adjust to the increase in demand. However, with short run profits appearing, new firms are attracted into the industry. Thus, as a second step in the adjustment process, supply increases (SS to S'S') as new firms enter the market. Figure 10.7b is deliberately drawn to show an excess of the new supply relative to the increase in demand. Remember, this is a trial-and-error process much as is our speculation as to the future share prices in the high-tech stock markets. Thus, the excess of supply (S'S' relative to D'D') leads to price decreasing to P''$_E$, which is lower than average cost, which translates into losses. Then, as a third step, some firms realizing losses will exit from the market and eventually, the new equilibrium (shown as E''') will reflect this decrease in supply (from S' to S'') resulting in the same equilibrium of P$_E$ and X$_E$ as in the original equilibrium.

This process of adjustment means that efficiency is produced in the long run under conditions of perfect competition. Microeconomics or price theory or the economics of the firm has as its major focus the allocation of resources to their most preferred and productive uses. Perfect competition, although only a model, creates the conditions and the pressures for this allocation process. Thus, in the long run (when supply fully adjusts to changes in demand) efficiency is attained. At the beginning of this chapter, there is reference to efficiency. At equilibrium, in the long run, P = minimum average cost, P = MR and P = MC. Each firm operates at this level of output, each firm is a price-taker (the market dictates the price), which means there is no rent seeking or other distortions of the market efficiency. With P = minimum average cost, the firm has zero economic profits with just the return on investment that it could receive elsewhere at a similar level of risk. This means we, as consumers, pay the minimum price (considering the firm's opportunity or implicit costs) to maintain the firm producing the goods and services that we desire with P = MC; the consumer pays a price exactly equal to the extra cost incurred by the firm.

The supply curve for the firm is more elastic in the long run (LR) than in the short run (SR). The basis for this is that the firm has more possibilities for substituting among input choices, i.e., labor substituting for capital and vice versa, the longer the time period.

Summary

The perfectly competitive market is characterized by a large number of sellers, availability of perfect substitutes, perfectly elastic demand function, price-takers, no barriers to entry or exit, efficiency, normal (zero) economic profits, and pricing at marginal cost and at minimum average cost in the long run.

The major criterion for determining the optimal (best) output for the firm operating under perfect competition, in the short run, is to produce that level of output at which MR = MC. The specific criteria and steps to determine the best output are:

1. The firm will produce, in the short run, as long as price is greater than or equal to average variable cost (AVC). If price is less than AVC, the firm should shut down and take as losses its total fixed costs.
2. The firm (if number 1 is satisfied), will produce up to the level of output at which MR = MC. This will either maximize profits or minimize losses.

The evaluation of perfect competition in the long run would reveal that firms are operating efficiently by utilizing the available technology with zero economic profits, price equal to minimum average cost and price equal to marginal cost (socially efficient pricing). Firms are directed by the market in their pricing (price-takers).

The adjustment of firms from the short run to the long run is accommodated by absence of barriers to entry or exit. The entry of new firms attracted by short run profits and exit of firms discouraged by losses ultimately results in the restoration of market equilibrium with the ensuing results described in the previous paragraph.

Terms

Economic Efficiency   the allocation of resources to most productive and desired uses

Profit Maximizing (loss minimizing) Criterion   the level of output at which marginal revenue (MR) equals marginal cost (MC)

Shut-Down Criteria   in the short run, the firm should shut down when price does not cover average variable cost (AVC)

Formulas

$P < AVC$ firms shut down in the short run

$P = MR$ perfectly competitive firm's demand function

$MR = MC$ profit maximizing criterion

$P = MC$ socially optimal price (under perfect competition in the long run); efficiency

P = minimum average cost in the long run for a perfectly competitive firm

Multiple-Choice Review Questions

1. The individual firm, operating under perfect competition is characterized as:

   A. a price-maker.
   B. one of a few sellers.
   C. a price strategist.
   D. a price-taker.
   E. interdependent.

2. Firms maximizing their profits by producing a level of output at which

   A. MC = AFC.
   B. MC = MR.
   C. P = ATC.
   D. MR = AVC.
   E. P = AVC.

3. In the short run, the shut down price is equal to

   A. minimum point on average total cost.
   B. maximum point on average total cost.
   C. minimum point on average variable cost.

   D. maximum point on average variable cost.
   E. minimum point on marginal cost.

4. The demand curve for the firm operating under perfect competition is

   A. upward sloping to the right.
   B. downward sloping to the right.
   C. perfectly vertical line.
   D. perfectly horizontal function.
   E. concave to origin.

5. Which of the following is not correct for the perfectly competitive firm, in the long run?

   A. price = minimum average cost.
   B. price = marginal revenue.
   C. price = minimum average variable cost.
   D. price = marginal cost.
   E. normal profits.

MULTIPLE-CHOICE REVIEW ANSWERS

1. **A**   2. **B**   3. **C**   4. **D**   5. **C**

Free-Response Review Questions

1. Using the table below (this table was developed progressively in the chapter on costs (Chapter 8, Tables 8.2, a & b)) and assuming that these cost data are for a firm in perfect competition for the short run, determine the best (optimal) output *and* the total amount of profits or losses at that output for *each* of the following prices:

Price	Best Output	Total Profits or Losses
a. $60.00		
b. $130.00		
c. $230.00		

Output	TC	AFC	AVC	ATC	MC
1	$ 500	$400	$100	$500	$100
2	550	200	75	275	50
3	610	133	70	203	60
4	690	100	73	173	80
5	800	80	80	160	110
6	940	67	90	157	140
7	1,120	57	103	160	180
8	1,350	50	119	169	230
9	1,640	44	138	182	290
10	2,000	40	160	200	360

2. Perfect Competition Questions: By Reference to Figure 10.8 and Symbols

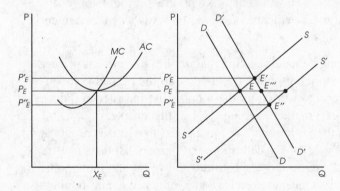

Fig. 10.8

A. What is the effect of the shift of DD to D'D' on:
   1) profits
   2) entry/exit of firms
B. What is the effect of the shift of SS to S'S' on:
   1) profits
   2) entry/exit of firms
C. At LR equilibrium, what is the:
   1) significance of P = minimum AC
   2) significance of P = MC
D. Where would you place (draw on graph) supply curve S″ such that the original equilibrium price, P_E would be restored?

FREE-RESPONSE REVIEW ANSWERS

1. A. Zero output, P < AVC. Total losses = $400
   B. Five. Highest level with MR > MC. Total losses = $150 Q(ATC − P) or 5(160 − 130) = $150.
   C. Eight. Total profits = Q(P − ATC) or 8(230 − 169) = $488 (or $490.00); TR − TC = $1840 − 1350. Differences are due to rounding.

2. A. The shift from DD to D'D' increases profits and encourages entry of new firms.
   B. The shift from SS to S'S' decreases profits or incurs losses for some firms. It would encourage firms to exit.
   C. The significance of P = minimum AC is that there is efficiency, i.e., lowest price consistent with zero economic profits. P = MC is the optimal or socially efficient price.
   D. The supply curve S″ would be drawn in between and parallel to SS and SS′ and intersect point E‴.

CHAPTER
11 Monopoly

Introduction

While it is important to know monopoly in terms of a definition—a market structure where one firm constitutes an industry and where no close substitutes exist for consumers, it is also important to know that a potential monopoly power can be found under oligopoly and monopolistic competition. Thus, firms can acquire power in imperfectly competitive markets if they can consistently price their goods in excess of marginal costs. Indeed, the Lerner Index (P – MC)/P is one method that economists use to ascertain this pricing power (the greater the value of the index, the greater the market power), including its duration and how the ratio compares among firms we distinguish "price-takers" in perfect competition, that is, the market dictates the price to the firms, from the "price-makers" in imperfect competition who are exemplified by monopoly pricing power. Alternatively, economists use the *Herfindahl Index*, the sum of the squares of the market shares of firms in a particular market or industry, to measure the concentrated power or power generated by shares of the market. In turn, these forms of monopoly reflect the characteristics of monopoly as illustrated in Table 9.1 in Chapter 9.

Things to Know

Even though we will examine the major concepts in some detail as we progress through this chapter, the following are important things to know as evidenced on previous Advanced Placement exams:

1. The monopolist faces a downward sloping demand function that implies that price is greater than marginal revenue, which implies a pricing policy (in contrast to the perfect competition) that could actually lead to a lowering of price by the monopolist in order to induce more sales in a relatively elastic (demand) market (see Fig. 11.1 in this chapter).
2. What follows from number 1 above is the notion that the monopolist maximizes profits at the optimal (best) level of output (MC = MR). By definition, the monopolist does control the supply of a product for which there are no close substitutes; however, the monopolist does not control the demand for the product but can exercise some influence on the amounts demanded by lowering or raising the price relative to price elasticity of demand. Also, the consumer can decide not to buy any of the monopolist's products. In other words, the monopolist can charge "what the traffic will bear."
3. Unregulated monopoly (see Figure 11.3) may lead to
    a. higher than competitive prices
    b. lower than competitive prices

      c.   misallocation of resources, inefficiency, and dead-weight loss

      d.   rent seeking

4. Regulated monopoly (Figure 11.3) can lead to

      a.   move toward outputs that are more efficient (as under competitive markets) through subsidies that rise as output rises.

      b.   "fair" rate of return (as would prevail under competitive markets); P = ATC

      c.   a socially optimal price and output; P = MC, which would require subsidies

5. It is important to know how to distinguish the various forms of monopoly regulated and unregulated, on a graph (see Figure 11.3), particularly in reference to the Basic Concepts listed here.

6. It is important to know the characteristics of monopoly. You may make reference to these characteristics in Chapter 9 on the introduction to product markets. The rest of this chapter on monopoly is primarily devoted to the development of these characteristics and their significance.

The Nature of Monopoly and Its Types

Monopoly can be identified by its definition and, more importantly, by its power. By definition, a monopoly is both an industry and a firm; that is, a single firm sells a product for which there are no close substitutes. Thus, the firm *is* the industry (product market). This definition is significant in theory and also in practice as one end of the market structure spectrum. As we know the perfectly competitive firm as the most competitive market structure, we know monopoly as the other end of the market structure spectrum (as indicated in Chapter 9 on the introduction of product markets) or as the very antithesis of a competitive market structure. In policy settings, such as antitrust cases, we know that a potential merger between two large firms could move the industry to be "less competitive" or to have a "tendency toward monopoly" with perfect competition and monopoly serving as "bookends" of market structure. A purely structural approach to antitrust policy would suggest that the above-cited merger be prevented. More importantly, monopoly can exert itself as a pricing power and/or as a determinant of output restrictions. This monopoly power need not exist only in definitional monopoly, i.e., monopoly pricing power can and does take place in other imperfectly competitive structures such as oligopoly and monopolistic competition. Two forms of monopoly power, pricing and market share, are measured in the Lerner Index and the Herfindahl Index, respectively, as identified at the beginning of this chapter. We discuss this pricing power more extensively in the following chapter.

    The demand curve facing the monopolist is downward sloping to the right implying that P > MR and a pricing strategy ensues. The monopolist determines price and output (optimal or best) at the intersection of MR and MC.

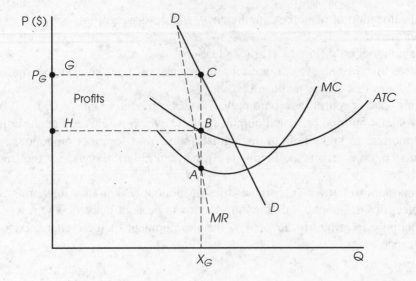

* One firm constitutes the market

Fig. 11.1 Firm/Market*

If a vertical line is drawn at the intersection of MR and MC (point A) and extended up to the demand function (point C) and then horizontally to the vertical or price axis (point G), we find the price to be P_G and if a line is dropped perpendicular from A to the horizontal axis we find the optimal output to be X_G. Profits are maximized at P_G, X_G and are measured as the rectangular area, HGCB (P-ATC)Q. The per unit profit at the optimal output of X_G is C-B or the per unit price minus the per unit cost. Total profits would be price per unit minus average total cost times the number of units of output.

In contrast to perfect competition, the monopolist is likely to realize economic profits and be able to set a price where MC = MR and P > MC, the latter being symptomatic of monopoly pricing power. Also, output is restricted as compared to perfect competition. The price is higher and the output is lower than the competitive counterpart leading to a misallocation of resources; the monopolist extracts a profit and restricts output that leads to a reduction of consumer surplus. Consumers receive fewer goods at higher prices and the monopolist receives a rent; he receives more than he contributes to production at the margin of the effort of the monopolist. Part of the reduction of consumer surplus accrues not to the monopolist as profits but the other part of the reduction accrues to no one or to a *dead-weight loss*, which is another form of resource misallocation in which resources could have been utilized to produce goods and services and are, instead, totally wasted. We measure this loss in terms of the loss of those goods and services that could have been produced. All of this is illustrated below. This graph assumes, for simplicity, that for the relevant range of costs, MC = AC.

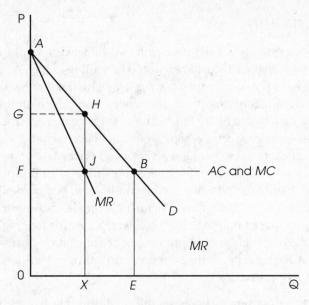

Fig. 11.2 Dead Weight Loss

In the graph above:

1. The original consumer surplus is ABF (formed by the amount of total utility area under the demand curve up to the amount of output consumed, OE, at price OF). This would occur in competitive markets.

2. Enter the monopolist who seeks economic profits. The monopolist will maximize profits with the optimal or best output. This level of output (OX) occurs at MC = MR (J). The line XH connects the intersection of MC and MR (J) with X, and H of this line XH is perpendicular to the horizontal axis at X (output OX) and connects with the demand function at H. Drawing a horizontal line from H to the vertical axis identifies OG as the monopolist's price. Therefore, the profit area is FGHJ, which is taken from the consumer surplus, leaving triangle JHB as an area that represents a further reduction in the consumer surplus but accrues to no one, not even the monopolist. Thus, the triangle JHB is a dead-weight loss representing neither a transfer to the monopolist from the consumer or a gain for society. It does represent resources that could have increased profits or that could have produced additional goods and services. There is an efficiency loss and a misallocation of resources.

3. Adverse effects of monopolists. As discussed earlier, the contrast can be made between perfect competition and monopoly with use of this same graph, namely:

	Perfect Competition	Monopoly
Price	Lower (OF)	Higher (OG)
Output	Higher (OE)	Lower (OX)

and the dead-weight loss to society of monopoly.

4. Thus, monopolies are likely to show some inefficiency relative to the efficient model of perfect competition.

Price Discrimination

If a monopoly or any imperfectly competitive firm had its way, it would charge each customer exactly the maximum price that each customer would be willing to pay. As a practical matter, this would be very difficult or impossible to do since the firm would not know the maximum price for each customer (the costs of identifying these differences would be high relative to any information revealed) and the policy would likely fall victim to some customers discovering they had paid more than others for the same product. Perhaps, you should not ask other passengers on an airline what they paid for their tickets unless you got a very good price.

Since the above suggests perfect price discrimination with perfect information about each consumer, we can still find many examples of price discrimination. For example, movie theaters may charge less for an afternoon (matinee) movie than for a movie in a more popular time such as evening or night. Senior citizens may be charged lower prices for lodging, museum attendance, and transportation. Some discounts simply promote better allocation of scarce commodities such as space on highways at commuter rush times or one's time. Price discrimination works best if the following conditions are operative:

1. Separate markets for consumers based on different price elasticities of demand. This really means that customers with higher price elasticities of demand have more choices of substitute products. Customers with lower price elasticities have less sensitivity to price of a particular product since they have fewer substitute choices.
2. There must not be opportunities for the resale of the product.
3. The price differences are not based on cost differences.
4. The firm is a price-maker—it has a pricing strategy that looks to charge a higher price and realize more profits.

QUICK CHECK QUESTION

Suppose that a private university has six colleges in the areas of liberal arts, veterinary medicine, business, education, law, and music. Also suppose that the college of veterinary medicine is one of only 16 in the entire United States and that the college of business competes with only three other business schools for its students. The liberal arts college competes with 1,000 other colleges in its standing in the nation. The college of music is ranked among the top three music schools. The colleges of education, law, and liberal arts are consistently undersubscribed, while the colleges of business, veterinary medicine, and music are consistently oversubscribed with many highly qualified students rejected.

What might you suggest as a pricing (tuition) policy for these six schools of the university. Explain. Is there any other additional information that you may wish to know? Why?

Answer: See Free-Response Review Answer, page 126.

Types of Monopolies and Their Potential Regulation

1. Natural monopoly
2. Unregulated monopoly
3. Regulated monopolies
   a. "fair" rate of return
   b. optimal pricing
   c. subsidized

NATURAL MONOPOLY

The original theory was that certain industries could best operate as monopolies, since to require or allow competition would negate the major economies of scale inherent in the nature (hence, natural) of these industries. For example, the electrical industry requires massive generating plants and a complex network of transmitting and distributing electrical energy. Therefore, smaller competitive firms would be less efficient and more costly. There would be unnecessary duplication of terminal facilities, electrical lines causing inefficiency. The traditional public policy for these natural monopolies was to create a power authority and/or a public service commission in each state that would approve the creation of a monopoly to an electrical generating private company for a particular region or city, but the company would yield the right to price its services without public utility commission approval. Recently, states have been experimenting with deregulation of the electric industry with respect to the generating function. The transmission and distribution functions would remain under control of a power or public authority.

REGULATED MONOPOLY

In Figure 11.3 below, the traditional regulation of a natural monopoly would be to allow prices that offer a "fair rate of return," which would allow a price of P_B (at the intersection of average cost with demand at point B). This price would be approximately the price of the perfectly competitive firm; it would "cover" average costs, including implicit costs that represent what would have been earned elsewhere with the same resources; so, the notion of a "fair return" follows. The utility firm needs to get a return on its investment at least equal to what investors could receive elsewhere at the same level of risk.

You will observe that as a result of this regulation, the price of P_B is lower than that of unregulated monopolist (P_A) but higher than that of a competitive firm (P_C). The output of the regulated monopolist (X_B) is less than that of the competitive firm (X_C) but greater than that of the unregulated monopolist (X_A). Thus, the regulation of the natural monopoly increases output and reduces price. However, in practice, the costs of the regulated electric utility were higher than expected with all sorts of inefficiencies present leading to calls for deregulation of the electrical generation function.

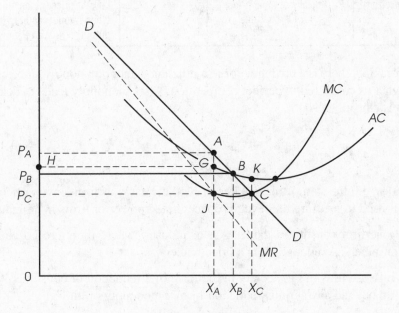

Fig. 11.3 Monopoly

UNREGULATED MONOPOLY

Again with reference to the same graph (Figure 11.3), we can see the different price and output effects of the unregulated monopolist. This monopolist is a profit maximizer. A profit maximizer prices and determines output at the level of output where MC = MR. This produces a price of P_A (higher than the competitive price of P_C) and an output of X_A, which is lower than that of the perfect competitor X_C. The profits of the monopolist are $HP_A AG$. Note then, the "fair return" price of P_B has zero economic profits.

OTHER REGULATED MONOPOLIES

Another possibility, at least in theory, would be to price at C (P_C), which is the price that is equal to MC. This would be the socially optimal price. When P = MC, as it does under perfect competition, the producer is having the extra cost incurred in producing one more unit "valued" at that cost by the consumer who is able to "coax" this extra unit from the producer or supplier. This represents efficiency at the margin of providing an additional unit of a good. Indeed, in antitrust cases, the question is often asked about the ability of the firm to consistently price goods *above* MC as an indication of monopoly power. However, if a producer sold goods at P_D with an output of X_C, the firm would incur a loss of (K-C) per unit of production times OX_C units of output. Since no profit-seeking firm would price at this level of losses, the government could provide subsidies for increasing units of output until the desired level of output (X_C) was attained. In summary:

TABLE 11.1

Type	Price	Quantity	Comment
Unregulated Monopoly	P_A (Profit Max. Prices)	X_A	Price highest output, lowest economic profits
Regulation of Natural Monopoly	P_B (Pricing for "fair return")	X_B Unregulated	Lower prices than monopolist. Higher output than unregulated monopolist. More efficient
Regulation (subsidized)	P_C (Socially optimal price)	X_C	Lowest price, highest output of three types. Would require subsidy to move output to X_C with P_C.

Generally speaking, there is a tendency for less efficiency under monopoly since output is lower and price is higher as compared to perfect competition. Also, monopoly leads to dead-weight loss and resource misallocation.

Terms

Herfindahl Index   the sum of the squares of market shares of firms in a particular market or industry. This is used to measure the level of concentrated power of firms in an industry

Monopoly   one firm constitutes the market or industry where there are no close substitutes available for consumers. A monopolist is a price maker

Dead-Weight Loss   the loss to society in the form of a reduction of consumer surplus from a competitive norm beyond any surplus reduction from a monopoly profit

Price-Discrimination   This practice charges different customers with different prices for the same product

Natural Monopolies these are monopolies for which competition would prevent the benefits of economies of scale

Formulas

MR = MC, profit maximizing level of output

Lerner Index = (P − MC)/P

Regulated Monopolies (pricing at):
    a. Fair Rate of Return:

        Price = average cost (at intersection of demand curve and average cost curve)

    b. Socially optimal price:

        Price = marginal cost (at the intersection of demand curve and marginal cost curve)

Multiple-Choice Review Questions

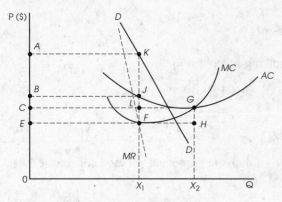

One firm constitutes the market

Fig. 11.4

For Fig. 11.4, answer Questions 1 and 2.

1. The total profits for this monopolist are identified by

    A. CEFL.
    B. ABJK.
    C. BCLF.
    D. CEHG.
    E. BEFJ.

2. The total costs for the monopolist are identified by

    A. CEFL.
    B. CEHG.
    C. ABJK.
    D. EOX_1F.
    E. BOX_1J.

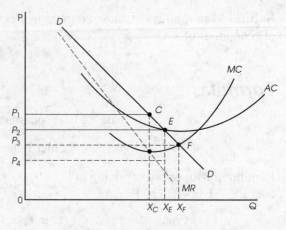

Fig. 11.5

For Fig. 11.5, answer Questions 3, 4, and 5.

3. The socially optimal price would be

    A. P_3.
    B. P_2.
    C. P_1.
    D. P_4.
    E. None of the above.

4. The unregulated monopolist's price would be

    A. P_3.
    B. P_2.
    C. P_1.
    D. P_4.
    E. None of the above.

5. The "fair return" price of the regulated monopolist would be

    A. P_3.
    B. P_2.
    C. P_1.
    D. P_4.
    E. None of the above.

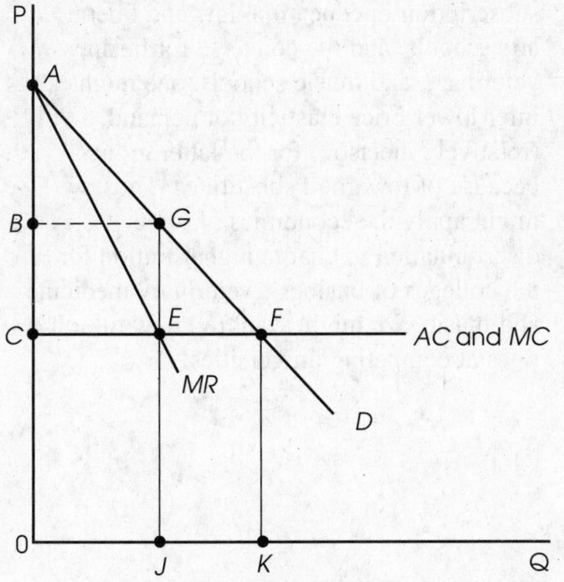

Fig. 11.6

For Fig. 11.6, answer questions 6, 7, and 8.

6. The original consumer surplus is

    A. ABG.
    B. ACF.
    C. BCEF.
    D. COKF.
    E. GEF.

7. After the monopolist enters, the consumer surplus is

    A. ABG.
    B. ACF.
    C. BCEG.
    D. COKF.
    E. GEF.

8. The dead-weight loss is

    A. ABG.
    B. ACF.
    C. BCEG.
    D. COKF.
    E. GEF.

MULTIPLE-CHOICE REVIEW ANSWERS

1. **B**	3. **A**	5. **B**	7. **A**
2. **D**	4. **C**	6. **B**	8. **E**

Free-Response Review Question

The free response question for this chapter is found inside the chapter. The question is based on price discrimination, page 120.

FREE-RESPONSE REVIEW ANSWER

Because of the greater number of choices for students and the consequent under subscription in education, law and liberal arts schools, and the converse for business, veterinary, and music schools, one might infer lower price elasticity of demand, (relatively inelastic) for the latter group because of few good substitutes. Thus, we might apply the economics of price discrimination to charge higher tuition for the colleges of business, veterinary medicine and music. We might want to know tuition rates at competing universities.

CHAPTER
12 Imperfect Competition: Monopolistic Competition, Oligopoly

Introduction

In the two previous chapters, we have reviewed "the bookends" of market structure: perfect competition and monopoly. Even though we have identified different forms of monopoly, monopoly is most importantly characterized for its monopoly pricing power (its sustainability of maintaining price over marginal cost) and its inefficiency compared to perfect competition. That is, the monopolist charges a higher price and restricts output to maximize profits as compared to the perfect competitor. Also, these restrictive actions of the monopolist as "price-maker" result in a "deadweight" loss to society. The monopolist is the prototype of a rent seeker causing misallocation of resources away from more productive uses. Monopoly is the very antithesis of perfect competition. You are advised to refer to the comparative characteristics of different market structures in Chapter 9 on market structures. Perfect competition provides a theoretical model. Firms and industries become more or less competitive as their behavior approaches or departs from the competitive model. Perfect competition sets the standard for efficiency. Thus, oligopolies and monopolistic competitors are inefficient since they are imperfect competitors. Monopolistic competition develops or fosters excess capacity in which there is underutilization of resources or inefficiency. Oligopolies, collusive and noncollusive, tend to set prices in such a way that P > MC, which is the standard identification and measure of monopoly pricing and rent seeking.

This chapter on monopolistic competition and oligopoly provides more real-world models and examples in between the "bookends" of perfect competition and monopoly. There are many more monopolistic competitors than there are oligopolies but oligopolies represent the most dominant industries in terms of market share, assets and control over prices, outputs, and allocation of resources. They are the best examples of "price-makers" and "rent seekers."

THINGS TO KNOW
Based on the most frequently asked questions on previous Advanced Placement exams, the following are the most important concepts. In the balance of this chapter, we will expand on these and other concepts and examples.

1. In the long run, monopolistic competition will be inefficient mainly due to excess capacity.

2. There is a long run tendency under monopolistic competition for zero economic profits. However, zero economic profits do not imply the efficiency of perfect competition (long run). The monopolistic competitor has zero economic profits when average total cost (ATC) equals price at the profit maximizing level of output but not at minimum average total cost, implying the inefficiency due to excess capacity as identified in number one above.

3. Inefficiency (allocative inefficiency) of monopolistic competition is also identified by price > marginal cost (P > MC). Unlike perfect competition, there is a tendency to price goods and services at a higher level than the costs to produce additional units.

4. Monopolistic competition is also inefficient compared to perfect competition since the monopolistically competitive firm restricts output level in order to maximize profits. In other words, optimal output is at the level at which MR = MC, which results in a higher price and less output as compared to perfect competition in the long run.

5. While the barriers to entry in the industry are not as formidable under monopolistic competition as under oligopoly, barriers to entry become a device for some monopolistic competitors to earn economic profits in the long run. Remember, as in number 2 above, there is a tendency for profits to be zero in the long run.

6. Monopolistic competition is characterized by non-price competition (advertising, unique products, warranties, coupons, appeal to brand or store name, etc.), differentiated products, innovation, large number of buyers and sellers, few barriers to entry and exit.

7. The profit-maximizing output and price for a firm under monopolistic competition is that level at which MR = MC. Also, unique to monopolistic competition is the long run tendency for zero economic profits but with the ATC curve tangent to the demand function at the level of output at which MR = MC. However, ATC is higher than the minimum average cost (see Figure 12.2).

8. Under oligopoly, there is more likely to be *interdependence* of the firms as contrasted to the price-takers of perfectly competitive markets and the price-makers of monopoly power. This, at least, holds for the noncollusive model of oligopoly. It maintains itself by rivals matching decreases in prices but not matching price increases. Even the collusive oligopolists are somewhat constrained in price-making by the interdependence of the market.

9. Oligopolists, like other imperfect competitors, may charge higher prices than needed to maximize profits. This is often reflected in monopoly pricing power or pricing where P > MC.

10. When merger activity increases, the structure, behavior (conduct), and performance of oligopolists comes into play on policy decisions. Refer to Chapter 11 on monopoly for pricing power and rent seeking.

11. Oligopolists can be noncollusive (see kinked demand curve, Figure 12.3c) and collusive. In both models, an action of one rival is interdependent on the action of other rivals.

Monopolistic Competition

There are many sellers and buyers under monopolistic competition; thus, it is difficult for any firms to emerge as price-makers or to seek rents. In order for a firm to gain an advantage in a market, it is often necessary to innovate or otherwise find a niche in the market. In other words, if a monopolistic competitor is able to distinguish its products or services from rivals, the firm will be successful. Most of any success for monopolistic competitors derives from non-price competition, such as brand name, store name, shoppers' cards, rewards for frequent customers, special amenities in lodging, etc. Wegman's Food Markets, a large and highly successful chain of stores in upstate New York is known for its ability to attract customers on the basis of its varied and attractive displays of food and merchandise. The customers are not interested only in prices but almost everything else. Since the barriers to entry are relatively weak, rivals must continuously innovate to survive. There are many other fine supermarkets in upstate New York including Tops, P&C, Price Chopper, A&P, and others. There is a highly competitive atmosphere with customers quite sensitive to prices since there are many good substitutes available and a relative easy of entry into the industry. Thus, each of these fine competitors has to find ways to distract the customers from prices and attract them to specialty features such as in-store brands of high quality, in-store bakeries, bulk food, etc.

These firms have downward sloping demand curves and they are characterized, as in monopolies, by price > marginal revenue and price > marginal cost.

SHORT RUN

In the short run, there are dynamic shifts in demand in an intense competitive environment. Thus, we can expect that some firms will realize profits as demand for their products increases, sometimes at the expense of rival firms, some of which will incur losses even to the extent of leaving the industry. Thus, in the short run, we can illustrate both situations with the following graphs:

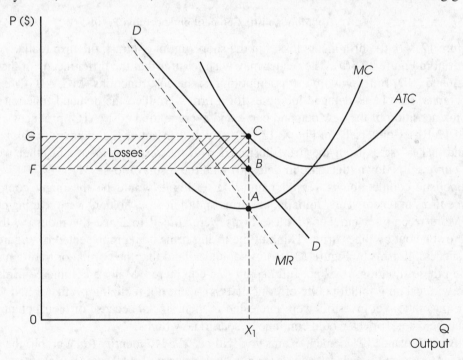

Fig. 12.1(a) Monopolistic Competition Short Run Losses

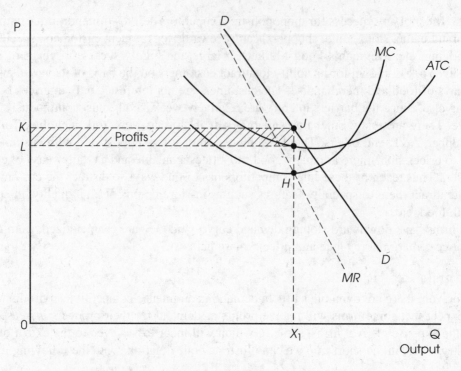

Fig. 12.1(b) Monopolistic Competition Short Run Profits

In Figure 12.1(a), the firm incurs losses in the short run; in contrast, the firm realizes profits in the short run in Figure 12.1(b). The reader may wish to infer that the difference is in the location of the demand (DD) function with the assumption that the cost functions (MC, ATC) are identical in both graphs. That is, as demand increases for a firm's product, the demand function shifts so that the juxtaposition of the new demand curve and average total cost (ATC) produces a profit as in Figure 12.1(b). Conversely, in Figure 12.1(a), a rival firm enters the industry (weak barriers to entry) and "takes" sales from the firm illustrated with the result of losses, in other words, the demand curve shifts down (decrease in demand) with the result of losses.

Monopolistic competition is very dynamic. An example would be the many competing e-commerce firms in recent years. Initially, the firms and their stockholders were reaping enormous profits. More recently, a number of these firms were forced to leave the industry; they were simply crowded out by other firms. Think of the losing firms being represented by Figure 12.1(a) and the successful firms by Figure 12.1(b). Also, understand that the normal or traditional way of illustrating these situations does not fully apply to e-commerce. Many e-commerce firms, except for those with exciting initial public offerings (IPSs), were not realizing profits or had very high price/earnings ratio, yet investors were interested in their stocks because of their potential or the sense that their stock prices would continue to soar to new highs.

Usually, on Advanced Placement exams you will be asked to identify (on a graph) the presence of profits or losses and which rectangular area is the measure of total losses or profits at the optimal (best) output level. The best output level is that output at which MR = MC. Thus, in Figure 12.1(a), there are losses at the best output, OX_1, or the output at which total losses are minimized in the short run. The total losses rectangular is identified on the graph as GCBF. The distance, CB, is the measure of the per unit loss at OX_1 or C-B. The per unit loss times the number of units of output, OX_2, yields the total loss rectangle. In Figure 12.1(b), there are profits at the best output, OX_1 (the ATC curve is below the demand function at the level of output, OX_1), which is the output level at which MR = MC. This is the output that would maximize total profits. It is measured by the rectangle KJIL. The best output and its price, OL, are located by first finding the intersection of MR and MC, which is identified on Figure 12.1(b) as "H". From H, a line is drawn perpendicular to the horizontal axis at OX_1 (best output). From H, also, a vertical line is drawn to the intersection of the ATC curve (I) and to the intersection of the demand function at J. Drawing a horizontal line from J to the vertical axis identifies the price (OK) as the price at best output. The related per unit cost is OL (distance between J and I). Thus, the reader needs to know that MR = MC is the level of best or optimal output and how to identify losses or profits at that level of output.

LONG RUN EQUILIBRIUM—MONOPOLISTIC COMPETITION

Since the nature of monopolistic competition is one of constant change, it is quite difficult to attain the status of long run equilibrium in practice, if not also in theory. However, a long run tendency emerges that allows us some ability to have a standard against which we can compare and contrast monopolistic competition with other forms of market structure, particularly perfect competition, which is definable in theory. We can then say that there is some inefficiency in monopolistic competition when compared to efficiency in perfect competition. This comparison has many applications in practice, such as, antitrust, market concentration, and innovation versus barriers to entry, etc.

There is a long run tendency for monopolistic competition to produce at zero or normal economic profits but not at minimum average total cost. This is an indication of some inefficiency in monopolistic competition as compared to perfect competition where long run equilibrium is at the efficient level—price equals minimum average total cost. The basic difference is that producing at less than minimum average total cost reveals inefficiency mainly in the form of excess capacity or underutilization of resources. One might visualize four gasoline stations on the four corners of a busy highway, an intersection. The total demand, on average, for gasoline is considerably less than the available supply; therefore, each station is not able to utilize all of its pump capacity. Each station does not sell enough gasoline to spread its high fixed costs over the gallons of gasoline sold, so the stations quickly exhaust any economies of scale and do not reach minimum average total costs. This is a classic case of underutilization or excess capacity. Suppose that two gasoline stations would have the right capacity to handle the demand. They could then spend the fixed costs over a greater number of gasoline and achieve some efficiency. With easy entry, there tend to be too many competitors given a certain demand. This is illustrated in Figure 12.2 below.

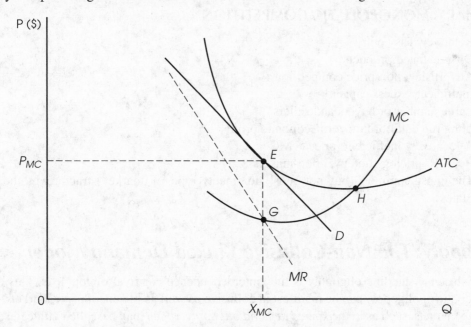

Fig. 12.2 Monopolistic Competition* Long Run Tendency
*Long run *tendency* to zero economic profits

In this graph, the best or optimal output is at OX_{mc} where MR = MC. Economic profits are zero or normal since the point of tangency of ATC and the demand curve (D) at E coincides with the level of best output (MR = MC). However, this point of tangency is higher on the demand curve than the minimum level of ATC at H. Therefore, the monopolistic competition is not achieving efficiency. The comparable point of efficiency for a perfect competitor would be at H with a higher output and a lower price. Also, observe that P > MC and P > MR. These are indications that there is some monopoly pricing power (P > MC) and some pricing strategy or policy (P > MR). To summarize the differences between monopolistic competition and perfect competition, review the table below.

TABLE 12.1
LONG RUN EQUILIBRIUM

	Pure Competition	**Monopolistic Competition**
Profits (Economic)	Zero Price = Minimum ATC	Zero Price = ATC (*not* at minimum)
Efficiency/Inefficiency	Efficient = Market prices weed out the inefficient firms	Inefficient (excess capacity, underutilization of capacity)
Product Differentiation	None. Products are homogeneous (identical in each product market)	Differentiation is necessary for survival.
Price/Non-Price Competition	*Only price* competition. Firms are "price-takers."	Non-price competition is common.
P and MC	P = MC (socially optimal) efficient allocation of resources. Price (consumers) = MC (produces at extra cost)	P > MC. Allocatively inefficient. Consumer pays more than extra cost of production.
P and MR	P = MR. No pricing strategy. All firms take prices from the market.	P > MR. Pricing strategy. Some extent of price making.

SUMMARY: MONOPOLISTIC COMPETITION

1. Relatively easy entry
2. Differentiated products
3. Advertising, non-price competition
4. Inefficient, excess capacity
5. Large number of buyers and sellers
6. Long run equilibrium: zero economic profits
7. Allocatively inefficient: price > MC
8. P > MR: pricing strategy, price-makers
9. The most common (but not most dominant) type of market structure in the United States)

Oligopoly: The Non-Collusive Kinked Demand Model

The key to understanding oligopoly is the "interdependence" of rival oligopolists. This defining characteristic of oligopoly can be manifest in collusive as well as in noncollusive markets. In non-collusive markets, such as in the *kinked demand oligopoly*, rivals may base their strategies, in part, on the anticipated reactions of other firms. For example, one firm may want to raise its prices in order to increase profits. However, if a second firm is expected to lower its prices to undercut the sales of the first firm, then the first firm may not raise its prices in the first place. The second firm may employ a similar strategy depending on the anticipated reactions of the first firm. This non-collusive interdependence may actually lead to lower prices or, at least, no increases in prices. It may be apparent to the reader that the firms would want to have an understanding that both firms would increase prices to maximize their profits. However, one firm could cheat on the agreement and corner more profits for itself. The firms could have a "price war" in which there would be the possibility of both firms being worse off, even to the extent of substantial losses. However, if one firm raises its prices, the rival firm may not match the price increase so that it could capture market share from the other firm. Thus, it is assumed for noncollusive oligopolists that, often, rivals will follow (match) price decreases by a firm but not follow (match) price increases. The kinked demand curve illustrates both the concept of interdependence and the notion of following price decreases and not following price increases of a rival.

The kinked demand curve takes on the following assumptions or conditions:

1. There are no collusive activities among the rival oligopolists.
2. There is no price leader.
3. There are relatively equal market shares among the rival oligopolists.

These are not mutually exclusive conditions. They are stated individually here to emphasize their simplifying nature and to capture the essence of interdependence. As we later critique the kinked demand curve, we will introduce more reality into the model of oligopoly; we will then arrive at the collusive model or the "wannabe a monopolist" oligopolists.

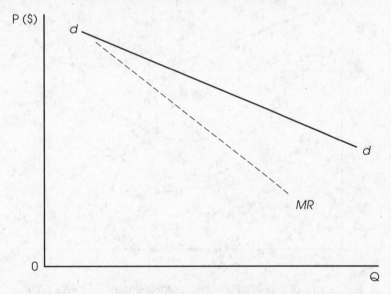

**Fig. 12.3(a) Rivals Following Price Changes of Oligopolist (*dd*) Oligopoly—
Formation of Kinked Demand Curve**

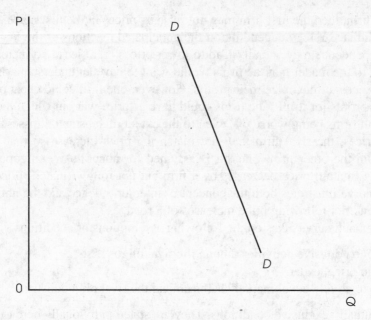

Fig. 12.3(b) Rivals *Not* Following Price Changes of Oligopolist (*DD*) Oligopoly—Formation of Kinked Demand Curve

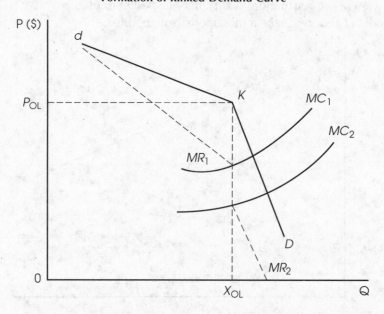

Fig. 12.3(c) Oligopoly—Formation of Kinked Demand Curve (*dD*)

To develop the kinked demand curve model of oligopoly, we will first construct two demand curves faced by the oligopolist. One possible demand curve will be that of rivals following the price changes of the oligopolist, whether it is a price increase or a price decrease (dd function on Figure 12.3(a)). The other demand curve will be that of rivals not following the price changes of an oligopolist, whether it is price increase or a price decrease (DD function on Figure 12.33(b)). The final kinked demand curve will have segments of both the dd and DD curves. The intersection of the two curves at the kink (K on Figure 12.3(c)) marks the point of discontinuity in the final demand curve. That is, the demand curve of kinked oligopoly is illustrated in Figure 12.3(c) as dD. The Dk segment of the dD demand curve is derived from the dd demand curve that the oligopolist faces when rivals follow price changes. The KD segment is derived from the DD demand curve that the oligopolist faces when rivals do *not* follow price changes. Thus, these two segments represent the relevant portions of the two demand curves.

The price that occurs at the kink (K) is P_{ol}. The kink is formed at the intersection of curves dd and DD. So, if rivals follow a price decrease, the relevant demand curve *below* price P_{ol} is DD. If rivals do not follow a price increase *above* price P_{ol}, the relevant demand curve is dd.

The significance of the kink is that rivals are more likely to follow price decreases and *not* follow price increases. Intuitively, we would expect the rivals to follow price decreases in order to maintain or increase market share. Conversely, we would not expect rivals to follow price increases since they would want to exploit the possibility that the oligopolist who raises prices would *lose* market shares to the benefit of rivals who did not raise prices. Thus, in such a situation we have the combination of the two demand curves as illustrated in Figure 12.3(c). There you will see the kinked demand curve as dKD. The segment dK is derived from demand curve dd (Figure 12.3(a)) and the segment KD is derived from demand curve DD (Figure 12.3(b)).

Example

As an example, some years ago a major breakfast cereal corporation (oligopolist) decided to lower its prices of leading cereals. Its decision was based in part on the fact that it could locate its price and quantity produced so that MC and MR would be equal anywhere between MC_1 and MC_2 (see Figure 12.3(c)). It might expect some rivals to lower their prices but the oligopolist would not expect rivals to raise their prices if the oligopolist decided to raise its prices. Thus the demand curve dKD becomes relevant if marginal costs of the cereal oligopolist were between MC_1 and MC_2.

Alternatively, we might explore other oligopoly models that might represent reality better than the kinked demand curve. That is, the conditions or assumptions that we stated earlier in this chapter (see page 133) may lack some theoretical or empirical bases. Theoretically, business may be defined as Nobel Prize economist George Stigher described it "as the whole set of activities designed to overcome barriers to profits." The kinked demand curve suggests that prices of oligopolists will remain (without shifts of demand or changes in costs) at the kink without the prospect of price-making that would allow excess profits (above normal or economic profits) or even rents to be paid to the oligopolists. Empirical evidence is to the contrary and economic theory indicates a desire on the part of firms to maximize profits. The following are examples of other models of oligopoly that are evidenced by structure and behavior of oligopolistic markets:

1. Price leadership. We assumed this possibility away for the kinked demand model. If there is a price leader or dominant firm among other oligopolists, the leader can "set" price to maximize profits and the other firms simply price at the same level since they are virtually unable to gain market share by maintaining price. The other firms in the oligopoly market face smaller profits given their lower volume of production.
2. Cooperative noncollusive activities. Here there are tactic understandings about the value of limited advertising, promotion, etc. Much of this is based on the *interdependence* of oligopolists.
3. Collusive oligopolies. These oligopolists may decide that if "you can't beat them competitively, you might join them." That is, rivals may divide markets among themselves according to regional areas (you cover the Northeast; I'll cover the Southwest, etc.), or product specializations. Collusive activities also include agreements to charge the same or higher prices. An airline may enter a contract with an airplane producer if the airplane producer agrees *not* to produce airplanes for other airlines or to charge them higher prices. Many such collusive activities are illegal in the United States. Cartels, such as OPEC—Organization of Petroleum Exporting Countries—may have production limits or price agreements among its members in an effort to set or control prices. These agreements can be maintained most

easily if there are few members and if the cartel controls a major share of the supply of the product. Cartels are clearly price-makers and not price-takers.

SUMMARY: OLIGOPOLY

1. Formidable barriers to entry
2. Differentiated or similar product
3. Interdependence
4. Few firms, controlling major shares of market
5. Allocatively inefficient: price > marginal cost, excess profits
6. Price > marginal revenue indicating pricing strategy and non-price competition
7. Price-makers
8. Collusive activities and cooperative arrangements
9. The dominant type of market structure in U.S. industry
10. The kinked demand curve illustrates how an oligopolist's actions may be influenced by the likely actions of rivals. Also, firms more likely to follow a price decrease but *not* follow a price increase.

Terms

Monopolistic Competition this form of market structure is characterized by many medium-sized firms that need to innovate and differentiate their products in both price and non-price competition

Oligopoly this form of market structure is characterized by relatively few sellers who act interdependently and/or collusively to be price-makers. There are strong barriers to entry and exit

Kinked Demand Curve this curve illustrates the interdependence of rivals under non-collusive oligopoly in which rivals match price decreases but do not match price increases of an oligopolist

Inefficiency this is the expected outcome of monopolistic competition derived from underutilizing capacity

Formulas

MR = MC profit maximizing criteria for monopolistic competition and oligopoly

P > CM relationship between price (P) and marginal cost (MC) for both monopolistic competition and oligopoly

P = average cost tendency for monopolistic competition in the long run

Multiple-Choice Review Questions

1. Which of the following is *not* a characteristic of a kinked demand curve?

   A. A range of marginal costs over which MR = MC.
   B. P < MC.
   C. Interdependence of rivals.
   D. Pricing at the kink.
   E. Demand curve discontinuous at the kink.

2. Which of the following is a characteristic of monopolistic competition?

   A. P > MC.
   B. Efficiency.
   C. Mostly price competition.
   D. P = MR.
   E. Homogenous or similar products.

3. Which of the following is *not* a characteristic of oligopoly?

   A. P = MC.
   B. Price-maker.
   C. Strong barriers to entry.
   D. Few firms.
   E. P > MR.

4. Which of the following is a characteristic of monopolistic competition?

   A. Economically efficient in the long run.
   B. Pricing at minimum ATC in long run.
   C. Excess capacity.
   D. Very few competitors.
   E. Most dominant market structure in United States.

5. Which of the following illustrates the demand curve facing an oligopolist when rival firms follow a price decrease but *not* a price increase?

   A. Perfectly horizontal demand curve.
   B. Highly inelastic demand curve.
   C. Highly elastic demand curve.
   D. A demand curve that is to the average total cost curve.
   E. A demand curve consisting of two discontinuous segments.

MULTIPLE-CHOICE REVIEW ANSWERS

1. **B**   2. **A**   3. **A**   4. **C**   5. **E**

Free-Response Review Question

1. Compare perfect competition to monopolistic competition in terms of efficiency.

FREE-RESPONSE REVIEW ANSWER

1. In the long run under perfect competition, the firm demonstrates efficiency in the following ways:

   A. price is at minimum average cost which means the consumer obtains goods and services at the lowest costs of production. It also means the producer must sell at this low price or not be able to compete with other firms who sell at this market price. This demonstrates efficiency.

   B. Zero economic profits or normal profits. These profits include the implicit costs or that the producer (firm) is being paid the value of its resources if they were employed elsewhere. This is just a minimum payment to the firm to ensure continuing service.

   C. Price is equal to marginal cost. This is the socially optimal price. The consumer is able to coax out one or more units of a good from the producer at exactly the marginal cost of producing that unit.

2. In the long run under monopolistic competition, the firm is inefficient compared to the perfect competitor in the following ways:

   A. Price is at average cost but *not* at minimum average cost. This is an indication of inefficiency resulting from under-utilization of capacity or excess capacity.

   B. P is greater than marginal cost; thus, socially optimal (efficient) pricing (P = MC) is not attained.

CHAPTER
13 Resource Markets with Applications to Labor

Connections Between Product Markets and Resource Markets

There is a symmetry between product markets and resource markets; further, there are direct connections between the two markets. In Chapter 8, Costs, Production, Supply, we discussed total physical product, average physical product, and marginal physical product (TPP, APP, MPP) in addition to their relationship to costs, especially for APP and MPP compared to AC and MC (see Figure 8.1 in Chapter 8 for the symmetry). The product markets and the resource markets are most directly linked by derived demand. For example, the demand for shoemakers (resource/labor market) is derived from the demand for shoes (product/shoe market). This relationship is significant since it ties together (not necessarily in a proportional manner) the elasticity of product markets with that of resource markets. Theoretically, it sets limits on the demand for pay increases by labor. Moreover, income distribution to labor depends on labor's contribution to increases in productivity—increases in marginal physical productivity became the basis for wage or salary increases. Of course, there are many other factors that can distort this basis for income distribution, including imperfect markets, discrimination, changes in product markets (including pay for workers), investment in human capital, etc. These factors will be discussed in this chapter as we apply the basic economic concepts of resource markets to labor.

Much of the material of resource markets is somewhat mechanical if not abstract. That is, the basic concepts can be explained in equations and graphs. The good side of this approach is that the student can condense much of what has to be learned into a few important relationships. The applications seem to flow easily from the knowledge of these basic concepts. For example, many of the questions on resource markets from past Advanced Placement examinations require the knowledge of marginal revenue product (MRP) as equal to marginal physical product times the marginal revenue or price of the product. The firm wants to pay labor no more than it contributes to the value of the product at the margin of adding one more unit of labor. So, if either the productivity of labor (MPP) increases, or the price of any good produced by labor increases, the MRP will increase. If we know that MRP equals the demand for labor, then with the increase of the MPP or the price of the product, the demand curve will shift to the right (an increase). Thus, the basic relationship of the marginal productivity of labor to the price of the good produced is important.

IMPORTANT CONCEPTS

Based on the most frequently asked questions on previous Advanced Placement exams, the following are the most important concepts. In the balance of this chapter, we will expand on these and other concepts and examples.

1. Extending the knowledge of production, costs and supply of Chapter 8, we need to know that marginal revenue product (MRP) of a resource such as labor represents the demand for labor. It is a downward sloping demand curve that tells the firm hiring labor what labor contributes to the revenue of the firm at the margin of each unit of labor (L) added. Thus, $MRP_L = MPP_L \times MR_x$ (or P_x in perfectly competitive product markets), where x = product produced. If product price is constant at all levels of output, we know that it is a perfectly competitive market.

2. Number 1 above tells us what labor contributes to the revenue of the firm; now, we need to know the related cost of labor. Essentially, marginal factor cost (MFC) is the cost of each additional unit of labor hired by the firm. In perfectly competitive labor markets, the price of labor is constant and MFC = price of labor, average cost of labor or the wage rate. $MFC = P_L$, AC_L or W_L.

3. If demand for labor is the marginal revenue productivity (MRP) of labor, and if the cost of hiring additional units of labor is the marginal factor cost (MFC) of labor, then the firm maximizes its profits in the hire of labor by continuing to hire labor as long as MRP > MFC up to the level of hiring at which MRP = MFC. This is the summary of the criterion for profit maximization for the hiring of one resource such as labor.

4. Criterion for profit maximization in the hire of more than one resource:

$$\frac{MRP_L}{MFC_L} = \frac{MRP_K}{MFC_K} \cdots \frac{MRP_N}{MFC_N} = 1$$

   P_L or wage rate can substitute for MFC if there is a perfectly competitive resource market. (L = labor; K = capital; N = number of resources).

5. Criterion for cost minimization (least-cost) for more than one resource:

$$\frac{MPP_L}{MFC_L} = \frac{MPP_K}{MFC_K} \cdots \frac{MPP_N}{MFC_N}$$

   P_L or wage rate can be substituted for MFC if there is a perfectly competitive resource market.

6. Derived demand. The demand for a resource is derived from the demand for the product produced, in part, by the resource. This concept, in turn, assists us in determining the wage elasticity of demand for labor. We will extend this discussion later in this chapter.

7. Government and market imperfections or interference with resource markets. This is about price ceilings and price floors; also, we examine the effects of trade unions and buyers of labor in a single market for labor. By name, these are imperfections in resource markets, including monopsonies that lower wage rates and hire fewer workers than competitive markets.

8. The bases for wage inequality. There are usually a few questions about this on the Advanced Placement exam. The factors responsible include risk (some jobs, such as repair of skyscraper buildings, carry higher levels of risk), attractiveness of job, human capital investment, discrimination, immobility, etc. We will discuss these factors in this chapter.

Additionally, we will discuss "rents," those payments received by workers that are in excess of what they could have earned elsewhere or what would minimally be necessary to attract or maintain workers. When workers receive in pay what they could have earned elsewhere, they are paid the value of the market or transfer earnings.

9. Factors that cause shifts in demand and supply for resources. For example, an increase in wage rates by a firm could attract more workers to that firm.

Derived Demand: Wage Elasticity of Demand

As noted above, the demand for labor (resource) is derived from the demand for the product that labor helped produce. The three laws of derived demand are based on the definition of wage elasticity of demand:

$$\frac{\%\Delta \text{ Quantity Demanded of Labor}}{\%\Delta \text{ wage rate}}$$

where Δ = change in.

The three laws of derived demand are:

1. *The higher the price elasticity of demand for the product, the higher the wage elasticity of demand.* For example, in the 1960s and part of the 1970s, the Big Three of the automobile industry—Ford, Chrysler, and General Motors—produced over 90 percent of the automobiles purchased in the United States. Further, General Motors had the dominant share of the market and clearly was the price leader. Thus, the price inelasticity (few substitutes and similar prices) allowed General Motors to administer prices to allow generous profits. The only real constraint was a change in consumer income. Therefore, the auto industry could afford to pay the union its demands or the industry had an inelastic resource to demands for wage demands. The Big Three could "pass on" much of the increases of wages to consumers who are more affected by their rising incomes than the rising prices of the autos. However, with the increasing competition from automobile companies of Japan, Germany, and other countries starting in the late 1970s and continuing into the twenty-first century, price elasticity of demand increased dramatically (the Big Three could no longer set prices since there were many lower-priced, fuel-efficient cars from overseas). Adding to the competitive intensity, many European and Japanese auto manufacturers began to produce their cars in the United States, hiring American workers and operating within the U.S. tariff area. An accompanying increase in the wage elasticity of demand also took place. The Big Three could no longer pass on union wage demands to the consumers in the form of price tag increases on their products. The history of the modern automobile industry affords us with many applications of the economics of product markets, resource markets, and elasticity.

2. *The higher the proportion of labor costs relative to total costs of production, the higher will be the wage elasticity of demand.* If we compare the higher education industry to the oil refinery industry, we can note the significance of the proportion of labor costs to total costs. In higher education, even with rising use of computer technology, usually 80 to 85 percent of the total budget of a college or university is in the form of salaries and wages, including fringe benefits (an ever-increasing proportion of total labor costs). Indeed, the increase in computer use has required additional labor costs for computer personnel. If we keep in mind the nature of derived demand, a relatively high labor cost would mean that firms would be resistant to a more than moderate pay increase. In the oil refining industry, labor costs are a relatively small proportion of total costs. Thus, even a more than modest pay increase is more likely to be tolerated as contrasted with the higher education industry.

3. *The greater the number of substitute resources available and the degree to which they are substitutable, the higher will be the wage elasticity of demand.* Related to this factor is the time period. We are subsuming the time period into the "greater availability of substitutes." That is, a longer time period typically allows the development of more substitutes, such as robotic or automated machinery. However, at least some resources are complements with other resources, as in the example of capital development of resources often requiring some additional labor to be hired. There is in this general discussion of derived demand the significance of more substitutes leading to more competition that, in turn, is reflected in greater elasticity. There is a symmetry on these linkages between product markets and resource markets; the more a firm can identify resources to substitute for labor, the more resistant (elastic, sensitive) the firm can be to suggestions for wage increases.

The Demand for a Resource (Labor)

The demand for labor is derived from the demand for the product. However, this is not a *per se* demand; firms do not determine the wage rates they are willing to pay only on labor's physical contribution to the final product, such as the marginal physical product (MPP), but also on what this extra product will sell for in the marketplace. Thus, the worker could be very productive or actually increase her marginal products, but if the product price decreases, her effort might not be fully valued in any consideration of a wage increase. (Remember: Marginal Revenue Product, MRP, = Marginal Physical Product, MPP, times Marginal Revenue$_x$ or price$_x$ where x = product). To illustrate the demand for a resource (labor), see Figure 13.1.

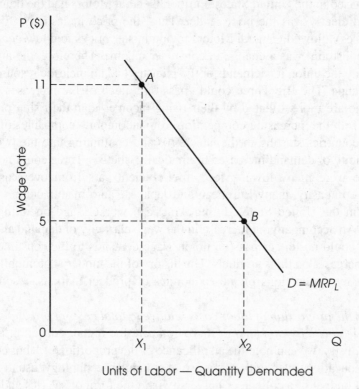

Fig. 13.1 Demand for Labor (Resource)

The demand curve is downward sloping to the right, which demonstrates the inverse relationship between the wage rate and the quantity of labor demanded by the firm. If the wage rate is at $11, the firm is willing to hire X_2 units of labor. At a wage rate of $5, the firm is willing to hire a larger quantity, X_2 units of labor.

The firm's demand schedule is equal to the marginal revenue productivity (MRP) of labor as defined above. Think of this schedule as an indication to the firm of the addition to the firm's revenue with each additional unit of labor employed. Think of the wage rate at the point of deciding to hire one more unit of labor as the marginal factor cost (MFC). Thus, the firm that wants to maximize its profits in the hire of labor will continue to hire labor as long as the marginal revenue product (MRP_L) is greater than the marginal factor cost MFC_L up to the level of hiring at which the $MRP_L = MFC_L$. First, we will look at a perfectly competitive labor market.

PERFECTLY COMPETITIVE LABOR MARKET

In a perfectly competitive labor market, the wage rate is determined in the market where all buyers and sellers of a particular type of labor, such as economists, meet. Each year, the Applied Social Services Association has a placement service in the city where its convention is held. Buyers (universities and other institutions) hold interviews with sellers (economists interested in securing research and teaching positions). While this is not an example of a perfectly competitive market, it does suggest a market or a place where buyers and sellers of a labor service meet. A firm that hires labor in a perfectly competitive labor (resource) market must pay its hired workers the going or market-determined wage rate. The firm is a price-taker as in the symmetrical case of the firm in a perfectly competitive product market. In other words, the firm cannot afford to pay a higher wage rate than the market-determined wage and if the firm wants to pay less, any potential workers would simply move to another employer who pays the market wage rate. This is illustrated below in Figure 13.2.

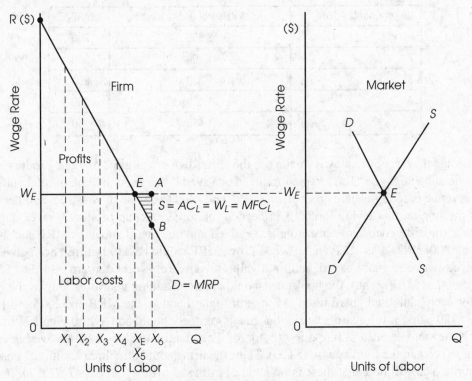

Fig. 13.2 Perfect Competition—Labor (Resource) Market

The hiring employer (firm) must pay the going wage of W_E, that is, the firm is a price (wage)-taker, $A + W_E$. Therefore, $W_E = AC_L = Supply = MFC_L$, where L = labor. Since the wage rate is dictated by the market, it becomes a perfectly horizontal supply (S) function, which means that the average cost of labor (AC_L) or the wage rate equals the marginal factor cost of labor (MFC_L). Regardless of the number of units of labor the firm wants to hire, the wage rate of labor stays the same—at X, X_2, X_3 ... X_6, the wage rate remains at the market given rate of W_E. Thus, the firm will continue to hire workers as long as the marginal revenue product (MRP) for each additional unit is greater than the associated marginal factor cost (MFC). For *each* of X_1, X_2, X_3, X_4, the $MRP_L > MFC_L$. That means with a wage rate of W_E, the firm adds more revenue at the margin of an additional unit of labor than it adds to its cost. This addition of smaller and smaller units of profits continues as long as $MRP_L > MFC_L$. At the level of hiring for which $MRP_L > MFC_L$, (level of X_5, or five units of labor), profits will be maximized in the hire of labor. You will note on Figure 13.2, the total profit triangle of REW_E and the total labor cost rectangle of W_EEX_E0. The total profit is the difference between MRP_L and MFC_L (or wage rate in this perfectly competitive market) for each unit of labor up to the five units hired at equilibrium ($MRP_L = MFC_L$). The cost rectangle is the result of the wage rate (W_E) times the number of units of labor hired (X_E or X_5). Also, observe what happens if the employer wants to hire one additional unit (the X_6 unit) of labor. This would result in a per unit loss of EAB, and this would reduce the total profits by the area of EAB. On Advanced Placement exams, there are often questions based on the above. For example, a bookstore observes that for each additional security guard hired, there is some reduction in the number of books stolen. Using an average retail price of books, the store devised the following schedule. The security guards are paid $120 per day (eight-hour shift times $15 an hour).

TABLE 13.1
SECURITY GUARDS

No. of Guards Added	Total Value of Books Saved	MRP_L
1	$ 800	800
2	1,100	300
3	1,300	200
4	1,400	100
5	1,450	50

A table like the one above may not even use the term MRP or marginal revenue product; instead, the table heading might be "Total Value Produced or Saved." You need to think of total value saved as total revenue or total revenue product, and also, you need to devise or construct another column such as the one on this table (Table 13.1) headed marginal revenue product. For example, you would take the difference between zero guards added and one guard added as MRP and the result would be $800 in row 1 as MRP. In the second row, MRP would be $300 (difference between total value saved with one guard added, and total value saved with a second guard added or $800 and $100 or $300 as MRP). Thus, the bookstore would continue adding guards as long as the $MRP_L > MFC_L$ for each additional guard hired. At the third guard added, the MRP of $200 is still greater than the $120 paid for the guard's work; thus, the bookstore should add a third guard. What would happen if the store decided to hire a fourth guard? The marginal value of $100 saved is *less than* the marginal cost of the fourth guard ($120). Thus, the firm should hire three additional guards, but not a fourth. You will note that there is no level of hiring at $MRP_L = MFC_L$. *This is an important note!* Some of the questions you will get will not have a level of resource (labor) use at which $MRP_L = MFC_L$. Therefore, choose the highest level of labor units at which $MRP_L > MFC_L$. In this particular example, the answer is three guards, which is the highest level of hiring additional guards for which MRP_L ($200) = MFC_L ($120). At the hiring level of a fourth guard, $MRP_L > MFC_L$ or

$120 > $100. The firm saves less than it costs to hire another guard. At the end of this chapter, there is an exercise on MRP_L to complete. Remember, whenever the wage rate or resource price (cost) is constant, there is a perfectly competitive resource (labor) market.

IMPERFECTLY COMPETITIVE LABOR (RESOURCE) MARKET (MONOPSONY)

We may find that some product markets are intensely competitive such as textiles, especially with competition from China. However, the resource or labor market may not be very competitive. Take the example of a U.S. textile company located in a small town with little or no sources of jobs outside the textile mill. The owner of this textile company is a monopsonist or a single buyer of a particular supply of labor, in this case textile workers. Given their skills as experienced textile workers and given no other viable employment opportunities, these workers can "sell" their labor to only one buyer, the textile mill. So, in this case the marginal factor cost (MFC_L) curve will vary from the average cost (AC_L) or supply (S) curve. Each time, the firm wants to hire an additional unit of labor and is forced to pay a higher wage rate to attract labor, $MFC > AC_L$ or wage rate (W_E). The firm would then have to pay the higher wage to all of the existing workers at the same skill level in order to maintain their services. To illustrate this, see Figure 13.3 below.

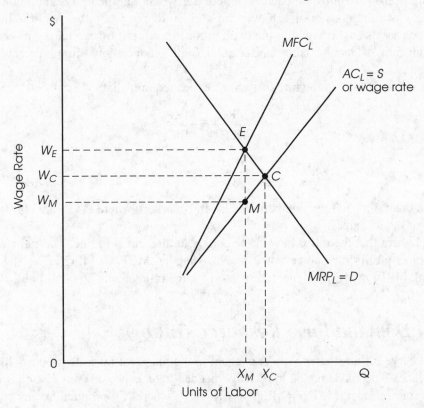

Fig. 13.3 Monopsony

In Figure 13.3, $MFC_L = MRP_L$ at E on the graph. However, we need to drop a line perpendicular to the horizontal axis to find the units of labor (X_M) that would maximize profits. At M this line intersects the supply curve (S) or average cost of labor (AC_L) at M from which we read the wage rate (W_M) that the monopsonist pays. Note that this wage rate, W_M is less than the value of the marginal revenue product at E (only wage rate, W_E, would be equal to MRP at X_M level of employees). Also note that the monopsonist pays a lower wage, W_M, than the competitive labor market. The competitive firm would pay W_C. Also, the monopsonist hires only X_M workers compared to the X_C level of a competitive labor market firm.

COST MINIMIZATION (LEAST COST COMBINATION) AND PROFIT MAXIMIZATION IN THE HIRE OF MORE THAN ONE RESOURCE

1. Cost minimization or least cost combination of resources for a given level of output. The basic concept here is that the firm will find the least cost combination of two resources when the marginal physical product (MPP_L) of one resource, labor, per its marginal factor (MFC_L) is equal to the marginal physical product (MPP_K) of another resource, capital (K) per its marginal factor cost (MFC_K)

$$\frac{MPP_L}{MFC_L} = \frac{MPP_K}{MFC_K}$$

or where P_L and P_K are constant factor costs in perfectly competitive resource markets.

$$\frac{MPP_L}{P_L} = \frac{MPP_K}{P_K}$$

You may find a few questions on this cost minimization on the exam. The important thing to note is that the *ratios* are equal, not necessarily the marginal physical products. In other words, cost minimization is achieved for a given output when the extra product produced by labor per its cost is equal to the extra product produced by capital per its cost. No other combination of inputs, labor and capital, will produce any improvement in resource efficiency.

2. Profit maximization in the hire of two resources requires that

$$\frac{MRP_L}{MFC_L} = \frac{MRP_K}{MFC_K} = 1$$

$$\frac{MRP_L}{P_L} = \frac{MRP_K}{P_K} = 1$$

(when there is a perfectly competitive resource market), where P_L, P_K are constant prices or costs of the resources.

Note here that the ratios have to be equal but also equal to one. The rationale is that to maximize profits for one resource (such as labor), $MRP_L = MFC_L$. The same holds for capital, $MRP_K = MFC_K$. Hence, the reason for the ratios being equal to one.

Shifts in Demand for a Resource (Labor)

The demand curve for a resource (labor) is equal to the marginal revenue product (MRP_L) of the resource of labor. The fundamental knowledge needed here, especially for test questions, is that marginal revenue product (MRP_L) = $MPP_L \times MR_X$ or P_X where X = product. So any condition that causes MPP_L or P_X to *increase* will cause an increase in demand for labor or a shift to the *right* in the demand curve. Conversely, any condition that causes MPP_L or P_X to *decrease* will cause a decrease in demand for labor or a shift to the *left* in the demand curve. For example, workers begin to produce more per hour because of a training program for workers. Even if the price of the product that they produce stays constant, the fact that the workers produce more per hour should increase their attractiveness to employers. If the price or the product the workers produce falls, then we expect, *ceteris paribus*, that the demand for labor will shift to the left or a decrease in demand for labor.

Other factors related to shifts in demand for labor include the number of buyers of the resource, for example, many firms in addition to high-tech firms are now hiring computer-trained personnel for the many computer-assisted tasks of industry. Such an increase in the number of firms demanding computer people would cause the demand curve for labor to shift to the right or an increase in demand for labor. Also the prices and availability of substitutes for labor will be a factor. Will distance learning eventually replace faculties of schools and universities? Some suggest that increases in the minimum wage caused more automated gasoline sales, and movie theaters without ushers. The availability and the technology of substituting capital goods for labor services may be more extensive in the long run than in the short run.

Supply of Resources

We might need to take a look at supply of resources such as labor. Then we will look at factors causing supply curves to shift. The normal upward sloping supply curve is contrasted with the backward bending supply curve in the following illustration.

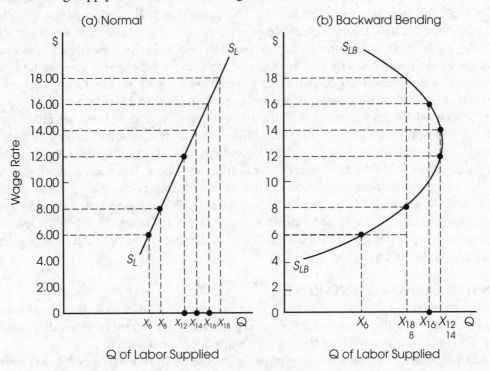

Fig. 13.4 Supply of Labor

In the normal supply curve Figure 13.4(a), the amount of labor willing to be supplied varies directly with the wage rate, in other words, as the wage rate increases from $6 an hour to $8 an hour, the labor supplied increases from X_6 to X_8 on the horizontal axis. The higher the wage rate, the higher the amount of labor supplied on the horizontal axis representing the minimum wage that will be acceptable for each of the amounts of labor indicated on the horizontal axis. **Caution:** "Minimum wage" used in the context has nothing to do with a federal- or state-mandated minimum wage.

In the backward bending supply curve, Figure 13.4(b), the amount of labor willing to be supplied as the wage rate rises varies differently at different wage rate levels. At first, as the wage rate increases from $6 an hour to $8 an hour, the amount of labor supplied increases from X_6 to X_8 on the horizontal axis. However, once the wage rate reaches $12 an hour, there is *no increase* in the labor supplied when the wage rate then rises to $14 an hour; the horizontal axis marking of X_{12} and X_{14} at the same point indicates this constant level of amounts supplied (the curve is relatively vertical between $12 and $14). Further, when the wage rate increases from $14 to $16 and from

$16 to $18, the amounts of labor willing to be supplied *decrease*! This is the "backward bending" portion of the labor supply curve S_{LB}.

All of this suggests that labor supplied curve "a" (normal) might better apply to some labor force participants, and labor supplied curve "b" would better apply to others. This is a *labor-leisure trade-off*. Think of income from supplying labor enabling workers to increase their ability to buy goods and services. However, these workers might also like to have some leisure. Given a finite number of hours in a week (say 60 or 70 hours) in which to exercise an option to forego more consumption of goods and services, any additional hour of leisure (as a commodity) consumed will mean one less hour of work. So, if my wage rate increases from $6 an hour to $8 an hour, it costs me *more* now (at $8) to have an additional hour of leisure than when I was paid $6 an hour.

Intuitively, one would expect me to work the hour since I am now able to buy more goods and services at $8 than when the wage rate was $6. This is the substitution effect (when the "price" of the alternate commodity—leisure increases (opportunity cost), I would be expected to supply more labor). We might think of the normal supply curve as applicable to low-income, discriminated (age, race, gender) workers with low amounts of labor force experience. They cannot "afford" more leisure. This scenario would also seem more likely to apply to young, large families with home mortgages, home equity loans, debts, and even with children in college.

The "backward bending" curve would most likely apply to workers who are older, more experienced, and who have amassed some wealth including a mortgage-free house, perhaps a second home, and maybe, a bumper sticker on a mobile home reading "We are spending our kids' inheritance." These folks are more likely to look differently at the labor-leisure trade-off than the group we described as being applicable to the normal supply curve. These workers can now "afford" more leisure and if they consider leisure (over goods and services) as a superior good, we have the perfect recipe for a changed mix of leisure and work to favor relatively more leisure. This is the income effect that suggests the backward bend of the supply function; this income effect suggests leisure as the superior good.

TRANSFER EARNINGS AND RENTS

Now, we can explain a few additional aspects of the supply of labor including transfer earnings and rents. Also, we will examine an axiom of economics about supply and then discuss shifts in supply. The final section will be on the bases of wage differentials.

The axiom alluded to above fits nicely into a discussion of transfer earnings and rents. The axiom is that we must pay the supplier his or her costs in order to expect the supplier to continue the supply of goods or services and/or to expect continuing or new competition for price discipline. If we pay these costs including the value of what could be earned elsewhere with the same resources, we would be paying a transfer earning (the value of alternative use of the resources of suppliers). We discussed this definition of economic costs/profits in Chapter 8 on costs, production, and supply. The transfer earning is the minimum price we must pay, as consumers, in order to assure a continuing supply of goods and services. Rents are those payments that suppliers receive that are in excess of transfer earnings or are in excess of those suppliers could earn elsewhere. These rents cause a reallocation of resources away from more productive uses of resources. We pay more for our goods and services than we would value in terms of transfer earnings.

Shifts in Supply

The following factors are determinants of shifts in the supply curve of resources. An increase in supply would be a shift to the right of an upward sloping supply curve. A decrease in supply would be a shift to the left of the supply curve. The factors:

1. *Attractiveness of an occupation.* It appears that we get more people interested in business careers, particularly in finance, as we have a boom in the economy and in the stock market. Also, entrepreneurs are encouraged to enter the business world through e-commerce and with venture capitalists opening their coffers. This would be represented by a shift to the right of a resource supply curve.
2. *The number of suppliers.* Computer scientists have a bright future, not only because of the rise in number of high-tech companies but also because of the extended use of computer technology in virtually every small and large-size companies. Thus, we would expect an increase supply of computer scientists.
3. *The relative prices of competing uses of a resource such as labor.* If electrical engineers discover that their services are more valuable as computer scientists than in more conventional electrical uses, the supply of computer scientists will increase (shift to the right) and the supply of electrical engineers will shift to the left (a decrease in supply).

The Bases of Wage Differentials

This is a particularly interesting topic since it relates well to the overall increases in wages in the United States over time, but also it is helpful in any discussion of the widening inequality in income distribution. The treatment in this chapter is a sketch but will outline the important bases of wage differentials. The bases:

1. *Not all jobs/occupations are equally attractive.* Being averse to the sight of blood, I am not about to consider a career in surgery. On the other hand, many would find the occupation of college professor to be uninspiring. Therefore, we may need to pay people in certain professions more than would be ordinarily necessary since there may be an insufficient supply of people into a particular occupation based on its sometimes unattractive nature.
2. *Innate differences.* All of us do not possess the necessary combination of skills, aptitude, and experience for all jobs. Thus, the fact that certain combinations of these traits are necessary for some high-paying jobs leads to wage differentials.
3. *Human capital.* Some workers have higher stocks of human capital (investment in education, job training and experience, health, etc.). Higher investment in human capital for some workers leads to higher returns in income over time.
4. *Compensating wage differentials.* Some workers are paid more than others because of special characteristics of the jobs such as risk. Take the example of two outside window washers. Both of these workers possess the same skills, aptitude, and experience. One worker washes the outside windows of very tall (skyscraper) windows, and the other worker washes the outside windows of one-story buildings. Besides, the obvious inability of the skyscraper washer to "step back and admire" his or her work, there is a considerable difference in risk between the two workers. We would expect this difference to be reflected in a wage differential with the higher-risk job receiving higher pay.
5. *Psychic income.* A college professor with both a Ph.D. and an M.B.A. might choose to be an academic (teaching) economist utilizing the Ph.D. but would receive a lower monetary income than if he or she entered the finance world with an M.B.A. The choice to teach may be based on the higher psychic income (attractive lifestyle) of the teaching career. We might qualify or measure that psychic income by that monetary income difference between the two occupations, for example, the opportunity cost. On balance, one might say that the monetary income and the higher psychic income of the college professor would equal the monetary income of the finance career.

6. *Discrimination*. It is accurate to say that many wage differentials are due to discrimination based on age, gender, sexual orientation, and race. It is beyond the scope of this book to have an extensive discussion of this extremely important topic.

7. *Immobility*. Because of sociological ties to an area, tenure/union seniority, lack of knowledge of job opportunities, and/or financial inability to seek opportunities, wage differential exists. We do not all move to the best jobs.

8. *Labor market imperfections*. Monopsonists (single buyers of labor) pay lower wages than do more competitive labor market employers. Some unions, during certain periods of time, are able to extract rents for their union members.

9. *Government interference*. The imposition of minimum wage laws, licensing requirements, and government wage subsidies can create differentials.

Summary

- Marginal Revenue Product (MRP) of a resource represents the demand for labor and *marginal factor cost* (MFC) of a resource represents the cost of labor.
- The firm maximizes its profits by hiring the number of units of employees at which MRP = MFC.
- The demand for a resource is derived from the demand for a product to which the resource has contributed.
- The three laws of derive demand are: (a) The higher the price elasticity of demand for a product, the higher the wage elasticity of demand; (b) the higher the proportion of labor costs relative to total costs of production, the higher will be the wage elasticity of demand; and (c) the greater the number of substitute resources available and the degree to which they are substitutable, the higher will be the wage elasticity of demand.
- The firm in the perfectly competitive labor (resource) market is a price-taker in terms of wage rate paid by the firm for its workers. The supply (of workers) curve is perfectly horizontal at the competitive market wage rate.
- The supplier of goods or services must be paid his or her costs including the opportunity costs or transfer earnings that could have been earned in alternative use of the supplier's resources.
- The factors that determine the shifts in the supply of labor as a resource include the attractiveness of an occupation, the number of suppliers and the relative prices of competing uses of labor.
- The bases of wage differentials include innate differences of workers, the unequal attractiveness to varying occupations, the amount of invested human capital, compensation for risk, psychic income, discrimination, immobility, labor market imperfections, and government interference.
- The "backward bending" supply curve for labor reflects changing ratios of labor/leisure. As workers reach certain goals of income, wealth, and goods, they begin to value leisure as a superior good and to substitute leisure for work.

Terms

Derived Demand   the demand for a resource such as labor is derived from the product that the resource helps to produce

Wage Elasticity of Demand   the percentage change in quantity demanded of labor in response to a percentage change in a wage rate

Marginal Revenue Product (MRP)   the addition to the firm's revenue as the result of an additional output for an additional unit of labor

Marginal Factor Cost (MFC)   the additional cost for each additional unit of labor hired

Marginal Physical Product (MPP)   the additional output produced as one more unit of labor (resource) is added

Monopsony   a market in which there is a single buyer of labor

Human Capital   the investment in people that increases their future monetary and psychic income

Compensating Wage Differentials   the differences in wages due to higher pay for workers who have higher risks inherent in their work or for other work conditions such as a highly structured job

Formulas

$$\frac{MRP_L}{MFC_L} = \frac{MRP_K}{MFC_K} \cdots \frac{MRP_N}{MFC_N} = 1$$

Profit maximization in the hire of more than one resource.

$$\frac{MPP_L}{MFC_L} = \frac{MPP_K}{MFC_K} \cdots \frac{MPP_N}{MFC_N}$$

Criterion for cost minimization (least-cost) for more than one resource.

$$\frac{\% \Delta \text{ Quantity Demanded of Labor}}{\% \Delta \text{ Wage Rate}}$$

Where Δ = change in wage elasticity of demand.

Multiple-Choice Review Questions

Labor Units	Total Output	MPP	Output* Price	TR	Labor** Price	MRP
1	5	5	10	50	60	
2	20	15	10	200	60	
3	30	10	10	300	60	
4	35	5	10	350	60	
5	35	0	10	350	60	

* Output price constant at $10 indicates a perfectly competitive product market, $P_X = MR_X$ where X = output product.
** Labor price constant at $60 indicates a perfectly competitive labor market, $P_L = W_L = MFC_L$ where L = labor, P = price of labor, W_L = wage rate of labor, and MFC_L = marginal factor cost of labor.

1. With the data in the table above, how many units of labor would the employer hire?

   A. 1
   B. 2
   C. 3
   D. 4
   E. 5

2. The basis for the answer in number 1 is

   A. P or wage rate of labor > MRP of labor and with one additional unit of labor, wage rate < MRP.
   B. P or wage rate of labor < MRP of labor and with one additional unit of labor W_L > MRP.
   C. total revenue is at a maximum.
   D. total output is at a maximum.
   E. marginal physical product is at a maximum.

3. Which of the following is *not* the basis for a wage differential?

   A. Higher risk job.
   B. Investment in human capital.
   C. Increase in production of SUVs.
   D. Racial discrimination.
   E. Psychic income.

4. A monopsonist is identified by one of the following:

   A. A wage payment lower than the marginal revenue product of labor.
   B. Employment level greater than that of a competitive labor market.
   C. A wage payment higher than that of a competitive labor market.
   D. A single seller of labor services.
   E. A marginal factor cost curve lower than the supply curve.

5. If for two resources, Labor (L) and Capital (K), the ratios of their marginal physical products are

$$\frac{MPP_K}{P_K} > \frac{MPP_L}{P_L}$$

   the firm should
   A. hire more capital (K) until the ratios are equal.
   B. hire more labor (L) until the ratios are equal.
   C. lower the price of capital (P_K).
   D. lower the price of labor (P_L).
   E. seek union membership for labor (L).

6. The backward bending supply curve is characterized by which of the following?

   A. As wage rates rise, the quantity of labor supplied continues to rise at every wage rate increase.
   B. The labor-leisure trade-off continues to favor the supply of more jobs, or the substitution effect.
   C. The labor-leisure trade-off favors the income effect or more leisure at higher wage rates.
   D. inexperienced, low-income, younger workers at the backward bending portion.
   E. discriminated workers.

MULTIPLE-CHOICE REVIEW ANSWERS

MRP in table going down the column starting with labor unit 2: 150, 100, 50, 0.

1. **C** 3, MRP (100) > labor price (60);
   at 4 labor units, MRP (50) < labor
   price (60).

2. **B** (see explanation in 1)
3. **C**   4. **A**   5. **A**   6. **C**

MODEL ADVANCED PLACEMENT EXAMINATION IN MICROECONOMICS

Answer Sheet

1. Ⓐ Ⓑ Ⓒ Ⓓ Ⓔ	16. Ⓐ Ⓑ Ⓒ Ⓓ Ⓔ	31. Ⓐ Ⓑ Ⓒ Ⓓ Ⓔ	46. Ⓐ Ⓑ Ⓒ Ⓓ Ⓔ
2. Ⓐ Ⓑ Ⓒ Ⓓ Ⓔ	17. Ⓐ Ⓑ Ⓒ Ⓓ Ⓔ	32. Ⓐ Ⓑ Ⓒ Ⓓ Ⓔ	47. Ⓐ Ⓑ Ⓒ Ⓓ Ⓔ
3. Ⓐ Ⓑ Ⓒ Ⓓ Ⓔ	18. Ⓐ Ⓑ Ⓒ Ⓓ Ⓔ	33. Ⓐ Ⓑ Ⓒ Ⓓ Ⓔ	48. Ⓐ Ⓑ Ⓒ Ⓓ Ⓔ
4. Ⓐ Ⓑ Ⓒ Ⓓ Ⓔ	19. Ⓐ Ⓑ Ⓒ Ⓓ Ⓔ	34. Ⓐ Ⓑ Ⓒ Ⓓ Ⓔ	49. Ⓐ Ⓑ Ⓒ Ⓓ Ⓔ
5. Ⓐ Ⓑ Ⓒ Ⓓ Ⓔ	20. Ⓐ Ⓑ Ⓒ Ⓓ Ⓔ	35. Ⓐ Ⓑ Ⓒ Ⓓ Ⓔ	50. Ⓐ Ⓑ Ⓒ Ⓓ Ⓔ
6. Ⓐ Ⓑ Ⓒ Ⓓ Ⓔ	21. Ⓐ Ⓑ Ⓒ Ⓓ Ⓔ	36. Ⓐ Ⓑ Ⓒ Ⓓ Ⓔ	51. Ⓐ Ⓑ Ⓒ Ⓓ Ⓔ
7. Ⓐ Ⓑ Ⓒ Ⓓ Ⓔ	22. Ⓐ Ⓑ Ⓒ Ⓓ Ⓔ	37. Ⓐ Ⓑ Ⓒ Ⓓ Ⓔ	52. Ⓐ Ⓑ Ⓒ Ⓓ Ⓔ
8. Ⓐ Ⓑ Ⓒ Ⓓ Ⓔ	23. Ⓐ Ⓑ Ⓒ Ⓓ Ⓔ	38. Ⓐ Ⓑ Ⓒ Ⓓ Ⓔ	53. Ⓐ Ⓑ Ⓒ Ⓓ Ⓔ
9. Ⓐ Ⓑ Ⓒ Ⓓ Ⓔ	24. Ⓐ Ⓑ Ⓒ Ⓓ Ⓔ	39. Ⓐ Ⓑ Ⓒ Ⓓ Ⓔ	54. Ⓐ Ⓑ Ⓒ Ⓓ Ⓔ
10. Ⓐ Ⓑ Ⓒ Ⓓ Ⓔ	25. Ⓐ Ⓑ Ⓒ Ⓓ Ⓔ	40. Ⓐ Ⓑ Ⓒ Ⓓ Ⓔ	55. Ⓐ Ⓑ Ⓒ Ⓓ Ⓔ
11. Ⓐ Ⓑ Ⓒ Ⓓ Ⓔ	26. Ⓐ Ⓑ Ⓒ Ⓓ Ⓔ	41. Ⓐ Ⓑ Ⓒ Ⓓ Ⓔ	56. Ⓐ Ⓑ Ⓒ Ⓓ Ⓔ
12. Ⓐ Ⓑ Ⓒ Ⓓ Ⓔ	27. Ⓐ Ⓑ Ⓒ Ⓓ Ⓔ	42. Ⓐ Ⓑ Ⓒ Ⓓ Ⓔ	57. Ⓐ Ⓑ Ⓒ Ⓓ Ⓔ
13. Ⓐ Ⓑ Ⓒ Ⓓ Ⓔ	28. Ⓐ Ⓑ Ⓒ Ⓓ Ⓔ	43. Ⓐ Ⓑ Ⓒ Ⓓ Ⓔ	58. Ⓐ Ⓑ Ⓒ Ⓓ Ⓔ
14. Ⓐ Ⓑ Ⓒ Ⓓ Ⓔ	29. Ⓐ Ⓑ Ⓒ Ⓓ Ⓔ	44. Ⓐ Ⓑ Ⓒ Ⓓ Ⓔ	59. Ⓐ Ⓑ Ⓒ Ⓓ Ⓔ
15. Ⓐ Ⓑ Ⓒ Ⓓ Ⓔ	30. Ⓐ Ⓑ Ⓒ Ⓓ Ⓔ	45. Ⓐ Ⓑ Ⓒ Ⓓ Ⓔ	60. Ⓐ Ⓑ Ⓒ Ⓓ Ⓔ

Model Advanced Placement Examination in Microeconomics

Two hours are allotted for this examination: 1 hour and 10 minutes for Section I, which consists of multiple-choice questions; and 50 minutes for Section II, which consists of three mandatory essay questions.

Section I—Multiple-Choice Questions

Time—1 hour and 10 minutes
Number of Questions—60
Percent of Total Grade—66²/₃

DIRECTIONS

Each of the questions or incomplete statements beginning on page 160 is followed by five suggested answers or completions. Select the one that is best in each case and then fill in the corresponding oval on the answer sheet.

1. Which of the following is NOT a characteristic of perfectly competitive industry?

   A. Free entry into the industry.
   B. Product differentiation.
   C. Perfectly elastic demand curve.
   D. Homogeneous products.
   E. Many sellers and many buyers.

2. Which of the following is a characteristic of monopolistic competition in the long run?

   A. Strong barriers to entry.
   B. Homogeneous products.
   C. Zero economic profits.
   D. Minimum average total cost equals price.
   E. Efficiency.

3. Which of the following is characteristic of oligopoly?

   A. Weak barriers to entry.
   B. Perfectly elastic demand curve.
   C. Interdependence among sellers.
   D. Price less than marginal cost.
   E. Price equal to marginal revenue.

4. Which of the following is a characteristic of monopoly?

   A. A single firm in the industry.
   B. Price equal to marginal revenue.
   C. Perfectly elastic demand curve.
   D. Weak barriers to entry.
   E. Zero economic profits.

5. Compared to perfect competition in the long run, monopoly has

   A. more choices of products for consumers.
   B. more efficiency.
   C. lower prices.
   D. higher output.
   E. price greater than marginal revenue.

6. With the presence of a negative externality, which of the following would internalize (or correct) the externality?

   A. A government subsidy.
   B. A government tax.
   C. A lower price.
   D. A higher level of output.
   E. A government-created task force.

7. With the presence of a positive externality, which of the following would correct the externality?

   A. A government subsidy.
   B. A government tax.
   C. A higher price.
   D. A lower level of output.
   E. A government-created task force.

8. Which of the following is true?

   A. A marginal social cost = marginal private cost + marginal social benefits.
   B. Value of externality = marginal social costs.
   C. Value of externality = marginal private costs.
   D. Marginal social cost = marginal private cost + negative externality.
   E. Marginal social cost = marginal private cost + positive externality.

9. Which of the following is true?

   A. Average total cost = total fixed costs divided by the number of units produced.
   B. Average total cost = average variable costs divided by the total number of units produced.
   C. Average total cost = average variable cost plus marginal cost.
   D. Average total cost = average variable cost plus average fixed cost.
   E. All of the above.

10. Which of the following is true about the relationship of the average total cost (ATC) curve and the marginal cost (MC) curve?

    A. ATC and MC are always equal.
    B. ATC and MC are never equal.
    C. The ATC curve intersects the MC curve at the minimum point of the MC curve.

D. The MC curve intersects the ATC curve at the minimum point of the ATC curve.

E. The MC curve intersects the ATC curve at the maximum point of the ATC curve.

Question 11 is based on the figure below:

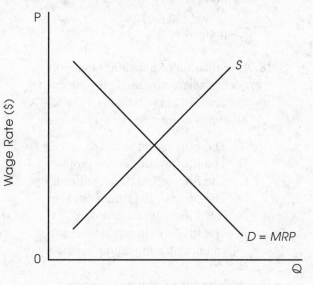

Number of Workers

11. Which of the following will happen when a new computerized system for a firm increases the marginal productivity of its workers?

   A. The marginal revenue product curve will shift to the left, which will cause the wage rate to decrease.

   B. The supply curve will shift to the right, causing the wage rate to decrease.

   C. The marginal revenue product curve will shift to the right, causing the wage rate to increase.

   D. The supply curve will shift to the left, causing the wage rate to increase.

   E. The marginal revenue product curve will shift to the right and the supply curve will shift to the left, leaving the wage rate unchanged.

12. Which of the following is true about a price floor?

   A. It is used to correct government policy.

   B. It is used when the equilibrium price is too high.

   C. It will be located above the equilibrium price.

   D. It will be located below the equilibrium price.

   E. It is when the stock market has closed at a new low.

13. Which of the following is true about a price ceiling?

   A. It is used to correct government policy.

   B. It is used when equilibrium prices are too low.

   C. It will be located above the equilibrium price.

   D. It will be located below the equilibrium price.

   E. It is when the stock market has closed at a new high.

14. Which of the following situations best exemplifies the concept of consumer surplus?

   A. It refers to a consumer who no longer has any outstanding debts.

   B. The federal government has taken in more revenue than it has paid out in expenditures.

   C. A consumer pays *more* for a pizza than she thought it was worth at the margin of the purchase.

   D. A consumer pays *less* for a pizza than she thought it was worth at the margin of the purchase.

   E. A consumer pays exactly what she thinks the pizza is worth at the margin of the purchase.

TABLE 1

Number of Workers	Pair Sets Produced per Two Weeks
1	40
2	70
3	95
4	115
5	130
6	130

15. Given the data in the table above, and knowing that workers are paid $1,250 every two weeks and that the pair sets are sold to retailers at $50, how many workers would be hired?

A. Two
B. Three
C. Four
D. Five
E. Six

Questions 16–19 are based on the figure below:

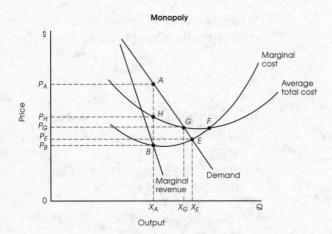

16. An unregulated monopoly would

A. sell at price, P_A and produce output at X_A.
B. sell at price, P_G and produce output at X_G.
C. sell at price, P_E and produce output at X_E.
D. sell at price, P_B and produce output at X_A.

E. sell at price, P_B and produce output at X_A.

17. A regulated monopoly could occur at

A. point A, G, or E.
B. point A or G.
C. point A or F.
D. point G or E.
E. point B or A.

18. If regulation of a natural monopoly occurs where marginal cost intersects the demand curve, which of the following is correct?

A. The firm would be taxed.
B. The firm would realize profits.
C. The firm would be subsidized.
D. The price of the firm would be equal to marginal revenue.
E. The firm would produce less than an unregulated natural monopoly.

19. Which of the following is correct about the profits of an unregulated monopolist?

A. The profits are the rectangle $P_A AHP_H$.
B. The profits are the rectangle $P_H ABP_B$.
C. The profits are less than those of a regulated monopoly.
D. The profits are less than at a socially optimal output.

Questions 20–23 are based on the figure below:

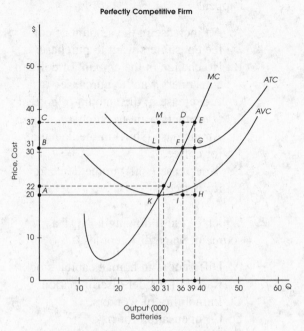

Perfectly Competitive Firm

Output (000)
Batteries

20. At a market price of $37, maximum profits are

   A. CBLM
   B. CBFD
   C. CBGE
   D. BAKL
   E. CAHE

21. At a market price of $19, how many batteries will the firm produce?

   A. 20,000
   B. 29,000
   C. 36,000
   D. 28,000
   E. Zero

22. At a market price of $22, how many batteries will the firm produce?

   A. 20,000
   B. 26,000
   C. 31,000
   D. Zero
   E. 10,000

23. At the market price of $22, the output will result in

   A. economic losses.

   B. economic profits.
   C. normal profits.
   D. business profits.
   E. shut-down.

24. If the government announces that the drinking of red grape juice reduces the risk of heart attacks, which of the following is correct?

   A. The amounts demanded of red grape juice will increase.
   B. The amounts demanded of red grape juice will decrease.
   C. The demand for red grape juice will increase.
   D. The demand for red grape juice will decrease.
   E. No change in demand or amounts demanded.

Questions 25–28 are based on the figure below:

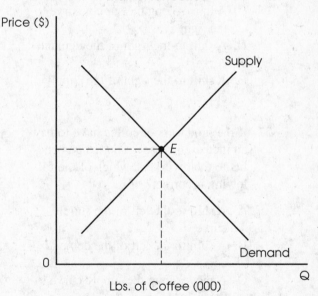

Market for Coffee

Lbs. of Coffee (000)

25. Using the figure above, which of the following is correct for the market for coffee?

   A. If both the demand for and the supply of coffee increases, both the price of coffee and the quantity sold of coffee will increase.

B. If both the demand for and the supply of coffee increases, the quantity of coffee sold will increase.

C. If the demand for coffee decreases while the supply of coffee increases, the price of coffee will increase.

D. If both the demand for and the supply of coffee decreases, both the price of coffee and the quantity sold of coffee decrease.

E. If the demand for coffee increases, and the supply of coffee increases, the price of coffee will increase.

26. If the government provides a subsidy to the producers of coffee, which of the following will occur?

A. A shift to the left of the supply curve.

B. A shift to the left of the demand curve.

C. A move along the supply curve to the right.

D. A shift to the right of the demand curve.

E. A shift to the right of the supply curve.

27. If the producers of coffee have to pay an increase in wages and fringe benefits to their workers, which of the following is correct?

A. A shift to the left of the supply curve.

B. A shift to the left of the demand curve.

C. A move along the supply curve to the right.

D. A shift to the right of the demand curve.

E. A shift to the right of the supply curve.

28. If the price of coffee increases, which of the following is most likely to happen?

A. An increase in the amount of coffee consumers want to purchase.

B. No change in the amount of coffee consumers want to purchase.

C. A decrease in the amount of coffee consumers want to purchase.

D. An increase (shift) in the demand for coffee.

E. A decrease (shift) in the demand for coffee.

29. Which of the following is NOT a source of wage differentials?

A. Differences in human capital stock.

B. Racial or gender discrimination.

C. Immobility of workers.

D. Compensation for risk.

E. Decrease in the birth rate.

Questions 30–31 are based on the figure below:

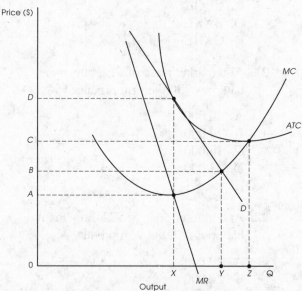

30. For this firm operating under monopolistic competition, which of the following is the profit-maximizing output and price?

A. OX output and OA price.

B. OX output and OD price.

C. OX output and OB price.

D. OZ output and OC price.

E. OZ output and OA price.

31. At the profit-maximizing output, which of the following is correct?

A. Economic profits are zero and the firm is operating efficiently.

B. Economic profits are above normal and output is greater than under perfect competition.

C. Economic losses are present.

D. Price is less than marginal cost.

E. Economic profits are zero and the firm is operating inefficiently.

32. Which of the following best exemplifies economies of scale?

A. As a firm's output decreases, average costs for production decreases.

B. As a firms output increases, average costs for production increases.

C. As a firm's inputs triple, its output quadruples.

D. As a firm's inputs triple, its output doubles.

E. As a firm's inputs triple, its output stays constant.

33. Which of the following is correct?

A. In the long run, all inputs are variable.

B. In the short run, all inputs are variable.

C. In the long run, supply is not able to adjust fully to changes in demand.

D. In the short run, supply is able to adjust fully to changes in demand.

E. A short run is any distance less than one mile.

34. If a firm decreases its prices by 15 percent and its total revenue increases by 30 percent, which of the following is correct?

A. The price elasticity of demand is unit elastic.

B. The price elasticity of demand is inelastic.

C. The price elasticity of demand is elastic.

D. The numerical coefficient of elasticity is equal to one.

E. The numerical coefficient of elasticity is less than one.

35. If one person has the only original signed copy of *The Wealth of Nations* by Adam Smith, which of the following would illustrate this situation?

A. A downward sloping demand curve.

B. An upward sloping supply curve.

C. An invisible hand.

D. A perfectly vertical supply curve.

E. A perfectly horizontal demand curve.

36. When marginal cost equals price in a perfectly competitive product market at long run equilibrium, which of the following is NOT correct?

A. There is a socially optimal or efficient output and price.

B. Other product markets are inefficient by contrast.

C. It is a sign of high concentration among sellers.

D. The value placed on the product by the buyer is equal to the cost of production of the seller at the margin of an additional sale.

E. Marginal cost equals minimum average total cost.

37. Which of the following is a correct statement?

A. Average total cost equals marginal cost plus average fixed costs.

B. Average total cost equals marginal costs plus average variable costs.

C. Average total cost equals average fixed costs plus average variable costs.

D. Total fixed costs vary with output.

E. Total fixed costs equal total variable costs at zero output.

38. Which of the following correctly identifies the condition that explains inefficiency for firms in a monopolistically competitive industry?

A. Higher output than competitive industries.
B. Lower price than competitive industries.
C. Price equals marginal cost.
D. Price equals marginal revenue.
E. Excess capacity compared to competitive industries.

Questions 39–41 are based on the figure below:

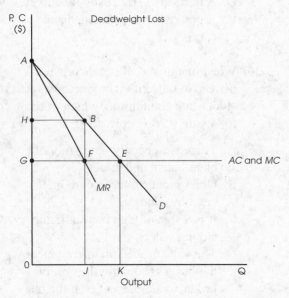

39. The original consumer surplus (before monopoly) is

A. AHB
B. BFE
C. AGE
D. HGFB
E. GOKE

40. The dead-weight loss as the result of monopoly is

A. AHB
B. BFE
C. AGE
D. HGFB
E. GOKE

41. The reduced consumer surplus as the result of monopoly is

A. AHB
B. BFE
C. AGE
D. HGFB
E. GOKE

42. If a merchant raises the price of her neckties and the consequent decrease in the quantity demanded of ties results in the total revenue of the merchant increasing, which of the following is correct?

A. The price elasticity of demand is elastic.
B. The price elasticity of demand is inelastic.
C. The price elasticity of demand is unit elastic.
D. The price elasticity of supply is elastic.
E. The price elasticity of supply is inelastic.

43. If the price of one good (A) increases and the quantity demanded of another good (B) increases, the two goods are

A. substitute goods.
B. complement goods.
C. inferior goods.
D. normal goods.
E. independent goods.

44. If, as the price of a particular good increases, the added satisfaction of each additional unit of this good for the consumer decreases, which of the following correctly identifies the concept?

A. Diminishing marginal productivity.
B. Diminishing marginal utility.
C. Increasing marginal utility.
D. Increasing marginal productivity.
E. Constant costs.

45. If, for each additional unit of a variable input, the increases in output become smaller, which of the following correctly identifies the concept?

    A. Diminishing marginal productivity.
    B. Diminishing marginal utility.
    C. Increasing marginal utility.
    D. Increasing marginal productivity.
    E. Constant costs.

46. Which of the following is correct about the demand for labor?

    A. The demand for labor is independent of the demand for other inputs or resources.
    B. The demand for labor is independent of the demand for the products produced by labor.
    C. The demand for labor is independent of the availability of other inputs or resources.
    D. The demand for labor is derived from the demand for the products produced by labor.
    E. The demand for labor is derived from the demand for labor unions.

47. The greater (higher) the wage elasticity of demand, the

    A. greater the proportion of capital costs to labor costs in the production of goods.
    B. greater the price elasticity for the product produced by labor.
    C. the smaller the number of substitutes for labor.
    D. the smaller the time period.
    E. the smaller the proportion of labor costs to total costs.

48. Which of the following is an example of a transfer earning?

    A. A superstar basketball player's $40 million earnings.
    B. A social security retirement income.
    C. A welfare payment from social services.

    D. A check to a college student from a parent or guardian.
    E. A cashier at a restaurant receiving the same $8 an hour that other cashiers receive.

49. Which of the following is an example of an economic rent?

    A. A superstar basketball player's $50 million earnings.
    B. A social security retirement income.
    C. A welfare payment from social services.
    D. A check to a college student from a parent or guardian.
    E. A cashier at a restaurant receiving the same $8 an hour that other cashiers receive.

50. Which of the following statements is NOT correct?

    A. The law of diminishing marginal productivity (returns) applies only to the short run.
    B. All resources or inputs are variable in the long run.
    C. Quantities of a variable resource or input are applied to a fixed quantity of another resource in the short run.
    D. The long run average total cost curve represents the lowest cost combination of resources for each level of output produced.
    E. In the long run, constant returns to scale always prevail.

TABLE 2
UNIT OF OUTPUT (PATIENT DAYS IN A HOSPITAL)

Labor (# of nursing staff)	Units of Capital (# of hospital beds in hundreds)		
	1	2	3
1	3,000	3,400	3,600
2	3,400	4,000	4,400
3	3,600	4,400	5,000

51. The table above shows the changes in total output (patient days in a hospital) that will occur as different combinations of the inputs (nursing staff as labor and hospital beds as representative of size or capital) are varied. Which of the following statements is correct?

A. In the long run, there are increasing returns to scale.
B. In the long run, there are decreasing returns to scale.
C. In the long run, there are constant returns to scale.
D. In the short run, there are increasing returns.
E. In the short run, there is no change in returns.

52. Which of the following statements is correct?

A. Economic Profits = Accounting Profits.
B. Economic Costs = Explicit Costs plus Implicit Costs.
C. Economic Costs = Explicit Costs minus Implicit Costs.
D. Opportunity Costs = Economic Profits.
E. Accounting Costs = Implicit Costs.

53. Which of the following is true for a firm operating under perfect competition in the long run?

A. The firm will engage in non-price competition.
B. The firm will realize economic profits.
C. The firm will incur economic losses.
D. The firm will realize zero economic profits.
E. The firm will have a price greater than its marginal revenue.

54. Which of the following conditions is characteristic of oligopoly?

A. A rival firm matches price decreases of rivals, but fails to match any price increases of rivals.
B. A rival firm matches price increases of rivals, but fails to match any price decrease of rivals.
C. A rival firm fails to match both price increases or price decreases of rivals.
D. Rival firms act independently of each other.
E. There is such a large number of firms that firms cannot exercise any price strategy.

55. With respect to the kinked demand curve, which of the following is NOT correct?

A. There is no price leader.
B. There are relatively equal shares of the market.
C. Price is greater than marginal costs.
D. It is a noncollusive model.
E. The demand curve is of one continuous function.

56. Usually, the supply curve of firms operating under conditions of perfect competition in product market would be identified as

A. perfectly vertical in the long run.
B. perfectly horizontal in the short run.
C. more elastic in the long run.
D. more elastic in the short run.
E. discontinuous in the long run.

57. Relatively free or easy entry (low or nonexistent barriers to entry) is best matched by which of the following?

A. More consumer choices, greater price elasticity of demand, more competitors.
B. More consumer choices, lower price elasticity of demand, more competitors.

C. More consumer choices, greater price elasticity of demand, fewer competitors.

D. Fewer consumer choices, lower price elasticity of demand, fewer competitors.

E. Fewer consumer choices, greater price elasticity of demand, more competitors.

58. Which of the following represents a measure of a firm's monopoly pricing or market power, i.e., the larger the value of the index, the greater the firm's market pricing power?

A. (MC-P)/MC
B. (MC-P)/P
C. (P-MC)/P
D. (P-MC)/MC
E. (P-MR)/MC

59. Which of the following correctly illustrates why price (P) equals marginal revenue (MR) under perfect competition, and why price (P) is greater than marginal revenue under monopoly or imperfect competition?

I. MR = P = demand on horizontal function for perfect competition.

II. P > MR as downward sloping functions for imperfect competition.

III. Demand and Price are represented as a vertical function for imperfect competition.

IV. Price equals MR in the long run for monopoly.

A. I, II, and III.
B. I and II.
C. I only.
D. I and III.
E. II only.

60. In the design of a competitive market system, which of the following does NOT describe how resources are allocated?

A. Price signals that guide producers on what, when, how, and for whom to produce goods and services.
B. Active government ownership and direction of production.
C. Voluntary market exchange between buyers and sellers.
D. Distribution of income and goods on the basis of contribution or productivity.
E. Profit motivation.

Section II—Free-Response Questions

Planning Time—10 minutes
Writing Time—50 minutes
Percent of Total Grade—33⅓

DIRECTIONS

You have 50 minutes to answer all three of the following questions. It is suggested that you spend approximately half your time on the first question and divide the remaining time equally between the next two questions. In answering the questions, you should emphasize the line of reasoning that generated your results; it is not enough to list the results of your analysis. Include correctly labeled diagrams, if useful or required, in explaining your answers. A correctly labeled diagram must have all axes and curves clearly labeled and must show directional changes.

Students should consider doing a "sketch" (main points, quick graph, etc.) of the answer before actually answering the free-response questions. Good luck! When you use graphs on the free-response questions, label the axes and make direct references to any symbols, e.g., MR, P, output, on the graphs when you respond to questions.

> **Note**: Recent Advanced Placement examinations require *three* questions. Some of the questions may be based on material covered in the common chapters, such as production possibilities frontier or curve when applied to international trade. For these questions, please refer to those chapters.

1. With the use of graphs, clearly labeled, explain the following:
   A. How price (P) and marginal revenue (MR) are differently related under perfect competition than under monopoly (or imperfect competition).
   B. *Explain* why these relationships between MR and P differ between perfect competition and monopoly.
   C. Identify a significant effect for pricing strategy of this relationship of P and MR in the two markets.

2. A. For a perfectly competitive firm and for an imperfectly competitive market, explain how the index (P-MC)/P demonstrates the degree of pricing or market power.
   B. What would be the significant consequences of the differences between perfectly competitive markets and imperfectly competitive markets?

3. Drawing graphs for the firm and for the market under perfect competition, show the process of adjustment from the short run and the long run. Assume that the only form of adjustment is the entry and exit of firms and that adjustment process does not alter the cost curves of the firms.

4. Butter and margarine are substitutes and are sold in perfectly competitive product markets. The Lots of Cream creamery company, one of 300 butter producers, develops a new automated churner that reduces costs.
   A. What will be the effect of this change on price, short-run profits, and the quantity of butter for the Lots of Cream Company? Explain your answer.
   B. If the other perfectly competitive firms use this same churner, what will be the effect on the price and quantity of butter produced in the market?
   C. What will be the effect of these changes in the butter market on the price and quantity produced of margarine?

ANSWERS AND ANSWERS EXPLAINED

MULTIPLE-CHOICE QUESTIONS— MODEL EXAM (MICROECONOMICS)

1. **B**	11. **C**	21. **E**	31. **E**	41. **A**	51. **C**
2. **C**	12. **C**	22. **C**	32. **C**	42. **B**	52. **B**
3. **C**	13. **D**	23. **A**	33. **A**	43. **A**	53. **D**
4. **A**	14. **D**	24. **C**	34. **C**	44. **B**	54. **A**
5. **E**	15. **B**	25. **B**	35. **D**	45. **A**	55. **E**
6. **B**	16. **A**	26. **E**	36. **C**	46. **D**	56. **C**
7. **A**	17. **D**	27. **A**	37. **C**	47. **B**	57. **A**
8. **D**	18. **C**	28. **C**	38. **E**	48. **E**	58. **C**
9. **D**	19. **A**	29. **E**	39. **C**	49. **A**	59. **B**
10. **D**	20. **C**	30. **B**	40. **B**	50. **E**	60. **B**

Answers Explained

1. **B** (Chapters 9,10) The other answers are all correct characteristics of a perfectly competitive industry. Products are homogeneous (the same, identical) under perfect competition.

2. **C** (Chapters 9,12) All of the other characteristics listed as choices are *not* appropriate for monopolistic competition. Choices **B**, **D**, and **E** are characteristics of perfect competition in the long run; choice **A** is characteristic of oligopoly and monopoly.

3. **C** (Chapters 9,12) For oligopoly, the other choices are not appropriate: **A** (weak barriers to entry) belongs to perfect competition; there are formidable barriers for oligopoly. **B**, rather than a perfectly elastic demand curve, oligopolists face a downward sloping demand curve.

4. **A** (Chapters 9,11) This is the most telling characteristic of monopoly; it defines monopoly. To change the other choices to fit monopoly, you would have to rewrite choices **B**, **C**, **D**, and **E** as follows:

B: P > MR (downward sloping demand curve)
C: imperfectly elastic demand curve
D: complete barriers to entry
E: usual presence of profits

5. **E** (Chapters 9,10,11) The other choices represent the "opposite" answers. Choice **A** should read fewer choices; choice **B** should read inefficiency; choice **C** should read higher prices; choice **D** should read lower output.

6. **B** (Chapter 7) The rule to follow is a tax for a negative externality and a subsidy for a positive externality. Both would internalize or correct the externality.

7. **A** (Chapter 7) See number 6.

8. **D** (Chapter 7) A negative externality is an outcome of a market transaction that is not "captured" by the price mechanism by the buyer or the seller and thus, it is incurred by other parties and is added to private costs.

9. **D** (Chapter 8) This is simply definitional. See the chapter on costs for other definitions (Chapter 8).

10. **D** (Chapter 8) This is a mathematical characteristic of average and marginal cost curves. See Chapter 8 on costs for other explanations.

11. **C** (Chapter 13) If you look at the graph for this question, you will see the demand for workers curve (D) is equal to the marginal revenue productivity (MRP) of the workers. $MRP_L = MPP_L \times P/$or MR_X). Thus, if the price for the product (P_X) stays constant and if the computerized system increases MPP_L (marginal physical productivity), then MRP_L will increase illustrated as a shift of $D(MRP_L)$ to the right (shift

to right, increase in demand for workers).

12. **C** (Chapter 4) The price floor is established since the market equilibrium price would be too low, e.g., when a $5 market wage (price) for labor is deemed insufficient. So, the government says no one can be paid less than $6 an hour (minimum wage).

13. **D** (Chapter 4) If interest rates for mortgage loans are 12 percent (market equilibrium) and the government says that this is too high, the government (state government under old usury laws) might establish a ceiling rate of 10 percent (below the equilibrium rate).

14. **D** (Chapter 6) A consumer surplus is established as the difference between the total utility (satisfaction) received and the price paid by the consumer. Because of diminishing marginal utility, consumers are able to buy a product at the price of the last unit sold (lower marginal utility) while the marginal utility of previous units would be higher.

15. **B** (Chapter 13) First, construct a third column headed marginal physical product (MPP) which would be the difference in pair sets for each additional worker hired (e.g., 30 MPP as the difference between 40 pair sets for one worker, and 70 pair sets for two workers) Second, construct a fourth column headed MRP_L (marginal revenue product) which is the function of $MPP_L \times P_X$. Then you will find the *number* of workers (first column) hired that will maximize the profits of the firm doing the hiring. This number will be the level of hiring at which $MRP_L \times P_L$ (or wage rate, which = $1,250). Thus,

TABLE 3

(1) Number of Workers	(2) Pair Sets Produced for Two Weeks	(3) MPP_L	(4) MRP_L (#3 × $50, P_X)
1	40		—
2	70	30	$1,500
3	95	25	1,250
4	115	20	1,000
5	130	15	750
6	130	0	—

Since the pair sets are sold at $50, column 4 is $MPP_L \times P_L$($50). The profit-maximizing level is three workers whose MRP_L is $1,250, which is equal to the wage paid every two weeks of $1,250 per worker. If there is no level at which the wage rate = MRP_L, then the firm would hire the highest level of workers where MRP_L is greater than the wage rate paid.

16. **A** (Chapter 11) The reference is to the graph supplied for Questions 16–19. The profit-maximizing (best) output and the selling price are determined by the intersection of marginal cost and marginal revenue (MR = MC). The price, P_A, is read from the demand curve or by extending a vertical line from the intersection of MR and MC to the demand curve (point A); the related point on the price axis is P_A. Similarly, the best output is X_A, which is found by dropping a vertical line from the intersection of MC and MR to the output (horizontal) axis.

17. **D** (Chapter 11) Point A is the unregulated position as described above in the response to Question 16. At "G" is the typical point for regulation of public utilities (at least, this was the case before deregulation of the generating function of these utilities); it is supposed to approximate the "fair return" for investors in public utili-

ties. In other words, price would be set at average total cost (ATC), which would include implicit costs or normal returns that would be equal to the returns in competitive, similar risk markets. The other form or regulation would require the government to subsidize firms to sell and produce at the socially optimal or efficient level of P = MC (point E).

18. **C** (Chapter 11) The firm would be subsidized at the point at which P = MC (socially efficient, see 17 above) or the point of intersection of MC with the demand curve.

19. **A** (Chapter 11) We start with point A and the related point P_A (see answer 16). Then to complete the rectangle, we extend a vertical line from point B (MC = MR) to its intersection with average total cost (ATC) to find the per unit cost at point H. We then extend a line horizontally from H to its intersection with the price (vertical) axis at point P_H; thus, the rectangle $P_A AHP_H$.

20. **C** (Chapter 10) The correct answer is CBGE in reference to the graph supplied for Questions 20–23. Profits for the perfectly competitive firm are at the level of MR = MC. Remember, with perfect competition P = MR for the firm. The demand function is horizontal (P = MR). Also, MC intersects ATC at the minimum point of ATC. Thus, profits are maximized (with a market price of $37) at output level of 39 batteries. Point E is where MR = MC and a line dropped perpendicular to the output axis indicates a level of output of 39.

21. **E** (Chapter 10) With a price of $19, price is less than AVC at all levels of output. The minimum price of AVC (average variable cost) is $20 (point K). If the price is less than

the average variable cost, the firm should shut down in the short run. Its best output would then equal its total fixed costs (TFC). Thus, the firm's best output is zero.

22. **C** (Chapter 10) At $22 (P = MR), MC = MR (intersection of MR ($22) with MC) at output level of 31,000 batteries. See point J.

23. **A** (Chapter 10) At a price of $22, P is less than ATC (see graph for Questions 20–23). This would result in a loss.

24. **C** (Chapter 4) Since tastes and preferences are held constant for a particular demand curve, the change would not be along a demand curve (change in amounts demanded) but rather a change in demand. In this case, the increase in preference would result in a shift (an increase) in demand.

25. **B** (Chapter 4) When there is an increase in demand for coffee, both the equilibrium quantity and equilibrium price increase with an increase in supply, the equilibrium quantity also increases while the price decreases. A suggestion for answering Questions 25–28: Draw the appropriate changes (e.g., shift in D and shift in S) and compare the results with the original equilibrium position. Use the graph supplied to make these comparisons.

26. **E** (Chapter 4) In the chapter on the basics of supply and demand (Chapter 4), there is a list of factors that will cause shifts in supply and demand curves (those determinants that we hold constant, *ceteris paribus*, when analyzing changes along a supply or demand curve). When the government provides a subsidy to the producer, there is a decrease (in effect) in the cost of production that encourages more

production (shift to the right of the supply curve).

27. **A** (Chapter 4) An increase in costs of production such as wage increases will lead to the opposite of answer 26, a decrease in supply.

28. **C** (Chapter 4) A change in the price of coffee, *ceteris paribus*, will be a change along a demand curve for coffee. A price increase would cause consumers to want to buy less coffee.

29. **E** (Chapter 13) All other factors could cause wages to differ among workers.

30. **B** (Chapter 12) This is a reference to the graph supplied for Questions 30–31. This is the typical tendency, in the long run, for monopolistic competitors—price equals average total cost (not at minimum ATC), allowing firms normal profits (zero economic profits). At MC = MR, price is at OD and output is at OX.

31. **E** (Chapter 12) See the answer for 30 above for zero economic profits. The firm operates inefficiently since ATC is above minimum level.

32. **C** (Chapter 8) With economies of scale, as production increases there are savings in average costs of production. When output increases more than proportionately to increases in input, the firm is getting more output per added input or, in effect, there is a decrease in cost of production.

33. **A** (Chapter 8) In other words (in contrast to the other answers or choices), supply is able to adjust fully to changes in demand in the long run. In the short run, all inputs are not variable; some are fixed in quantity. In the short run, supply is unable to adjust fully to the changes in demand.

34. **C** (Chapter 5) Elastic means a coefficient of elasticity greater than 1 or a more than proportional increase of quantity demanded to a decrease in price. Since P × Q = total revenue, if prices decrease by 15 percent and while total revenue increases by 30 percent, there is a factor of 2. That is, the response in quantity demanded was twice the percentage change in price, leading to an increase in total revenue. Price elasticity = 1 (unit elastic, proportional); Price elasticity > 1 (elastic, more than proportional); price elasticity < 1 (inelastic less than proportional).

35. **D** (Chapter 5) Only one copy available means the supply is fixed (vertical supply curve) and does not change with changes in price (perfectly inelastic).

36. **C** (Chapter 10) This is the only choice that is not a characteristic of perfectly competitive markets; instead, it is a characteristic of oligopolies or other forms of imperfect competition.

37. **C** (Chapter 8) This is purely definitional.

38. **E** (Chapter 12) None of the other choices is appropriate. Monopolistic competition is characterized by lower output, higher price than competitive industries. Price is greater than MR and greater than MC.

39. **C** (Chapter 11) Consumer surplus is that excess of utility over price paid for goods or services. If you measure total utility as the area under the demand curve up to the amount of output consumed (AEKO), and if you subtract the cost (GOKE), you are left with the consumer surplus,

triangle AGE. This is in reference to the graph for Questions 39–41.

40. **B** (Chapter 11) This occurs after the monopolist extracts HGEB as profits from the consumer surplus.

41. **A** (Chapter 11) The original surplus is AGE. If the monopolist's profit is HGFB and if the dead-weight loss is BFE, then the reduced consumer surplus must be the remaining triangle, AHB.

42. **B** (Chapter 5) As a device, consider the following table:

TABLE 4

P	Q	TR	Elasticity
increases	decreases	increases	inelastic, E = <1
increases	decreases	decreases	elastic, E = >1
increases	decreases	no change	unit elastic, E = 1
decreases	increases	no change	unit elastic, E = 1
decreases	increases	increases	elastic, E = >1
decreases	increases	decreases	inelastic, E = <1

43. **A** (Chapter 4) If the question had read "If the price of one good (A) increases and the quantity demanded of other good decreases," the answer would be **B**, complement goods. Review these definitions.

44. **B** (Chapter 6) This is definitional. You should review the other terms as well. One is in the next question.

45. **A** (Chapter 8) This is definitional. You can place "productivity" with inputs and outputs for firms or suppliers. You can place "utility" with satisfaction in purchases and consumers.

46. **D** (Chapter 13) This is a very important concept, derived demand.

47. **B** (Chapter 13) The key concept here is that the demand for labor is

derived from the demand for the product that labor produces. Thus, the greater the price elasticity of demand for the product, the greater the wage elasticity of demand for labor. Also, each of the other choices for this question are the opposites of the correct answer, for example, for **E** the answer should read "the greater the portion of labor costs to total costs." See Chapter 13, Resource Markets, for the complete analysis.

48. **E** (Chapter 13) A transfer earning is a reflection of a competitive labor (resource) market. It is the earning that could have been received elsewhere. A payment in excess of a transfer earning is called an *economic rent* (as in the next question).

49. **A** (Chapter 13) This is above the earnings of other basketball players and qualifies as a *rent*. See the explanation above for number 48.

50. **E** (Chapter 8) The question asks "which of the following is NOT correct?" All of the other choices (**A, B, C, D**) are correct statements about the law of diminishing marginal productivity and the differences between the short run and the long run. Indeed, in the long run, we may expect constant, decreasing, or increasing returns to scale. All of these can and do happen.

51. **C** (Chapter 8) To confirm this, examine the matrix in the question. First, allow only labor to change with capital fixed, then allow labor and capital to change and you will see the same pattern (constant) of returns to scale.

52. **B** (Chapter 8) This is definitional. Review the various definitions of economic (accounting) costs/profits

in Chapter 8, Costs, Production, Supply.

53. **D** (Chapter 10) This refers to a firm operating under perfect competition in the long run. For each firm in the long run, P = minimum average cost (zero economic profits). Also, P = MR; P = MC and all the competition is based on price.

54. **A** (Chapter 12) This refers to the interdependence characteristic of oligopoly. Price decreases are matched in the hope of maintaining or increasing market share. Price increases are *not* matched for fear of losing market share or having the possibility of gaining market share over the price-increasing rival.

55. **E** (Chapter 12) This refers to the question that asks "Which of the following is NOT correct (for the kinked demand curve)?" The major feature of the kinked demand curve is that it consists of two segments (one that indicates "following" and the other that "does not follow" the price changes of rivals), so that the demand function is discontinuous at the kink. See Chapter 12, Imperfect Competition, for the analysis.

56. **C** (Chapter 8) This refers to the supply curve of perfectly competitive firms in product markets. Elasticity tends to be greater in the long run since the firm will be able to adjust to changes in demand. The firm will have more options in availability of resources in order to substitute less expensive resources (inputs) for more expensive resources in the long run.

57. **A** (Chapter 9) This refers to "relatively free or easy entry." That is, if competitors are allowed easy entry, there will be more consumer choices. The increased choice for

consumers means that they will be more sensitive (elastic) to price increases. Review the table of characteristics of product markets in Chapter 9, Introduction to Product Markets.

58. **C** (Chapter 11) (P – MC)/P is the Lerner index of monopoly pricing power. The higher the value of this ratio, the higher the pricing power of a firm. In effect, the index measures the firm's ability to price its goods over marginal cost. If the socially optimal price for efficiency is P = MC, this ability to price greater than marginal cost suggests inefficiency.

59. **B** (Chapters 10,11,12) This fundamental difference between perfect competition and imperfect competition is crucial to success on the exam. It is often asked on free-response questions.

60. **B** (Chapter 4) This is in reference to "Which of the following does NOT describe how resources are allocated (competitive market)?" All of the other choices are related to allocation in a competitive market system. Active government ownership and direction of production is more akin to non-market systems such as socialism.

FREE-RESPONSE ANSWERS—MODEL EXAM (MICROECONOMICS)

For each of the free-response questions, we have provided answers that contain the significant concepts and their relationship to the question. We have also supplied the necessary graphs (labeled) with their relationship to the answer. For each of these suggested answers, you should refer to the question as asked in the free-response section of this model examination.

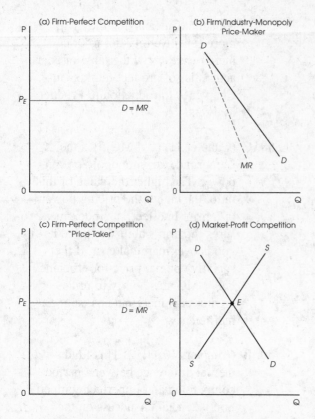

price, P_E, that each seller must use. The seller will not sell any goods at a price higher than the market price since buyers will then go elsewhere to buy the same product. To sell the product at a price below the market price of P_E, the seller would incur losses. Thus each additional unit sold adds the same amount (marginal revenue) to total revenue. This marginal revenue (MR) is equal to the price. This table illustrates this point:

TABLE 5
PERFECT COMPETITION

$P	Q	$TR	$MR
6	1	6	
6	2	12	6
6	3	18	6
6	4	24	6
6	5	30	6
6	6	36	6
6	7	42	6
6	8	48	6

1. A. Price (P) and Marginal Revenue (MR) are differently related under perfect competition and monopoly. Graph 1(a) shows the demand function as the marginal revenue curve, for perfect competition. That indicates that *P = MR under perfect competition*, e.g., Price at P_E in graph 1(a). For monopoly, P > MR (graph 1(b)). MR is derived from the downward sloping demand curve. As illustrated in graph 1(b), the marginal revenue function becomes more distant from the demand function as price decreases.

   B. These relationships between P and MR differ for the two markets basically on the basis of a firm being a price-taker (perfect competition) or a price-maker (monopoly). The perfectly competitive firm is a price-taker, for example, the market where all buyers and sellers meet determines the price. Graph 1, parts (c) and (d) illustrate this point. In 1(d), the market determines the

For monopoly or other forms of imperfect competition, there is a downward sloping demand curve that indicates that the seller can induce more sales of a product by lowering the price. Since marginal revenue is derived from the demand function or price, we find that P > MR. As illustrated below:

TABLE 6
MONOPOLY

$P	Q	$TR	$MR
10	1	10	
9	2	18	8
8	3	24	6
7	4	28	4
6	5	30	2
5	6	30	0
4	7	28	−2
3	8	24	−4

This indicates that the monopolist can be a price-maker.

C. All of the above suggests a significant effect on price strategy that will be different for the monopolist as contrasted with the perfect competitor. Essentially, the perfect competitor has no price strategy. As explained and illustrated above, the perfect competitive firm is a price-taker—accepts the price as determined by the market and does not vary price as more units are sold. P = MR is reflective of this. The price competitor's only market decision is how many units to sell. To attempt sales at a higher than market price would result in loss of sales to competitors; to attempt sales at lower than market price would result in losses in the long run.

For the monopolist, there is a pricing strategy. As explained and illustrated above, the monopolist faces a downward sloping demand function (P > MR) and can induce more sales by lowering the price. Thus the monopolist can be a price-maker. This power is enhanced by the monopolist having no competitors (within the industry) that have close substitutes. Of course, the price elasticities of demand can place limits on both the lowering of prices and the increasing of prices. The relationship among price, elasticity of demand, and marginal revenue is $MR = P[1 − (1/\eta)]$ where η = numerical coefficient of elasticity.

2. A. The ratio of (P − MR)/P demonstrates the degree of marketing power for firms, that is, the larger the value of the index, the larger the mark-up pricing power of the firm. The smaller the firm's demand elasticity at the profit-maximizing output, the greater the Price minus MC market-up and the greater the monopoly power. We start with the criterion for profit maximization being that level of output where MR = MC. As explained in essay number 1, P > MR for the imperfectly competitive firm and P = MR for the perfectly competitive firm. Therefore, for the monopolist P > MC. Thus, the numerator for the monopolist will be positive or greater than zero. However, for the perfectly competitive firm the index value of the ratio will equal zero. This follows from P = MR and MR = MC for perfect competition. All of this can be put to symbols and values of the ratio as follows:

For imperfectly competitive firms:

$\dfrac{(P − MC)}{P}$ → P > MC → positive value
→ positive since all prices are above zero. Thus, ratio is positive (follows from P > MC and MR = MC)

For perfectly competitive firms:

since P = MC and P = MR and MR = MC

$$\frac{(P − MC)}{P} = \frac{0}{>0} = 0$$

Therefore, since P > MC in imperfectly competitive markets and

P = MC in perfectly competitive markets, the pricing power is clearly that of monopolists or other imperfectly competitive firms. They can charge a price higher than their marginal costs.

B. The consequences of A are that the perfectly competitive firm must charge a price that is equal to marginal cost. This is a socially optimal or efficient price. In other words, the consumer is able to coax out an additional unit of a product at a price exactly equal to the added cost (MC) of the producer. Society pays what is minimally necessary to induce or maintain production of goods. Conversely, if consumers pay a price greater than marginal cost, consumers are paying a rent to the producer, a price *higher* than would be minimally necessary to induce additional production. The monopolist has pricing power, a price-maker, subject to constraints. The perfect competitor has no pricing power, or P = MC, P = MR.

3. For this question, we advise that you draw two graphs, side by side, as illustrated in graph 2(a) and (b).

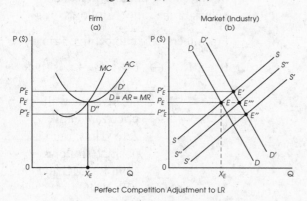

Perfect Competition Adjustment to LR

We begin at equilibrium with the market at price, P_E, and with each firm selling and producing at P_E. At P_E and associated output, X_E, each firm sells and produces its output where P = MC, P = MR, P = minimum average cost. Next, demand increases from DD to

D'D'. Each firm now sees its demand increasing to D'. Since MR = P, price (P_E) is now in excess of average cost and short run profits are realized. The profits induce new firms to enter in such a way that supply SS increases to S'S'. This excess supply suppresses prices to P''_E and firms incur losses (D''D'' lower than AC). Some (less efficient) firms exit and the consequent new equilibrium point (E''') is at the same level of price (P_E) as the original equilibrium.

Consequently, the old equilibrium of P_E and X_E are restored. Thus, in long run equilibrium under perfect competition, P = MC; P = MR; P = minimum average cost and profits are zero economic profits. The economy is operating efficiently and the socially optimal price, P = MC, obtains.

4. For the butter and margarine markets, the following graphs are provided.

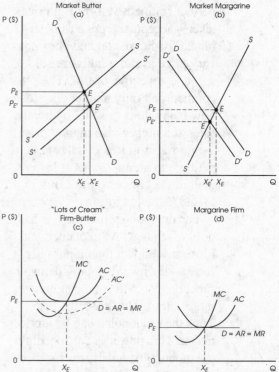

A. The new churner allows the Lots of Cream company to lower its average costs so that, given a market price of P_E, it will increase its short-term profits. The firm's price will stay the same since the price is set in the market (price-taker), but its profits will rise from zero to positive profits. The decrease in costs is illustrated as average cost moves from AC to AC'. Thus, economic profits exist as P stays the same and AC decreases. Before the cost decrease, P = minimum AC resulting in zero profits.

B. The effect of the other competitive firms adopting the same cost-saving technology is that the supply curve in graph 3(a) for the butter market would increase (shift in supply to the right), which is illustrated as a shift from SS to S'S'. The effect of this would be a decrease in the equilibrium price from P_E to P'_E and an increase in equilibrium quantity from X_E to X'_E. If costs of production decrease, the market would increase its supply of butter, *ceteris paribus*. This means that the price-cost ratio increases with price staying constant (competitive market) and costs decreasing so that suppliers are motivated to provide more products.

C. The effects of the above changes on the price and quantity of margarine would be that since margarine and butter are substitutes, and since the price of butter has decreased, the demand for margarine would decrease (from DD to D'D') resulting in a decrease in the equilibrium price from P_E to P'_E and a decrease in equilibrium quantity from X_E to X'_E as illustrated in Graph 3(b).

MACROECONOMICS

CHAPTER
14 The National Income and Product Accounts

The Accounts

The National Income and Product Accounts (NIPA) are a comprehensive group of statistics that measure various aspects of the economy's performance. For instance, if everyone's income in the United States was summed together, how much would that be? The figure for personal income in 1999 is $7,791.8 billion. What were corporate profits in 1999? $892.7 billion. Personal income and corporate profits are two examples of the hundreds of statistics included in NIPA.

NIPA includes a variety of measures of income and production. The most recent updates on these figures are published by the Department of Commerce in a periodical titled the "Survey of Current Business." On the World Wide Web, updates are available at *www.bea.doc.gov*, the home page of the Bureau of Economic Analysis (BEA), an agency within the Department of Commerce.

Gross Domestic Product

The premier statistic for measuring the overall performance of the economy is gross domestic product (GDP). GDP measures the dollar value of production within the nation's borders. Generally speaking, the more that is produced, the healthier the economy.

The BEA provides "flash" estimates of GDP for each quarter about 30 days after the quarter ends, but these rough estimates are subject to large revisions. The annual estimates of GDP are more reliable, but they too are subject to revision.

An amazing feature of these estimates is that they are available on such a timely basis. Consider all of the goods and services produced in the United States in a year, from toothpicks and space shuttles to haircuts and surgery. How does the BEA keep track of all this production? For 1999, GDP was estimated to be $9,256.1 billion.

How did the BEA arrive at this figure? A small army of statisticians and analysts keeps track of production and sales of a wide variety of goods and services. For instance, one person is responsible for Popsicle sticks, toothpicks, and tongue depressors. This person gets in touch with the major suppliers and retailers of these products. From this survey an estimate of the number of toothpicks sold is obtained. There is a difference between the number of toothpicks sold and the number produced, but this difference will be allowed for later. The survey of manufacturers and retailers also yields an average price of toothpicks. Then the number of toothpicks sold is multiplied by their price to get the dollar value of toothpick sales.

The dollar values of all other products sold are added to the figure for toothpicks to obtain an estimate of total sales of goods and services. The resulting figure is known as "final sales" and is part of NIPA. But it is not GDP. GDP measures *production* not sales. There may be goods that are produced but not sold. They will show up in inventories at the manufacturers or at the retailers. Therefore, the change in business inventories is added to final sales to arrive at GDP.

Table 14.1 shows the calculation of GDP for a hypothetical economy that produces only two products—pizza and soda. In the year 2000, 4 pizzas are produced at an average retail price of $10; 12 sodas are produced at a price of $2. GDP is $64. In the year 2001, pizza production is up to 5 pizzas and the price has increased to $11. Soda production is up to 15 units, but the price has fallen to $1. GDP is $70.

TABLE 14.1
CALCULATING GDP

Year 2000		
Production	Price	Value
4 Pizzas	$10	$40
12 Sodas	$2	$24
		GDP = $64
Year 2001		
Production	Price	Value
5 Pizzas	$11	$55
15 Sodas	$1	$15
		GDP = $70

This is a general overview of how GDP is estimated. In practice, many more complications arise. Some of these complications will come to light as we examine the expenditure and the income approaches to calculating GDP.

The Expenditures Approach

Consumption Expenditures
If you look up the estimates of GDP in the "Survey of Current Business," don't expect to see the dollar value of toothpicks sold or produced. That level of detail would require a publication much thicker than the metropolitan New York phone book. Instead, the BEA lumps together all the goods and services sold to households and calls this consumption expenditures.

Government Expenditures
However, state, local, and federal governments also make expenditures. The things that are produced and sold to governments are summed together and referred to as government expenditures. Some of the products that governments buy are unique to this category. For instance, fighter jets are sold to our federal government but not to individual households. On the other hand, our government purchases many of the same items bought by households, such as personal computers; but

the value of personal computers purchased by the government will be different than that of households.

Investment Expenditures

Expenditures by businesses on plant and equipment are called investment expenditures; thus, the term "investment" means something very different in its economic sense. It does not refer to households buying stocks or bonds. The complete definition of investment is business expenditures on plant and equipment plus the change in business inventories. The change in business inventories was mentioned in the previous section. It changes the figure for final sales into GDP. The BEA lumps the change in inventories in with business spending on plant and equipment to get what it calls investment.

Exports and Imports

Many goods and services are produced and sold abroad. These are called exports. It should be noted that some of the expenditures made by households, government, and businesses will be from abroad. These imports should not be included in our GDP since they represent production outside our nation's borders. That is why imports are subtracted from exports to get "net exports."

GDP represents production. Some of the goods and services produced go to households, some to government, some to businesses, and some are sold abroad. Imports are subtracted out because these products were not made domestically, yet they are counted in consumption expenditures by households, purchases by government, and investment by firms.

The expenditure approach to calculating GDP is often summarized with the formula:

$$GDP = C + I + G + X$$

where C is consumption expenditures by households

I is investment by firms

G is government purchases

X is net exports = exports − imports

The formula appears deceptively simple. Remember that to obtain the figure for C, consumption expenditures, quite a bit of effort is required. The average price and quantity sold of millions of products must be gathered. The same must be done for I, G, and X.

Table 14.2 shows the components of the expenditures approach to calculating GDP with their values for 1999. Notice that about two-thirds of all the goods and services produced go to households.

TABLE 14.2

THE EXPENDITURE APPROACH TO GDP—1999 (BILLIONS OF DOLLARS)

Consumption expenditures	6,257.3
Government expenditures	1,630.1
Investment	1,622.6
Net exports	−253.9
GDP	9,256.1

Source: U.S. Department of Commerce, Bureau of Economic Analysis

The Income Approach

The BEA takes the trouble to calculate GDP in a manner completely different from the expenditures approach outlined above. This second way of calculating GDP is known as the income approach. The income approach yields several statistics that are incorporated into NIPA and provides a check on the expenditures approach.

Theoretically, both techniques for calculating GDP will result in exactly the same figure because when anything is produced, whether it is a stick of gum or a skyscraper, just enough income is generated in the production process to equal the value of what is produced.

Consider a toaster that retails for $15. Suppose it costs $10 to manufacture it:

Labor	$6
Materials	$3
Overhead	$1

Since the toaster retails for $15, then $5 in profits were made when it was sold. So, if everyone who had anything to do with the manufacture of the toaster chipped in the income they made, it would equal $15 exactly. Workers made $6; raw material owners made $3; the utility company (overhead) made $1; and the owner of the toaster company made $5. Altogether, this comes to $15.

Notice that if the toaster sold for $15.01, then $5.01 in profits would have been earned and the principle would still hold true: Whenever anything is produced, just enough is earned to buy it back. Therefore, an alternate way to measure GDP, which measures production, would be to add up all the income that was earned in the economy. That is the income approach to calculating GDP.

Table 14.3 outlines the income approach for calculating GDP. Wages and salaries are the predominant type of income. But there is also proprietors' income, rental income, and interest income. Corporate profits must also be included because this represents corporate income and corporations are owned by their shareholders. There are some adjustments that must be made once all the types of income are summed together. Specifically, indirect business taxes (such as business licenses) and depreciation must be added in.

TABLE 14.3
THE INCOME APPROACH TO GDP—1999 (BILLIONS OF DOLLARS)

Wages and salaries	5,331.7
Proprietors' income	658.6
Rental income	145.9
Interest income	467.5
Corporate profits	892.7
Indirect business taxes	624.0
Depreciation	1,135.8
GDP	9,256.1*

* Does not sum exactly due to rounding
Source: U.S. Department of Commerce, Bureau of Economic Analysis

Adjusting for Price Changes

GDP measures production but one cannot conclude that more was produced simply because this year's GDP was greater than last because prices may have risen. The rise in prices could offset a decline in production volume, resulting in a higher figure for GDP. Clearly, if the prices of the goods and services produced changes, so will GDP, regardless of production.

There is, however, a simple way to correct for price changes: When calculating GDP for different years, use prices from just one of those years. This way the prices are constant from one year to the next and any change in GDP must be due to a change in production.

The BEA routinely makes this correction and the resulting figure is known as "real GDP," or "constant-dollar GDP." In order to make the distinction, regular GDP is sometimes referred to as "nominal" or "current-dollar GDP." The year from which prices are taken to calculate real GDP is called the base year. It does not matter which year is chosen as the base year. The important feature is that prices are held constant, so that any changes in real GDP are the result of changes in the amount of production.

Table 14.4 shows nominal and real GDP over the years. An astute reader could deduce that 1996 is the base year since real and nominal GDP are equivalent in that year. Once nominal and real GDP have been calculated, it is a simple matter to obtain a measure of price changes. But this statistic will be discussed in the next chapter when inflation and price indexes are taken up.

TABLE 14.4
NOMINAL AND REAL GDP

	Nominal GDP (billions of $)	Real GDP (billions of chained 1996 $)
1990	5,803.2	6,707.9
1991	5,986.2	6,676.4
1992	6,318.9	6,880.0
1993	6,642.3	7,062.6
1994	7,054.3	7,347.7
1995	7,400.5	7,543.8
1996	7,813.2	7,813.2
1997	8,300.8	8,144.8
1998	8,759.9	8,495.7
1999	9,256.1	8,848.2

Source: U.S. Department of Commerce, Bureau of Economic Analysis

The Underground Economy

Each year there are trillions of dollars of goods and services that are produced and never counted in GDP. All of this production falls into what is called the underground economy. The first thing that comes to mind with regard to the underground economy is illegal items and activities, but illegal production and ill-gotten income are the smaller part of the underground economy.

Marry your auto mechanic, the saying goes, and you will lower GDP. This is true because when you took your car to the shop to be repaired, the BEA was able to estimate the transaction and include it in GDP under household consumption. Now that the mechanic is your spouse, the auto repairs are done out back under the shade tree. The BEA does not attempt to measure this sort of production.

Anything households do for themselves and that does not pass through a market goes unmeasured. This amounts to quite a bit of production. The backyard gardens, the lawn maintenance, the cleaning, the baby-sitting, etc. One estimate of underground household production puts it at 30 percent of official GDP.

Illegal gambling services, prostitution, and drugs are not counted in official GDP estimates. The housepainter who insists on being paid in cash to avoid taxes is part of the underground economy.

Adding together the legal and illegal sides of the underground economy, some analysts get a figure that is 150 percent of the official figure. That implies that production in the United States in 1999 was closer to $13,884.2 billion than the official figure of $9,256.1 billion.

Other Things That Are Not Counted in GDP

The underground economy is a subset of total production that is not counted in GDP but, technically speaking, should be. The illegal nature of the goods and services involved often prohibits estimation. However, there is a list of things that are not counted in GDP and rightly so.

1. For instance, it would be incorrect to count secondhand sales in GDP. When you sell your 1997 Ford truck, this does not represent production in the current year. The truck was counted in the GDP of 1997 and there is no reason to count it, or any portion of it, again simply because it is being resold.
2. Transactions that are purely financial are not, and should not be, counted in GDP. If you buy 100 shares of IBM stock, this does not directly represent any new production. Someone got your money and got their shares of IBM. This swap does not affect GDP.
3. Intermediate sales are not included in GDP. These are sales to firms that will incorporate the item into their final product. An example will help here. When a corporation that makes Popsicles buys Popsicle sticks, this is an intermediate sale. When a person buys a Popsicle, he cannot avoid buying the stick as well. This latter transaction is counted in GDP and valued at the price of the Popsicle and the stick. So the stick would be counted twice if the purchase of sticks by the manufacturer was included in GDP and the final sale to the consumer was also counted.

   As another example of an intermediate transaction, the purchase of flour by a baker is not counted in GDP because the flour will get counted when the bread is purchased by a household. However, when a baker buys a delivery truck, this is not an intermediate transaction and the purchase gets counted in GDP under investment expenditures.

Other Measures in the National Income and Product Accounts

Table 14.5 highlights several other important measures in NIPA aside from GDP. Again, GDP measures overall production, and therefore income as well, in the economy. Net domestic product (NDP) takes into account the fact that a certain amount of plant and equipment is worn out in the production process.

TABLE 14.5
GDP AND OTHER MEASURES IN NIPA 1999 (BILLIONS OF DOLLARS)

Gross Domestic Product (GDP)	9,256.1
Minus depreciation	1,135.8
Equals Net Domestic Product (NDP)	8,120.3
Minus indirect business taxes	624.0
Equals National Income (NI)	7,496.3
Minus Social Security contributions	658.2
Minus corporate taxes	259.4
Minus retained earnings	224.4
Plus transfer payments	1,437.5
Equals Personal Income (PI)	7,791.8
Minus personal taxes	1,152.1
Equals disposable Personal Income (DPI)	6,639.7

Source: U.S. Department of Commerce, Bureau of Economic Analysis

Specifically, NDP is GDP minus depreciation. Depreciation, often referred to as the *capital consumption allowance*, is a dollar estimate of how much plant and equipment deteriorated in a given time period. Therefore, NDP represents how much was produced net of the capital that wore away in the process.

Another figure, national income (NI), measures the income earned by households and profits earned by firms after adjusting for depreciation and indirect business taxes. NI is often defined as the income earned by all the factors of production. The factors of production are land, labor, and capital.

NI represents the income earned by households and firms, but personal income (PI) represents the income received by households only. In order to derive PI from NI, the profits made and retained by corporations must be taken out. This can be tricky because some of the profits earned by firms are distributed to households in the form of dividends. Since dividends are part of household income, they should be included in PI, but other corporate earnings should be excluded.

These other corporate earnings take the form of corporate taxes, Social Security contributions, and retained earnings. Hence these forms of corporate earnings are taken out of NI to arrive at PI.

One other adjustment is necessary to reach PI. Transfer payments must be added in. Transfer payments are payments from the government to households in the form of Veterans' Benefits, unemployment compensation, various welfare benefits, and so forth. Transfer payments are a form of income to the households that receive them, so they should be included in PI. However, transfer payments are a form of "unearned" income, which is why they are not part of NI.

To summarize, PI is equal to NI minus Social Security contributions, corporate taxes, and retained earnings, plus transfer payments.

Finally, disposable personal income (DPI) is the income of households after taxes have been paid. It is easily derived by subtracting personal taxes from PI. Disposable income represents the discretionary income of households. It can be spent or saved.

Summary

- NIPA are a bank of internally consistent statistics that measure various aspects of the economy's performance. Basically, NIPA measure production and income in their various forms. An implicit assumption behind the statistics is that more production and more income means a better economy.
- Some economists have questioned this assumption. Are we really better off when we produce more gadgets and gizmos, and pollute the environment in the process? Is it possible for more to be produced and more income to be earned while the quality of life deteriorates? Another criticism of NIPA concerns leisure time. Don't rising production levels sometimes result in less leisure time? If so, this is not reflected in the statistics where the negative side effects of increased production levels are not taken into account.
- Despite these criticisms, NIPA are the best measures available for gauging the economy's health. One final note: Other nations have similar statistics, but they may not be defined or collected in the same way. There are, however, some organizations that generate and publish international data that are comparable across countries. Putting the statistics on a per capita basis also facilitates international comparisons.

TABLE 14.6
GDP AND GDP PER CAPITA FOR SELECTED COUNTRIES—1996

Country	GDP (billions of $)	GDP per Capita ($ per person)
Canada	645	21,529
Denmark	118	22,418
Japan	2,925	23,235
Switzerland	181	25,402
United Kingdom	1,096	18,636
United States	7,388	27,821

Source: Organization for Economic Cooperation and Development

Terms

Consumption Expenditures   all the goods and services sold to households

Disposable Personal Income (DPI)   the income of households after taxes have been paid

Government Expenditures   goods and services sold to governments

Gross Domestic Product (GDP)   dollar value of production within a nation's borders

Intermediate Sales   sales to firms that will incorporate the item into their final product

Investment Expenditures   expenditures by businesses on plant and equipment and the change in business inventories

National Income (NI)   the income earned by households and profits earned by firms after subtracting depreciation and indirect business taxes

National Income and Product Accounts (NIPA)   a comprehensive group of statistics that measures various aspects of the economy's performance

Net Domestic Product (NDP)   GDP minus depreciation

Net Exports   exports minus imports

Personal Income (PI)   income received by households

Real GDP   GDP adjusted for price changes

Transfer Payments   payments from the government to households that qualify for income support programs

Underground Economy   all the illegal production of goods and services and legal production that does not pass through markets

Formulas

$$GDP = C + I + G + X$$

$$GDP \text{ per Capita} = \frac{GDP}{Population}$$

Multiple-Choice Review Questions

D. B and C.
E. A and C.

6. National income measures

   A. household income in the nation.
   B. income earned by the factors of production.
   C. GDP minus depreciation and indirect business taxes.
   D. the income earned by households and profits earned by firms after adjusting for depreciation and indirect business taxes.
   E. B., C., and D.

1. GDP is calculated for each _____ by _____.

   A. quarter ; The Bureau of Economic Analysis
   B. week ; The Bureau of Economic Analysis
   C. month ; The Bureau of Economic Analysis
   D. month ; The Bureau of Labor Statistics
   E. quarter ; The Bureau of Labor Statistics

2. "Flash" estimates of GDP

   A. are subject to revision.
   B. do not require revision.
   C. are available after a thirty day lag.
   D. both A. and C.
   E. both B. and C.

3. According to the way in which economists use the word, the bulk of "investment" is done by

   A. households.
   B. businesses.
   C. government.
   D. foreigners.
   E. all of the above.

4. In the equation GDP = C + I + G + X, X stands for

   A. exports.
   B. expenditures.
   C. exports minus imports.
   D. imports minus exports.
   E. export taxes.

5. GDP measures

   A. production within a nation's borders.
   B. production by a nation's citizens wherever they may be.
   C. income earned by the factors of production plus depreciation and indirect business taxes.

7. Imagine an economy that produces only two goods, cheese and crackers. Calculate GDP for this economy if cheese retails for $3 a pound and 10 pounds are produced while crackers sell for $2 a pound and 20 pounds are produced.

   A. $35
   B. $1,200
   C. $70
   D. $150
   E. Not enough information is given to calculate GDP.

8. Assume Country Z only produces hot dogs and buns. Given the table below, what is the value of GDP in Country Z?

Production	Price
4 hot dogs	$1.00
4 buns	$0.50

   A. $1.50
   B. $12.00
   C. $6.00
   D. $8.00
   E. $4.50

9. If XYZ Corporation buys an original Matisse painting to hang in its board room, then

   A. GDP decreases by the amount of the purchase because C decreases.

B. GDP increases by the amount of the purchase because I increases.

C. GDP is unaffected because it is a second hand sale.

D. GDP decreases because I decreases.

E. I increases, but C decreases.

10. The cabbages you grow in your summer garden are

A. counted in GDP under C.

B. counted in GDP under I.

C. counted in GDP but not NDP.

D. not counted in GDP.

E. counted in final sales but not GDP.

11. Suppose transfer payments are greater than Social Security contributions, corporate taxes, and retained earnings combined. In that case,

A. NDP will be greater than GDP.

B. NI will be greater than GDP.

C. PI will be greater than NI.

D. DPI will be greater than PI.

E. PI will be greater than GDP.

12. GDP measures

I. production

II. income earned during the production process

III. spending by consumers, businesses, governments, and foreigners

A. Only I is correct.

B. Only II is correct.

C. Only III is correct.

D. Only I and II are correct.

E. I, II, and III are correct.

13. Real GDP

A. is actual GDP as opposed to the estimate made by the BEA.

B. is also called current-dollar GDP.

C. is GDP adjusted for price changes.

D. is not calculated for the United States.

E. B. and C. are both correct.

14. Which of the following events has no effect on GDP?

A. You buy a 1957 Chevy from a friend.

B. The Department of Transportation repaves a road.

C. Your friends make a music CD that doesn't sell any copies.

D. A college buys computers.

E. You buy a bottle of French wine.

15. Which of the following will have an effect on GDP?

A. You lose $50 betting with a friend.

B. You fix your brother's car without buying any new parts.

C. Your father's firm makes computers and exports them to China.

D. You buy 1,000 shares of stock in a corporation.

E. Your wealthy uncle buys a painting by Picasso.

MULTIPLE-CHOICE REVIEW ANSWERS

1. **A**	4. **C**	7. **C**	10. **D**	13. **C**
2. **D**	5. **E**	8. **C**	11. **C**	14. **A**
3. **B**	6. **E**	9. **C**	12. **E**	15. **C**

Free-Response Review Questions

I. Explain the difference between nominal GDP, real GDP, and GDP per capita.

II. Suppose that production and prices rise from one year to the next, but population stays constant. Will each of the three statistics above rise, fall, or remain unchanged? Explain your reasoning.

III. In what type of situation is GDP per capita more appropriate than nominal or real GDP?

IV. Is GDP an under- or overestimate? Explain.

FREE-RESPONSE REVIEW ANSWERS

I. Nominal GDP measures the production of goods and services within a nation's borders. Nominal GDP could increase because of an increase in output or an increase in the prices of the goods and services produced. Real GDP measures production, but adjusts for any price changes. Real GDP does not change if prices change because it values current output in terms of prices of the given base period. Only one thing can cause real GDP to change and that is a change in output. GDP per capita is production per person.

II. If production and prices rise while population stays constant then all three statistics, GDP, real GDP, and GDP per capita will rise.

III. GDP per capita is most appropriate for making international comparisons of GDP. The GDP of the United States is much greater than that of Switzerland, but production per person, and therefore living standards, are not all that different between the two nations.

IV. GDP is a vast underestimate of output because of all the production that is not counted. Items that do not go through standard markets are not counted. This includes illegal drugs and gambling, but also home car repair and household vegetable gardens. All of this uncounted production is known as the underground economy. Estimates are that the underground economy could be half the size of the official economy.

CHAPTER
15 Inflation and Unemployment

The Twin Evils

Both *inflation* and *unemployment* exert an enormous toll on the economy and, therefore, on our standards of living. The cost of unemployment is obvious. An important resource, labor, is being underutilized. This implies that we are not producing as much as if we were using our resources fully. In economic terms, we are producing inside the production possibilities frontier. Moreover, the households that are experiencing unemployment face real hardships.

The costs associated with inflation are less obvious. Many people understand that rising prices can hurt families on fixed incomes, but this is only a minor issue because most incomes keep pace with rising prices. When prices rise, someone benefits—the owners of the firms that produce the goods and services whose prices are rising. In general, rising prices imply rising incomes, so falling real incomes are not a major cost of inflation.

We will see that a more significant cost associated with inflation is the inefficiencies that ensue when people respond to rising prices. Again, we will be producing at a point inside the production possibilities frontier if we do not use our resources efficiently.

In addition, inflation arbitrarily takes purchasing power from some households and puts it in the hands of others. A massive redistribution of wealth is yet another cost of inflation.

The costs to society of rising prices are much more subtle than the blunt and obvious damages caused by unemployment. Nevertheless, it is unclear which economic evil is more pernicious. Only normative conclusions are possible on this question.

Inflation

HOW INFLATION IS MEASURED
Inflation is a sustained rise in most prices in the economy. The inflation rate is the rate at which prices are rising. It is much easier to define inflation than to measure it.

Each month the Bureau of Labor Statistics (BLS) checks prices on 90,000 items at more than 23,000 retail and service outlets. The BLS checks prices in urban, suburban, and rural areas. Because prices are liable to be different in different regions, the BLS must check prices on the same items in every part of the country.

The result of all this effort is the predominant measure of the cost of living in the United States—the consumer price index (CPI). The CPI measures the average change over time in the prices paid by urban consumers for a market basket of consumer goods and services. The BLS computes the CPI for each month.

Consider a simple example where the typical household in the economy consumes 5 packages of cheese and 8 boxes of crackers in a month. If the price of cheese rises to $2.25 from $2.00 and the price of crackers climbs to $1.50 from $1.25, then the CPI rises to 116.25 from 100. The calculations are shown in table 15.1. The assumption is that period 1 is the base period, the period to which all other periods are compared.

TABLE 15.1
CALCULATING THE CONSUMER PRICE INDEX

Period 1

Item	Price	Amount	Cost
Cheese	$2.00	5	$10.00
Crackers	$1.25	8	$10.00

Total cost = $20.00

$$CPI = \frac{\text{Total Cost this Period}}{\text{Total Cost Base Period}} \times 100 = \frac{20.00}{20.00} \times 100 = 100$$

Period 2

Item	Price	Amount	Cost
Cheese	$2.25	5	$11.25
Crackers	$1.50	8	$12.00

Total cost = $23.25

$$CPI = \frac{\text{Total Cost this Period}}{\text{Total Cost Base Period}} \times 100 = \frac{23.25}{20.00} \times 100 = 116.25$$

Period 3

Item	Price	Amount	Cost
Cheese	$2.35	5	$11.75
Crackers	$1.60	8	$12.80

Total cost = $24.55

$$CPI = \frac{\text{Total Cost this Period}}{\text{Total Cost Base Period}} \times 100 = \frac{24.55}{20.00} \times 100 = 122.75$$

In period 3, the CPI rises to 122.75. To calculate the inflation rate between any two periods, take the percentage change in the CPI. For example, the inflation rate between periods 2 and 3 is:

Inflation Rate = (122.75 − 116.25)/116.25 = .0559 = 5.59%

The inflation rate between periods 1 and 3 is:

Inflation Rate = (122.75 − 100.00)/100.00 = .2275 = 22.75%

These calculations indicate that the cost of living for a typical family in this economy increased 5.59 percent between periods 1 and 2 and 22.75 percent between periods 1 and 3.

In the real world, many complications arise when calculating the CPI that are not apparent in this simple example. For instance, what should be done when the quality of a product changes? The price of automobiles has risen dramatically since the 1950s, but so has the quality of the product. A new car these days comes with seat belts and air bags—safety devices that were not available in earlier versions of the product. Quality improvements such as this account for some portion of the price rise. The CPI overstates the amount of inflation since it does not account for all quality improvements.

This is just one example of how the CPI can overstate cost of living increases. A 1996 study from a bipartisan commission concluded that the CPI overstates inflation by more than one percentage point a year. The discrepancy is important because most income maintenance programs, such as Social Security, adjust their benefit payments with the CPI.

THE GDP DEFLATOR

Inflation can be measured with another statistic—the GDP deflator. In the previous chapter we discussed how GDP and real GDP are calculated. Both of these statistics can be used to obtain the GDP deflator through a simple formula:

$$\text{GDP Deflator} = (\text{GDP/Real GDP}) \times 100$$

In 1999 GDP was $9,256.1 billion, while real GDP equaled $8,848.2 billion. Therefore the GDP deflator for 1999 was 104.6 (= (9,256.1/8,848.2) × 100). Table 15.2 shows GDP, real GDP, and the GDP deflator over the years.

TABLE 15.2
GDP, REAL GDP, AND THE GDP DEFLATOR

$$\text{GDP Deflator} = \frac{\text{Nominal GDP}}{\text{Real GDP}} \times 100$$

$$\text{Real GDP} = \frac{\text{Nominal GDP}}{\text{GDP Deflator}} \times 100$$

Year	Nominal GDP	Real GDP	GDP Deflator
1990	5,803.2	6,707.9	86.5
1991	5,986.2	6,676.4	89.7
1992	6,318.9	6,880.0	91.8
1993	6,642.3	7,062.6	94.0
1994	7,054.3	7,347.7	96.0
1995	7,400.5	7,543.8	98.1
1996	7,813.2	7,813.2	100.0
1997	8,300.8	8,144.8	101.9
1998	8,759.9	8,495.7	103.1
1999	9,256.1	8,848.2	104.6

Source: U.S. Department of Commerce, Bureau of Economic Analysis

To calculate the inflation rate between any two years simply take the percentage change in the GDP deflator. By what percent did prices rise from 1993 to 1999? 11.3 percent (= (104.6 − 94.0)/94.0)). In other words, there was 11.3 percent inflation between 1993 and 1999.

The GDP deflator, like the CPI, measures the level of prices in the economy. The inflation rates derived from the GDP deflator, however, do not match the inflation rates obtained from the CPI. Both inflation gauges suggest the same general pattern of inflation over the years.

The GDP deflator ignores import prices. If the price of imported beer increased, the CPI would rise in response, but not the GDP deflator. Still, for most years the CPI and the GDP deflator do not differ markedly.

In some instances we may have data on the GDP deflator and GDP, then we can calculate real GDP with the following formula:

$$\text{Real GDP} = (\text{GDP/GDP Deflator}) \times 100$$

In 1998 GDP was \$8,759.9 billion and the GDP deflator equaled 103.1. Therefore, real GDP was \$8,495.7 billion (= (8759.9/103.1) × 100). (**Note**: Due to rounding this calculation is not exact.)

THE COSTS OF INFLATION

Many people think that the most damaging aspect of inflation is that it erodes purchasing power. It is true that any household whose income does not keep pace with inflation will be hurt. But for the vast majority of households, incomes keep pace with, if not exceed, price increases.

1. To understand why, consider the circular flow diagram presented earlier in the text (page 32). If the prices paid for goods and services produced by firms increases, firms take in more revenue. If this revenue is not passed back to households in the form of higher wages or rent, the firms make more profits. But someone owns the firms and the profits become their income. More specifically, the profits are returned to households in the form of dividends. So higher prices always translate into higher levels of income.

2. Inflation can be detrimental even if a household's income rises as fast as prices. This is because the value of savings accounts, trust funds, brokerage accounts, and other forms of financial wealth will be worth less than before the inflation. In other words, inflation erodes the purchasing power of savings. Savings play an important role in the economy. Households, businesses, and governments often need to borrow funds. Inflation discourages savings.

3. Another problem with inflation is the resources that are wasted dealing with higher prices. Firms have to print new brochures, restaurants need to produce new menus, and price lists in all the media will have to be revised. This takes time and effort. Resources that could have been used more productively are deployed to cope with rising prices. The misallocation of resources because of inflation is sometimes called "menu costs."

4. A final issue associated with inflation has to do with borrowing and lending in inflationary conditions. Lenders can be hurt by inflation because the dollars they loaned out are repaid at a later date with dollars that are not worth as much because of inflation. Imagine lending a friend \$100 for a year at 10 percent interest. A year later the friend repays you \$110. But suppose prices had risen 12 percent over the course of the loan. Your \$110 could not even buy what your \$100 could a year ago.

   By the same token, borrowers could benefit from inflation because they get to repay their borrowings with inflated dollars. Why don't banks get hurt by inflation? Aren't they big lenders? They are, but they are also smart enough to add an inflation surcharge onto the interest rate that they charge. When a bank lends \$100 dollars to your friend it might charge 22 percent—10 percent for their real return and 12 percent to cover the cost of inflation that they expect over the course of the loan.

   The idea that some lenders would protect themselves from inflation by charging higher interest on loans was codified into a formula by Irving Fisher in the early 1900s, the formula is known as "Fisher's Hypothesis":

$$\text{Nominal Interest Rate} = \text{Real Interest Rate} + \text{Expected Inflation}$$

   The nominal interest rate is the rate actually paid. The real interest rate is the actual return the lender receives net of inflation.

The end result is that lenders who do not anticipate inflation will be hurt, but the borrower would benefit in this case. The biggest lender in the economy is households if you consider putting money in a bank account a loan to the bank. Notice that the nominal interest rate paid by banks is not adjusted upward for expected inflation. Households are big lenders who do not anticipate inflation; therefore, they will be hurt by rising prices.

The federal government is the biggest borrower in the United States' economy. It stands to benefit from inflation because it can repay its borrowings with inflated dollars.

If you think about it, inflation works just like a tax because households are major lenders and the government is a major borrower. It is as if Uncle Sam reaches into your wallet every night while you sleep and slips out just a little cash so that you don't even notice. The inflation tax is the result of the federal government benefiting from inflation while households are harmed. This redistribution of wealth from lenders to borrowers is yet another cost of inflation.

The costs of inflation are summarized in Table 15.3.

TABLE 15.3
THE COSTS OF INFLATION

- Financial wealth is eroded
- Savings are discouraged
- Menu Costs—resources are misallocated with rising prices
- Inflation Tax—wealth is redistributed from lenders to borrowers

Unemployment

The costs associated with unemployment are obvious. Households will encounter hardships, maybe even hunger. Unemployment means that a resource, labor, is not being used to its fullest potential. We are producing inside the production possibilities frontier. We could be producing more and enjoying more goods and services.

Unemployment is a problem during recessions—periods when real GDP is declining. During a recession fewer goods and services are being produced. The amount of labor and other resources required for production is reduced and people find themselves out of work.

The unemployment rate is defined as the number of unemployed persons divided by the labor force. The labor force does not include retired persons, those too young to work, and anyone who has not been actively seeking employment. In order to be counted as unemployed you have to be out of work and looking for a job.

The Bureau of Labor Statistics (BLS) reports the unemployment statistics based on two broad surveys taken each month. One survey contacts employers and asks about employment levels at various business establishments, while the other survey interviews households.

Economists classify the unemployed into five general categories:

1. Those who are able to work, but not actively seeking employment because they are discouraged about their prospects for finding employment, are referred to as *discouraged workers* or the *hidden unemployed*. This situation is unfortunate because these people lack basic skills or suffer from other problems and have a difficult time finding work. Discouraged by their prospects, they no longer bother to pursue employment. These people do not show up in the unemployment statistics because they are not considered to be part of the labor force, thus the name "hidden" unemployment.

2. A form of unemployment that does show up in the official statistics is *structural unemployment*. The structurally unemployed are out of work because the economy is structured, or set up, to their disadvantage. For instance, there may be welders looking for work in Cleveland, but the welding jobs are in Dallas. Or welders may be out of work in Boston, but their are plenty of secretarial jobs open in that same area. Since it is often difficult for a person to relocate or retrain, structural unemployment is not easily remedied.

3. Some persons are able to find work for only a portion of the year due to the seasonal nature of their jobs. These individuals are considered to be *seasonally unemployed* as long as they actively look for work in the off-season. Farmers and construction workers may fall into this category.

4. As mentioned previously, unemployment rises during the contractionary phase of the business cycle. Individuals who lose their jobs during a recession and the corresponding slow-down in production are said to be *cyclically unemployed*. They are out of work specifically because of the business cycle. Hopefully, these people will be back to work when production picks up during the next expansion.

5. Finally, a number of persons are not working because they are in between jobs. Someone who is scheduled to begin a new job next month and does not presently hold a job is considered to be *frictionally unemployed*. It is unlikely that people will be able to switch jobs without some time off. Indeed, some people take advantage of this time to relax or move their households and get their affairs in order. Also, someone who quits one job to look for another is considered to be frictionally unemployed.

In 1999 the labor force was estimated to be 139.4 million persons, while the unemployed numbered 5.9 million. This implies an unemployment rate of 4.2 percent (= 5.9/139.4) Some analysts contend that the unemployment picture is actually much worse than this figure indicates. For one, the 4.2 percent does not count hidden unemployment. Remember, those too discouraged to look for work are not counted as being unemployed or even in the labor force. They are simply not counted.

Another factor to consider is that persons who are working part time are counted as if they are fully employed, even if they would like to have a full-time job. Again, the reported statistic of 4.2 percent understates the unemployment problem.

A related point to keep in mind is that 4.2 percent is the average unemployment rate across the nation. There are sections of the country where the rate is much higher and sections where it is lower. Moreover, it is well known that the unemployment rate is worse for certain groups within the population, such as teenagers.

Many of the people counted as being unemployed are merely frictionally unemployed. In fact, it is estimated that of the 5.9 million persons unemployed in 1999, anywhere from 2 to 4 million are frictionally unemployed. Indeed, economists consider the economy to be at full employment when the unemployment rate reaches the 4 to 5 percent range since the frictionally unemployed account for about that much of the unemployment rate. If the unemployment rate were to fall further, inflation would most likely be a problem. The full employment rate of unemployment is sometimes called NAIRU for the nonaccelerating inflation rate of unemployment.

Despite the criticisms of the unemployment statistic, the fact remains that it is tabulated in the same manner each time, so that a drop in the rate means more people are working or the labor force has shrunk. The unemployment rate is a useful statistic, but care should be taken with its interpretation.

Summary

- Inflation and unemployment are serious economic problems. Inflation causes the misallocation of resources and an arbitrary redistribution of income. Inflation is typically a problem when the economy is overheated—growing faster than normal. But inflation can also occur during recessions. Later we shall see why.
- Unemployment occurs when the economy is operating below its potential. Our most important resource is labor, and unemployment exists when this resource is not being fully utilized. We could have produced more and enjoyed more goods and services if not for the unemployment.
- We have reviewed the major statistics that measure unemployment and inflation and found that they are not perfectly accurate. It is important to understand how the numbers are generated so that their potential deficiencies can be anticipated. For instance, if the price of imported oil is rising rapidly, it is critical to know that the GDP deflator will not reflect this increase. The GDP deflator does not include the prices of imported products. The CPI does.

The most important question concerning inflation and unemployment has been ignored in this chapter: What causes inflation and unemployment? A complete answer is provided in the chapters ahead.

Terms

Consumer Price Index (CPI)   measure of the average change over time in the prices paid by urban consumers for a market basket of consumer goods and services

Cyclical Unemployment   loss of jobs by individuals during a recession and the corresponding slowdown in production

Fisher's Hypothesis   Nominal Interest Rate = Real Interest Rate + Expected Inflation

Frictional Unemployment   state of being out of work because the person is in between jobs

GDP Deflator   measure of the level of prices in the economy

Hidden Unemployment   describing those who are able to work but who are not actively seeking employment because they are discouraged about their prospects for finding employment

Inflation   a sustained rise in most prices in the economy

Menu Costs   the misallocation of resources because of inflation

Nonaccelerating Inflation Rate of Unemployment   the full employment rate of unemployment; when employment falls below this rate, inflation accelerates

Seasonal Unemployment   state of being out of work because of the time of year

Structural Unemployment   state of being out of work because the economy is structured, or set up, to a person's disadvantage

Unemployment Rate   the number of unemployed persons divided by the labor force

Formulas

$$CPI = \frac{\text{Total Cost this Period}}{\text{Total Cost Base Period}} \times 100$$

$$\text{Inflation Rate} = \frac{\text{CPI (this period)} - \text{CPI(previous period)}}{\text{CPI (previous period)}} \times 100$$

$$\text{GDP Deflator} = (\text{GDP/Real GDP}) \times 100$$

$$\text{Real GDP} = (\text{GDP/GDP Deflator}) \times 100$$

$$\text{Nominal Interest Rate} = \text{Real Interest Rate} + \text{Expected Inflation}$$

$$\text{Unemployment Rate} = \text{Number of Unemployed/Civilian Labor Force}$$

Multiple-Choice Review Questions

1. The CPI is calculated for each _____ by _____.

    A. week ; The Bureau of Economic Analysis
    B. month ; The Bureau of Economic Analysis
    C. month ; The Bureau of Labor Statistics
    D. quarter ; The Bureau of Economic Analysis
    E. quarter ; The Bureau of Labor Statistics

2. If the CPI goes to 150 from 120, then prices have

    A. risen 20 percent.
    B. risen 25 percent.
    C. fallen 30 percent.
    D. risen 30 percent.
    E. risen 150 percent.

3. According to experts, the CPI

    A. overstates increases in the cost of living.
    B. understates increases in the cost of living.
    C. accurately estimates changes in the cost of living.
    D. could over- or underestimate changes depending on the season.
    E. should be abandoned in favor of the GDP Deflator.

4. When products improve in quality the CPI will

    A. automatically increase.
    B. automatically decrease.
    C. become negative.
    D. overestimate the inflation rate.
    E. underestimate the inflation rate.

5. The GDP Deflator

    I. is used to calculate inflation rates.
    II. is an alternative to the CPI.
    III. is more accurate than the CPI.

    A. Only I is true.
    B. I and II are true.
    C. I and III are true.
    D. II and III are true.
    E. I, II, and III are true.

6. If nominal GDP equals $5,000 and real GDP equals $4,000, then the GDP Deflator equals

    A. 125
    B. 1.25
    C. 800
    D. .8
    E. 300

7. If nominal GDP equals $6,000 and the GDP deflator equals 200, then real GDP equals

    A. $30
    B. $3,000
    C. $12,000
    D. $1,200
    E. $1,200,000

8. Which of the following is NOT a major cost of inflation?

    A. Resources will be misallocated.
    B. Wealth will be redistributed.
    C. Savings will be discouraged.
    D. Real incomes will fall.
    E. Financial wealth will be eroded.

9. The term "menu costs" refers to

    A. less choices due to inflation.
    B. financial assets being worth less due to inflation.
    C. "à la carte" savings falling.
    D. food prices rising due to inflation.
    E. resource misallocation due to inflation.

10. Inflation

    A. encourages households to save more.
    B. does not affect savings in the economy.

C. forces households to save more.
D. forces households to save less.
E. discourages savings.

11. Rising prices are a problem because

A. money in household savings accounts can now buy fewer goods and services.
B. household incomes generally do not rise with prices.
C. the economy could run out of money.
D. borrowers have to repay loans with more dollars.
E. households are encouraged to save more.

12. Fisher's Hypothesis states that

A. the real interest equals the nominal interest rate plus the inflation rate.
B. the nominal interest rate equals the real interest rate minus the inflation rate.
C. the nominal interest rate equals the unemployment rate plus the real interest rate.
D. the nominal interest rate equals the unemployment rate minus the real interest rate.
E. the nominal interest rate equals the real interest rate plus the inflation rate.

13. Sue loses her job at a shoe factory when the economy falls into a recession. Sue is

A. frictionally unemployed.
B. cyclically unemployed.
C. seasonally unemployed.
D. structurally unemployed.
E. a discouraged worker.

14. There is a strong demand for welders in California but Bill, an unemployed welder, lives in New York. Bill is

A. frictionally unemployed.
B. cyclically unemployed.
C. structurally unemployed.
D. considered to be a hidden worker.
E. not counted in the ranks of the unemployed.

15. It is unlikely that the unemployment rate will ever fall to zero because of

A. frictional unemployment.
B. cyclical unemployment.
C. government policies.
D. corporate policies.
E. the aged and infirm in our population.

MULTIPLE-CHOICE REVIEW ANSWERS

1. C	4. D	7. B	10. E	13. B
2. B	5. B	8. D	11. A	14. C
3. A	6. A	9. E	12. E	15. A

Free-Response Review Questions

Inflation exerts significant costs on the economy. Specifically, explain how inflation

I.   causes a misallocation of resources.
II. discourages savings.
III. redistributes wealth from lenders to borrowers.

FREE-RESPONSE REVIEW ANSWERS

I.   Inflation causes a misallocation of resources. Resources are spent dealing with rising prices and the repercussions of rising prices. Instead, these resources could have been spent producing more goods and services for the constituents of the economy to enjoy. For example, some firms will have to print new catalogs and revise their web sites when the prices of their products change. This time and effort would not have been expended if prices had not risen. Some households will take the trouble to stock up on goods whose prices are expected to rise. The effort and storage costs are another misallocation of resources.

II. Inflation erodes the value of financial assets. Bank and brokerage accounts, trust funds, and other accounts cannot buy as many products when the prices of those products rise. Why save if inflation will simply eat away at the value of savings?

III. Inflation allows borrowers to repay their loans with dollars that are not worth as much as the ones they borrowed. Lenders, on the other hand, are being repaid with dollars that have lost some of their value. Shrewd lenders understand this and charge higher rates of interest to cover the inflation that may occur over the course of a loan. However, lenders who do not anticipate inflation will be hurt while those who borrow from them will benefit.

CHAPTER
16 Aggregate Supply and Aggregate Demand

Why the Economy Moves in Cycles

1. The average growth rate of the United States economy, as measured by the percentage change in real GDP, is just over 3 percent per year for the postwar period, yet only in a very few instances has the economy grown at its average rate. It typically grows faster than average and then in some years real GDP falls or shows negative growth. We call these negative growth periods *recessions*.

2. Capitalist economies experience fluctuations in economic activity—contractions and expansions. The ups and downs in economic activity are recurrent but do not conform to a uniform schedule. The longest recession lasted 16 months, the shortest just 6 months. The longest expansion is more than 10 years, while the shortest lasted only 12 months.

3. One business cycle is comprised of an expansion and a recession. The fact that business cycles do not conform to a time schedule and differ in other respects, such as their severity, makes them extremely difficult to predict. Economic forecasters get lower grades than the weatherman.

Our task in this chapter, however, is not to predict when the next recession will occur, but to explain *why* the economy moves in cycles. We will build a replica, or model, of the economy and see if that model moves in fits and starts like the real economy. Our model should also display other well-known characteristics of capitalist economies. For instance, large increases in income tend to result in inflation. Does our model confirm this? Technological advances tend to increase output while putting downward pressure on prices. Does our model explain this? Inflation and unemployment tend to be inversely related—when one is up, the other is down—but not always. Does our model explain this tendency and is it flexible enough to allow for exceptions to the relationship?

The name of the model that addresses all of these questions is the *aggregate supply/aggregate demand (AS/AD) model*. The AS/AD model highlights the factors that determine output, income, employment, and prices in the economy. Before we begin to build the model, we must consider what Classical economic theory indicates are the important factors determining output, income, employment, and prices in the economy.

Classical Economic Theory

Classical economic theory was the predominant paradigm in economic analysis from about 1800 until 1930. The basis of Classical thought is Say's Law—supply creates its own demand. As we pointed out earlier, whenever anything is produced, it generates an amount of income equal to its value. Say's Law indicates that it would be impossible to produce too much because of this fact. When something is produced (supplied), it generates enough income to purchase (demand) the item.

However, there is no rule that says the income generated in the production process must be used to purchase the item produced. Workers and managers may decide to save a portion of their earnings. Say had a response to this: The unpurchased items would collect in inventories. Swelling inventories would induce producers to lower prices, the items in inventory would now sell. In other words, even if wage earners do not use their incomes to purchase all that was produced, prices would adjust to ensure there was no excess production.

Therefore, demand for products was never a concern for Classical thinkers. There would always be enough demand. The most important factor determining output was supply. And the most important factors determining supply were the amount of resources in the economy and the state of technology. Classical analysis has a very simple response to the question what determines the amount of output in the economy? Resources and technology.

Given this analysis it is easy to understand why Classical theory fell out of favor in 1930 during the Great Depression. Here, output in the economy had fallen sharply, yet there was no decrease in the amount of land, labor, and capital available. What's more, the productivity of those resources had not diminished either. That is to say, the state of technology was not deteriorating. The Classical economists could not explain why output fell so precipitously during the Great Depression.

Keynesian Theory

In 1936 John Maynard Keynes (pronounced KANES), a British economist, published a book entitled *The General Theory of Employment, Interest, and Money*. The book pointed out flaws in Classical theory and went on to suggest another, more general, theory. Basically, Keynes suggested that the price adjustment the Classical economists relied upon to ensure that supply would always equal demand did not work under certain circumstances. Essentially, Keynes pointed out that Say's Law, the basis for Classical analysis, did not hold true in all cases.

Keynes' model of the way the economy works is handed down to us in the form of the AS/AD model. The model indicates that the Great Depression was caused by a lack of demand for goods and services. Based on this assessment of the situation, Keynes developed a brilliant remedy for the Great Depression. Unfortunately, the remedy Keynes suggested was considered too radical and the Great Depression lingered on until World War II when both Great Britain and the United States were forced to apply Keynes' remedy.

To truly appreciate Keynes' solution to the Great Depression (and to do well on the Advanced Placement exam) we have to build an AS/AD from scratch.

AGGREGATE SUPPLY

Aggregate means "sum total" and aggregate supply is the supply of all goods and services by all suppliers in the economy. In other words, aggregate supply is the supply of everything by all producers.

We are specifically interested in how the supply of everything by all suppliers is affected by the level of prices in the economy. We already know how the Classical economists viewed supply or output—output depends on the amount of resources available and the state of technology, not prices. So if we drew an aggregate supply curve in line with Classical reasoning it would be perfectly vertical, indicating that the price level in the economy can be high or low, it doesn't matter, because output or supply is going to be the amount indicated by where the vertical aggregate supply curve touches the horizontal axis. In Figure 16.1 the horizontal axis is labeled *Real GDP*. In many textbooks it is labeled *Quantity of Output* since real GDP is a measure of the quantity of output.

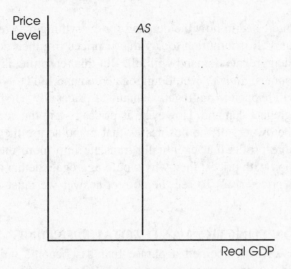

Fig. 16.1 A Classical Aggregate Supply Curve

If the aggregate supply curve is drawn as a vertical line as the Classical economists suggest, then the conclusions of Classical economic theory will be borne out by the AS/AD model. We shall see this in complete detail after developing the entire model.

There may be situations, however, where the price level in the economy does indeed affect the amount supplied by all producers. For instance, in recessionary or depressionary conditions an increase in prices may result in an increase in supply. This is because it is easy to increase supply during a recession when there are plenty of unused resources. The increase in prices induces suppliers to provide more output. This idea is reflected in an aggregate supply curve that slopes upward from left to right.

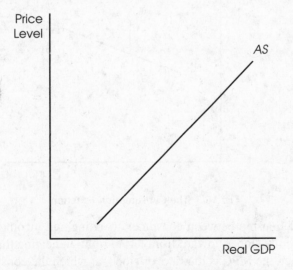

Fig. 16.2 A Keynesian Aggregate Supply Curve

If the aggregate supply curve is drawn as an upward sloping line, as Keynesians suggested, then the conclusions of Keynesian economic theory will be borne out by the AS/AD model. We shall see this in complete detail after developing the entire model.

AGGREGATE DEMAND (FIRST PASS)

The aggregate demand curve represents the demand for all goods and services by all households, businesses, governments, and foreigners. In other words, aggregate demand is the demand for everything by everyone.

We are specifically interested in how the demand for everything by everyone is affected by the price level in the economy. It is tempting to say that if prices rise then demanders will be turned off by higher prices and aggregate demand will fall. But this reasoning is incorrect because when all prices rise, so do incomes. So why would aggregate demand fall?

It is not clear what will happen to aggregate demand as prices rise. Higher prices by themselves would result in less aggregate demand. However, as prices rise in the economy, someone is benefiting. For example, the owners of the businesses that manufacture the products that are rising in price are making more profits that eventually translate into more income for the owners. If incomes rise in proportion with prices, then why would aggregate demand fall? Or will aggregate demand hold steady as prices rise? To see the correct answer we must analyze spending in the economy more closely.

THE CONSUMPTION FUNCTION AND TOTAL SPENDING

In *The General Theory*, Keynes coined a phrase that has become universally known among economists—the marginal propensity to consume or MPC: Given an extra dollar, how much is spent? Young people are well known to have MPCs equal to 1. But middle-aged persons thinking about retirement or their children's education may save 15 cents out of an extra dollar of income, giving them an MPC of .85.

The MPC is a critical concept for Keynesian economic analysis because it relates spending to income—and spending is even more critical to Keynesian analysis. According to Keynes, the Great Depression was caused by a lack of spending. So what determines the total amount of spending in the economy? Consumer spending is primarily determined by income.

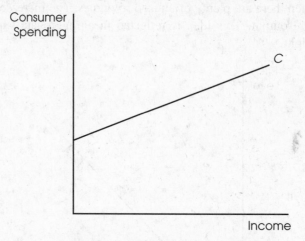

Fig. 16.3 The Consumption Function

The graph of the relationship between consumer spending and income (Figure 16.3) is called the *consumption function*. It slopes upward from left to right, indicating that spending increases as income increases. In fact, the MPC is the rate, or slope, at which the consumption function rises.

To keep things simple, suppose that business spending, government spending, and foreign spending do not depend in any way on the level of income, but on other factors. Then the total spending line will have the same slope as the consumption function, only it will lie above the consumption function (Figure 16.4).

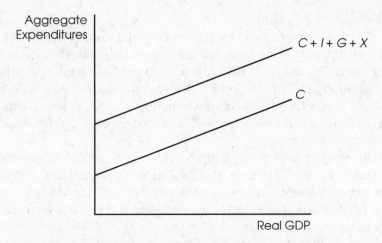

Fig. 16.4 The Consumption Function and the Total Spending Line

Total spending, or aggregate expenditures, includes spending from all sectors, not just consumers. Business spending on plant and equipment must be counted along with government spending and spending by foreigners. The components of aggregate expenditures (C + I + G + X) should look familiar since they are the same as the components of GDP. Notice that the label on the vertical axis has changed from consumer spending to aggregate expenditures to reflect this. There is also a label change on the horizontal axis from income to real GDP. Remember that GDP measures production and income as well, since everything that is produced generates an equivalent amount of income.

Break-even Point

If we consider a 45 degree ray from the origin along with the total spending line, we can make some interesting deductions. First notice that on any point along the 45 degree ray total spending exactly equals income. However, there is only one point on the total spending line that also lies on the 45 degree ray. That is known as the *break-even point*.

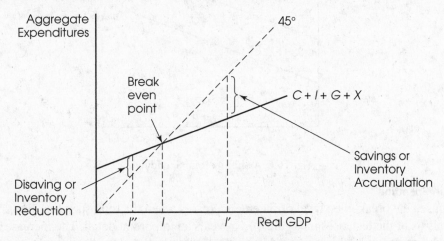

Fig. 16.5 The Break-even Point

All earnings are spent in an economy operating at the break-even point, and there will be a tendency for the economy to gravitate to this point. Consider a point to the right of the break-even point as income level I′ in Figure 16.5. Since the total spending line lies below the 45 degree ray we know that spending must be less than income at I′. When spending is less than income, there must be saving taking place. In fact, the distance between the total spending line and the 45 degree ray at I′ is equivalent to the amount of saving in the economy.

Inventory Accumulation

However, there is something more going on at income level I'. Since there is saving occurring we can also deduce that things are being produced that are not being bought by anyone—businesses, government, and foreigners included. This unpurchased production must be piling up in inventory. So to the right of the break-even point saving and inventories are accumulating. Inventory accumulation causes producers to cut back production levels and let some workers go. This, in turn, causes overall income in the economy to fall, indeed, income will fall back to I, the break-even level of income.

Just the opposite occurs when the economy is operating at an income level to the left of the break-even point such as I″ in Figure 16.5. At I″ total spending is more than income. We know this because the total spending line lies above the 45 degree ray at I″. Income and spending are equal on the 45 degree ray and here we are above the ray. How is it possible to spend more than was earned? Only by using previous savings.

When the economy operates at a point like I″ there will be dissaving (using savings for current expenses) in the economy. Moreover, inventories of products will be falling since spending is so great it is outstripping income. When inventories dwindle because spending is strong, producers respond by stepping up production levels. This means more workers will have to be hired and overall income in the economy will rise. We will move from income level I″ to income level I.

All of this analysis goes to show that the economy will tend to operate at the break-even point. Once the break-even level of income is achieved, this does not mean that the economy will remain there forever. The total spending line can shift up or down for a variety of reasons. For instance, if corporations expect sales to be higher next year and begin spending more right now on plant and equipment to prepare for those higher future sales, then the total spending line will shift up. This is shown in Figure 16.6.

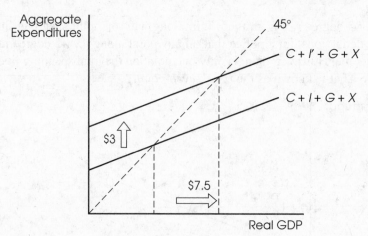

Fig. 16.6 A Shift in Total Spending

Increases in Spending

As you can see the break-even level of income increases when the total spending line shifts up. A careful analysis of the distances in Figure 16.6 reveals an important detail. The increase in income appears to be greater than the upward shift in the total spending line. So if businesses increased their spending on plant and equipment by $3 million, income looks to have gone up by more than that. This is because of the multiplier.

When businesses increase their spending by $3 million, this is just the beginning of the analysis. Other businesses must produce the $3 million of plant and equipment that was ordered. These firms will take in $3 million more in revenue and use that to pay their workers and managers, who in turn will spend a significant portion of their $3 million in extra income, each according to their MPC.

To keep the analysis manageable, let's assume that everyone in the economy has an MPC of .6. When businesses spend $3 million on plant and equipment, other firms must provide that plant and equipment and these suppliers make $3 million in revenues that are used to pay workers, managers, and owners. Now the workers, managers, and owners have $3 million more in income of which we know they will spend $1.8 million (= $3 × .6). Wherever they spend this $1.8 million, say buying food and clothing, it becomes someone's income. Now grocers and tailors have $1.8 million in extra income of which we know they will spend $1.08 million (= $1.8 × .6). And this process, known as the multiplier, goes on and on, until the change in the amount of spending falls to negligible levels.

There is formula to calculate the value of the multiplier:

$$MULTIPLIER = \frac{1}{1 - MPC}$$

In our example, the MPC was .6 so:

$$MULTIPLIER = \frac{1}{1 - .6} = \frac{1}{.4} = 2.5$$

This implies that any initial change in spending will be magnified 2.5 times. So if the total spending line shifts up by $3 million, then we can expect the level of income in the economy to increase by $7.5 million.

Total Change in Income = Initial Change in Spending × Multiplier
$7.5 million   = $3 million   × 2.5

Any initial change in spending in the economy will have a magnified effect on income. The degree of magnification is equal to the multiplier. It should be noted that the initial spending change can come from any sector of the economy; it need not be the business sector. For instance, an increase in government spending would shift the total spending line up as well. Any change in foreign tastes in favor of American products would shift the total spending line up. Table 16.1 provides an array of examples that would shift the total spending line.

TABLE 16.1
SHIFTS IN TOTAL SPENDING

Factor	Direction
Businesses expect higher future sales	Upward
Increase in consumer confidence	Upward
Increase in government spending	Upward
Foreigners develop preference for our products	Upward
Decrease in the money supply	Downward
Prices rise (Inflation)	Downward

The last factor mentioned in Table 16.1 will be important as we move forward. An increase in prices would shift the total spending line down. In the previous section we said it is not clear that spending will fall when prices rise because incomes rise in proportion with prices. So why would the total spending line shift down when prices rise? One reason is because foreign incomes do not rise when our prices rise. So foreign spending will be curtailed by rising domestic prices.

A more important explanation for the drop in total spending when prices rise involves Fisher's Hypothesis: When prices rise we have inflation and inflation induces lenders to raise the rate of interest charged on loans. With higher interest rates, consumers and businesses borrow and spend less. Thus, the rise in prices leads to a decline in total spending.

AGGREGATE DEMAND (SECOND PASS)

Now that we understand that the total spending line shifts downward with a rise in prices, we can derive an aggregate demand curve. Figure 16.7 stacks a total spending diagram on top of a graph with the price level on the vertical axis and quantity of output on the horizontal axis. Notice that the total spending diagram has been slightly amended. Since income equals production we may as well label the horizontal axis quantity of output. That will give us the same horizontal axes on our stacked diagrams.

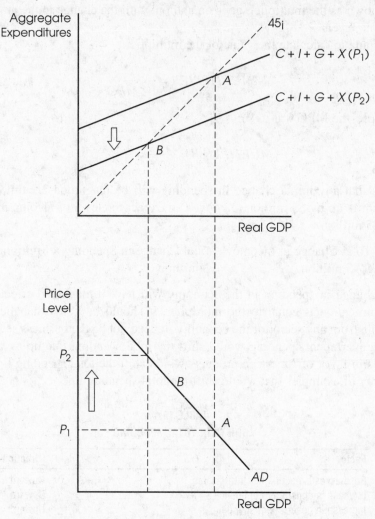

Fig. 16.7 Deriving the Aggregate Demand Curve

Beginning with the initial total spending line we have break-even point A. We can drop a plumb line from this point down to the vertical axis to see the level on income and production in the economy. Assume that the price level is Pa and drag the level of income down into the bottom diagram. This gives us a corresponding point A in the lower diagram. Now suppose prices rise to level Pb. A rise in prices would shift the total spending line down so that the new break-even point was point B. Again, drop a plumb line down to find the new, lower level of income and output. Dragging this level of output down into the lower diagram and noting that it corresponds with price level Pb gives us point B in the lower diagram. Connecting points A and B in the lower diagram give an aggregate demand curve that slopes downward from left to right.

The aggregate demand curve slopes downward because when prices rise, total spending falls even though incomes rise in proportion to the rise in prices. Total spending falls because foreign buyers of our products are not experiencing the rise in incomes and Fisher's Hypothesis. The rise in prices leads to a rise in interest rates that, in turn, cause consumer and business spending to decline.

AGGREGATE SUPPLY AND AGGREGATE DEMAND TOGETHER

The aggregate supply curves that we discussed earlier and the aggregate demand curve that we derived in the previous section all have the price level on the vertical axis and the quantity of output on the horizontal axis. We can, therefore, draw both curves on the same diagram.

You may recall that we discussed two different aggregate supply curves. Figure 16.8 uses a Keynesian aggregate supply curve. This supply curve slopes upward as opposed to the Classical aggregate supply curve, which is vertical. Later we will see how our analysis would be affected if we used a Classical aggregate supply curve.

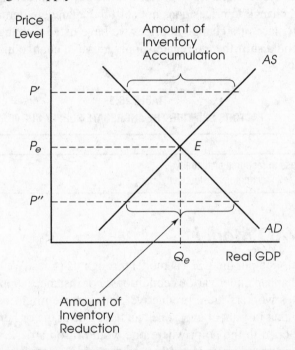

Fig. 16.8 Equilibrium of Aggregate Supply and Aggregate Demand

The economy will have a tendency to operate at point E in Figure 16.8 with a quantity of output of Qe and price level of Pe. Say the price level was not Pe but P'. At P' aggregate supply is greater than aggregate demand. This will cause inventories of products to bulge. Producers would respond by lowering prices.

A similar analysis suggests that if the price level was P" aggregate demand would exceed aggregate supply. Inventories would fall. Producers would realize that they could raise their prices. In short, surpluses and shortages will drive the price level to Pe and the quantity of output Qe. Only then will there be no surplus or shortage of output.

The economy will produce Qe and experience price level Pe until something changes. Specifically, the equilibrium point will change when the aggregate supply curve or the aggregate demand curve shifts. Table 16.2 lists an array of factors that shift aggregate demand or aggregate supply.

TABLE 16.2
FACTORS SHIFTING THE AGGREGATE DEMAND CURVE

Factor	Direction
Businesses expect higher future sales	Right
Increase in consumer confidence	Right
Increase in government spending	Right
Foreigners develop preference for our products	Right
Decrease in the money supply	Left
Reduction in taxes	Right

Notice that the first five factors that can shift the aggregate demand curve are identical to the factors that can shift the total spending line. Here, however, the direction is left or right, not up or down. Furthermore, a change in prices does not shift the aggregate demand curve as it would the total spending line. In place of a change in prices we have listed a change in taxes.

Only two factors could shift the aggregate supply curve: a change in technology and a change in resource availability.

TABLE 16.3
FACTORS SHIFTING THE AGGREGATE SUPPLY CURVE

Factor	Direction
Decrease in resource availability	Left
Increase in technology/productivity	Right

Using the AS/AD Model

We are now in a position to put the AS/AD model through its paces. We can use the model to help us analyze what will happen under various conditions. For instance, suppose there is a technological advance that makes workers more productive. An example might be the development of the personal computer so that just about everyone can have one at his or her desk. In the 1970s computers were not developed to the point where one would fit on a desk and the cost of owning a personal computer was prohibitive. Now that productivity-enhancing computers are just about everywhere, how would this affect the economy?

Remember that a technological advance shifts the aggregate supply curve to the right. This is shown in Figure 16.9.

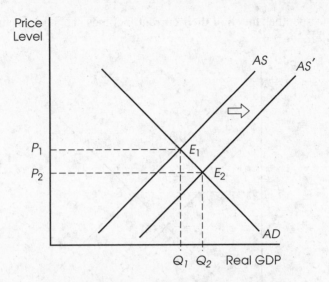

Fig. 16.9 The Effects of a Technological Advance

The original equilibrium is E1. After the technological advance, the new equilibrium is E2. Four specific conclusions can be made by comparing E1 to E2. First, prices are lower at E2. Second, real GDP is higher. We are at Q2 compared to Q1. Because real GDP is higher we can draw two further conclusions: Unemployment will fall and income will rise.

Our AS/AD model tells us that we can expect lower prices, more output, less unemployment, and more income after a technological advance. Would a Classical economist respond differently? Let's redo the analysis using a Classical aggregate supply curve.

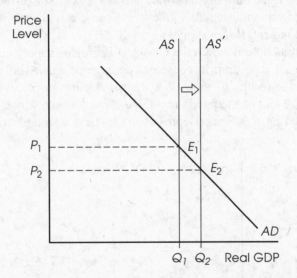

Fig. 16.10 The Effects of a Technological Advance with a Classical Aggregate Supply Curve

Figure 16.10 shows that an advance in technology would shift the Classical aggregate supply curve to the right. Comparing the original equilibrium, E1, with the new equilibrium, E2, gives the same results as when the aggregate supply curve was upward sloping: Prices are lower at E2 and real GDP is higher. Higher output means unemployment will be lower and income will be higher. The results are the same using either aggregate supply curve.

Let's try another example where the results will differ depending on what type of aggregate supply curve is used. This time let's consider the effects of a drop in consumer confidence on the economy. When consumers feel less confident about their future job prospects and income levels, they are not willing to spend as much of their current incomes. This causes the aggregate demand curve to shift to the left.

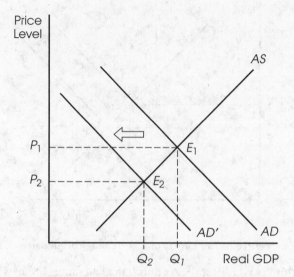

Fig. 16.11 The Effects of a Drop in Consumer Confidence

Comparing the initial equilibrium, E1, with new equilibrium, E2, in Figure 16.11 indicates that prices and real GDP will fall because of the decline in consumer confidence. Once real GDP falls we can conclude that unemployment will rise and income will fall. It seems that we have a self-fulfilling prophesy here. Consumers begin to think that the economic future will be bleak so they stop spending as much right now because they are not as certain of their job prospects in the future. Our AS/AD analysis indicates that this would cause a recession where output falls along with income and employment. Prices should also fall.

Would the same results hold if we used a Classical aggregate supply curve? Figure 16.12 indicates that they would not. The drop in consumer confidence again shifts the aggregate demand curve to the left, but the results of this are a steeper decline in prices than with a Keynesian aggregate demand curve and no change in real GDP. Now you see why Classical economic theory fell out of favor during the Great Depression. Classical economic theory cannot explain a depression.

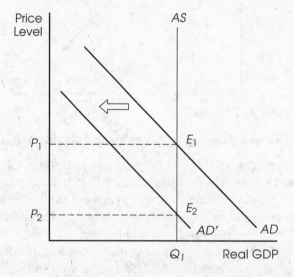

Fig. 16.12 The Effects of a Drop in Consumer Confidence with a Classical Aggregate Supply Curve

According to Classical analysis, when aggregate demand falls, prices fall and this drop in prices should help maintain spending levels. Therefore, real GDP does not fall with the decline in aggregate demand. When output fell during the Great Depression, Classical economists suggested that this was only temporary; falling prices would soon correct the problem. As we know today, they didn't.

Summary

At this point some readers may be thinking, "Why study Classical economic theory at all since it was wrong about the Great Depression?" The answer is that Classical theory is not always wrong and Keynesian theory is not always right. Most modern economists are eclectic, meaning willing to accept several theories with the understanding that some theories are appropriate under certain conditions, while other theories have better explanatory power under different conditions.

- Classical economic theory is most appropriate when the economy is operating at or near full capacity. Under these conditions, a change in aggregate demand will have more impact on prices and little, if any, impact on output. Also, a vertical aggregate supply curve seems to better represent the relationship between output and prices in the long run. Classical economic analysis gives predictions that are typically borne out over the years when the economy has time to adjust to price changes.
- Keynes is famous for saying, "In the long run, we are all dead." An upward sloping aggregate supply curve is more representative of an economy's behavior in the short run. And when we consider economies that are in recessions or depressions, operating well below full capacity, it is best to use a Keynesian aggregate supply curve.
- Sometimes, Classical and Keynesian economic analysis will yield the same predictions about how the economy will respond to a shock. Remember the analysis we conducted in Figures 16.9 and 16.10 where the economy experienced a technological advance. Both Classical and Keynesian theory predicted a fall in the equilibrium price level and an increase in output, income, and employment.
- The AS/AD model is a very powerful tool for thinking about how an economy will respond to given events, such as a technological advance or a dip in consumer confidence. If the economy under consideration is near full capacity, or you are interested in the long run effects, then it is best to use a vertical aggregate supply curve. Use a Keynesian aggregate supply curve in the opposite circumstances.
- The question we asked at the beginning of this chapter got lost in all the details: What causes business cycles? The AS/AD model suggests that shifts in the aggregate supply and demand cause fluctuations in economic activity. We listed the factors that could shift these curves. The resulting changes in equilibrium output and prices are the business cycles that we observe in the real world.

Finally, keep in mind that the AP exam in Macroeconomics emphasizes the material in this chapter. It will pay for you to become familiar with the graphs and understand what can cause the curves in each graph to shift. You may think about repeating the chapter if you do not do well on the sample multiple-choice and free-response questions.

Terms

Aggregate Demand   the demand for all goods and services by all households, businesses, governments, and foreigners

Aggregate Supply   the supply of all goods and services by all producers in the economy

Break-even Point   point where the consumption function crosses the 45 degree ray and income equals spending so that saving is zero

Business Cycle   a wave of economic activity comprised of an expansion and a recession

Classical Economic Theory   the predominant paradigm in economic analysis from about 1800 until 1930, based on Say's Law

Consumption Function   the relationship between consumer spending and income

Equilibrium Price Level   the price level that equates aggregate supply and aggregate demand, the average level of prices in the economy

Equilibrium Quantity   the amount of output that results in no shortage or surplus, the amount of goods and service bought and sold in the economy

Expansion   a sustained improvement in economic activity

Keynesian Theory   theory that opposes Classical theory by emphasizing the short run and focusing on economies that are operating below full capacity

Marginal Propensity to Consume (MPC)   idea that given an extra dollar, how much is spent?

Multiplier   an initial change in spending in the economy that will have a magnified, or multiple, effect on income

Recession   a sustained decline in economic activity

Say's Law   theory that supply creates its own demand

Formulas

$$\text{Marginal Propensity to Consume} = \frac{\text{Change in Spending}}{\text{Change in Income}}$$

Multiplier = $1/(1 - \text{MPC})$

Total Change in Income = Initial Change in Spending $\times$ Multiplier

Multiple-Choice Review Questions

1. Business cycles

   A. occur infrequently in capitalist economies.
   B. refer to reusing resources in production.
   C. are predictable ups and downs in economic activity.
   D. are each comprised of a recession and an expansion.
   E. are the same as depressions.

2. Recessions

   A. are a thing of the past.
   B. are very severe depressions.
   C. are marked by a sustained decline in output.
   D. are regular occurrences in capitalist economies.
   E. are typically accompanied by falling unemployment.

3. Say's Law

   A. is the basis of Keynesian economic analysis.
   B. is the basis of Classical economic analysis.
   C. states that demand creates its own supply.
   D. indicates that prices will be stable in capitalist economies.
   E. was verified by the Great Depression.

4. Keynes

   A. advanced Classical economic theory by making several refinements.
   B. showed how Say's Law operated in capitalist economies.
   C. was a great American economist.
   D. explained the cause of and cure for the Great Depression.
   E. advanced Classical economic theory by building on Say's Law.

5. Which of the following would NOT shift the aggregate supply curve?

   A. An increase in the price level.
   B. A decrease in the amount of resources in the economy.
   C. An increase in the amount of resources in the economy.
   D. An increase in technology.
   E. A decrease in productivity.

6. Which of the following would shift the aggregate demand curve to the left?

   A. An increase in consumer confidence.
   B. Business firms expect lower sales in the future.
   C. Foreigners develop a preference for our products.
   D. Government increases its level of spending.
   E. An increase in the money supply.

7. Which of the following would NOT shift the aggregate demand curve?

   A. A change in consumer confidence.
   B. A change in technology.
   C. A change in the money supply.
   D. A change in spending by state governments.
   E. A change in foreign tastes for our products.

8. What will happen to the equilibrium price level and the equilibrium quantity of output if the aggregate demand curve shifts to the right? Assume an upward sloping aggregate supply curve.

   A. The equilibrium price level increases while the equilibrium quantity of output decreases.
   B. The equilibrium price level decreases while the equilibrium quantity of output increases.
   C. The equilibrium price level and quantity of output increase.

D. The equilibrium price level and quantity of output decrease.

E. The equilibrium price level increases while the equilibrium quantity of output remains unchanged.

9. What will happen to the equilibrium price level and the equilibrium quantity of output if consumer confidence increases? Assume an upward sloping aggregate supply curve.

A. The equilibrium price level increases while the equilibrium quantity of output decreases.

B. The equilibrium price level decreases while the equilibrium quantity of output increases.

C. The equilibrium price level and quantity of output increase.

D. The equilibrium price level and quantity of output decrease.

E. The equilibrium price level increases while the equilibrium quantity of output remains unchanged.

10. What will happen to the equilibrium price level and the equilibrium quantity of output if the aggregate demand curve shifts to the right? Assume a Classical aggregate supply curve.

A. The equilibrium price level increases while the equilibrium quantity of output decreases.

B. The equilibrium price level decreases while the equilibrium quantity of output increases.

C. The equilibrium price level and quantity of output increase.

D. The equilibrium price level remains unchanged while the equilibrium quantity of output increases.

E. The equilibrium price level increases while the equilibrium quantity of output remains unchanged.

11. What will happen to the equilibrium price level and the equilibrium quantity of output if the aggregate supply curve shifts to the left? Assume an upward sloping aggregate supply curve.

A. The equilibrium price level increases while the equilibrium quantity of output decreases.

B. The equilibrium price level decreases while the equilibrium quantity of output increases.

C. The equilibrium price level and quantity of output increase.

D. The equilibrium price level and quantity of output decrease.

E. The equilibrium price level increases while the equilibrium quantity of output remains unchanged.

12. What will happen to the equilibrium price level and the equilibrium quantity of output if a major earthquake destroys much of the plant and equipment on the West Coast? Assume an upward sloping aggregate supply curve.

A. The equilibrium price level increases while the equilibrium quantity of output decreases.

B. The equilibrium price level decreases while the equilibrium quantity of output increases.

C. The equilibrium price level and quantity of output increase.

D. The equilibrium price level and quantity of output decrease.

E. The equilibrium price level increases while the equilibrium quantity of output remains unchanged.

13. What will happen to the equilibrium price level and the equilibrium quantity of output if the aggregate supply curve shifts to the left? Assume a Classical aggregate supply curve.

A. The equilibrium price level increases while the equilibrium quantity of output decreases.
B. The equilibrium price level decreases while the equilibrium quantity of output increases.
C. The equilibrium price level and quantity of output increase.
D. The equilibrium price level remains unchanged while the equilibrium quantity of output increases.
E. The equilibrium price level increases while the equilibrium quantity of output remains unchanged.

14. Total spending

A. is all of the spending done by all of the households in a nation.
B. slopes downward because less spending occurs when prices rise.
C. slopes downward because less spending occurs when income falls.
D. slopes upward because more government spending occurs when income rises.
E. slopes upward because more household spending occurs when income rises.

15. At the break-even point

A. the expenses of corporations just equal their revenues.
B. household spending equals household income.
C. total spending equals income.
D. dissaving occurs and inventories are accumulating.
E. saving occurs and inventories are accumulating.

MULTIPLE-CHOICE REVIEW ANSWERS

1. **D**	4. **D**	7. **B**	10. **E**	13. **A**
2. **C**	5. **A**	8. **C**	11. **A**	14. **E**
3. **B**	6. **B**	9. **C**	12. **A**	15. **C**

Free-Response Review Questions

I. Draw an aggregate supply/aggregate demand diagram. Label the axes of your diagram. Make the aggregate supply curve upward sloping. Show which curve shifts when foreigners suddenly develop a distaste for our products. What will happen to equilibrium output and the equilibrium price level in the short run?

II. Would you expect the same thing to happen to equilibrium output and the equilibrium price level in the long run? Redraw the aggregate supply/aggregate demand diagram using a vertical aggregate supply curve. Now what happens when foreigners develop a distaste for our products?

III. Explain why the long run aggregate supply curve is drawn as a vertical line and the short run aggregate supply curve is drawn upward sloping. Explain why the long run effects of a change in foreign tastes are different from the short run effects.

FREE-RESPONSE REVIEW ANSWERS

I. AS/AD Model when foreigners develop a distaste for our products

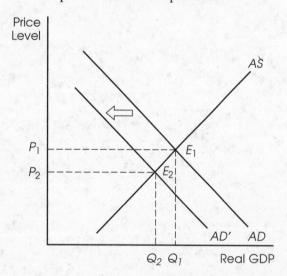

When foreigners develop a distaste for our products the aggregate demand curve shifts to the left. This causes the equilibrium price level and the equilibrium quantity of output to fall.

II. AS/AD Model when foreigners develop a distaste for our products (with long run aggregate supply curve)

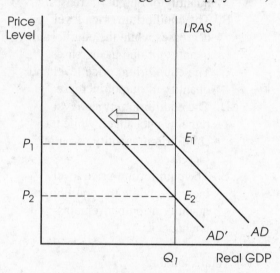

The long run, or Classical, economic analysis indicates that the equilibrium price level will fall when foreigners develop a distaste for our products, but the equilibrium quantity of output will remain unchanged.

III. The long run aggregate supply curve is drawn as a vertical line because aggregate supply is not affected by the price level in the long run. Only the amount of resources and the state of technology affect aggregate supply in the long run. In the short run, however, an increase in the price level induces suppliers in the economy to bring more product to market. Therefore, when foreigners develop a distaste for our products, prices fall and this reduces the amount of product that suppliers are willing to bring to market. But in the long run, the change in foreign tastes has not affected the amount of resources we have or our state of technology, so the quantity of output remains unchanged.

CHAPTER
17 Fiscal Policy

Keynes' Remedy for the Great Depression

Imagine an economy that is suffering from low levels of output and income. Unemployment is high and prices are falling. The AS/AD model (see Chapter 16) tells us that this is exactly what would occur in an economy where the aggregate demand curve has shifted to the left. Keynes concluded that the Great Depression was caused by a deficiency of spending, or aggregate demand, in our terms. His remedy was to get a boost in spending. But how? Consumers were tapped out and barely had enough to put food on the table. The unemployment rate was 25 percent in the United States. Why should businesses spend more on plant and equipment? Many of them were on the verge of bankruptcy. Maybe foreigners could be called upon to spend more? No, our major trading partners were experiencing depressions of their own.

Keynes recommended that the federal government boost its level of spending. That would shift the aggregate demand curve to the right where it belonged. The only catch was that the government couldn't tax more to pay for the increased spending. Increasing taxes would only shift the aggregate demand curve back to the left; the government would have to spend money it didn't have. It would have to run a deficit and borrow the money to increase spending. This was unheard of at the time. Prudent governments did not spend more than they took in by way of tax revenues.

In fact, during the Great Depression tax collections were down because so many businesses were not making any profits to tax and so many households were making no income to tax. There was talk of raising the tax rate. Our aggregate supply and demand model tells us that this is exactly the wrong thing to do—increasing taxes would only shift the aggregate demand curve further to the left.

No government was willing to try Keynes' radical new idea to remedy the Great Depression and the economic bad times persisted. It wasn't until the early 1940s that World War II forced many governments to spend more money than they had and borrow to make up the difference. That was how the Great Depression was finally put behind us.

Today, governments have gotten over their qualms about deficit spending. Governments have been known to deficit spend even when there was no recession. Keynes would be appalled. During expansions governments should spend less than they take in through taxes. Run a surplus. These surpluses could be used to pay off the borrowings from the deficits. To do well on the AP Macroeconomics exam you will have to understand how government spending and tax collections affect the economy.

Fiscal Policy

Fiscal policy is changes in government spending and taxes to fight recessions or inflations. To remedy recessions the government should increase its level of spending and/or reduce taxes. In other words, the government should run a deficit.

The aggregate supply/aggregate demand (AS/AD) model can be used to show how deficit spending would work to cure a recession. Consider Figure 17.1, which shows an economy experiencing a recession. The aggregate demand curve and the short run aggregate supply curve cross to the left of the long run aggregate supply curve. Remember that the long run aggregate supply curve is vertical at the quantity of output the economy could produce if it used its resources fully and efficiently. Since the short run equilibrium is to the left of the vertical long run aggregate supply curve, the economy must not be using its resources fully and/or efficiently.

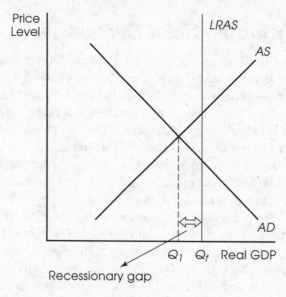

Fig. 17.1 A Recessionary Gap

The horizontal distance between the quantity of output the economy is producing, Q1, and its potential, Qf, is called the recessionary gap. The economy depicted in Figure 17.1 is experiencing a recession. Output is below potential and if output is low, so is income. And unemployment must be a problem if production is low. These are recessionary conditions.

Fiscal policy could be used to close the recessionary gap. An increase in government spending would shift the aggregate demand curve to the right. So would a decrease in taxes. Either of these policies would mean deficit spending on the part of the government. But when the aggregate demand curve shifts to the right, the recession is over. This is shown in Figure 17.2.

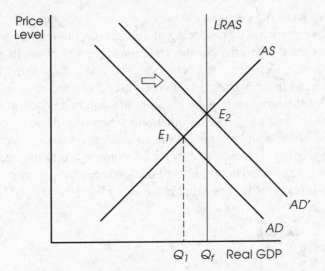

Fig. 17.2 Fiscal Policy to Close a Recessionary Gap

After the aggregate demand curve shifts to the right, the new equilibrium occurs where all three curves cross. The new quantity of output is Qf (f for full employment) and the recession is ended. Unfortunately, the price level is higher at the new equilibrium. This means the economy experienced some inflation as a result of the fiscal policy that cured the recession. Hopefully, the costs of this inflation were worth the benefits of ending the recession.

An economy can experience the opposite sort of trouble from a recessionary gap. An inflationary gap occurs when an economy is producing above its potential. Figure 17.3 illustrates this situation.

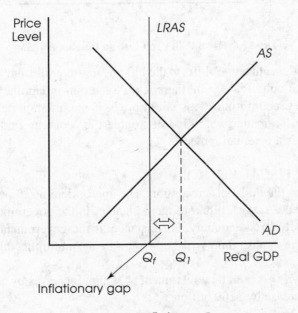

Fig. 17.3 An Inflationary Gap

The short run aggregate supply curve crosses the aggregate demand curve to the right of the long run aggregate supply curve. The quantity of output is Q1, which is more than the economy's potential, Qf. You may well ask how an economy can produce above its potential. One response is overtime. Resources are being worked more than full time. Another response is that unemployment is below 5 percent. Remember that full employment does not mean zero unemployment. We are at full employment when the unemployment rate reaches 5 percent or so. If the unemployment rate falls lower still, we can wind up producing more than our full employment potential.

The situation is not good when the economy is producing more than its potential. Inflation is typical during these times. Resources are being strained and the economy may be overheating. Prices are usually driven higher in these situations. That is why the distance between Qf and Q2 in Figure 17.3 is called the *inflationary gap*. Fiscal policy can be applied to resolve the problem.

The appropriate fiscal policy to close an inflationary gap is to decrease government spending and/or increase taxes. These policies would result in a surplus where government tax collections exceed government spending. This would slow the economy by curtailing the amount of spending that occurs. The aggregate demand curve shifts to the left when the government decreases its level of spending or raises taxes. This is shown in Figure 17.4.

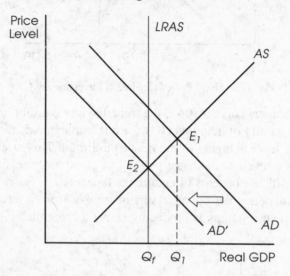

Fig. 17.4 Fiscal Policy to Close an Inflationary Gap

After the aggregate demand curve shifts to the left, the new equilibrium is where all three curves cross. The new level of output is Qf and there is no longer an inflationary gap; in fact, the price level is lower at the new equilibrium. This fall in prices is the inflation being cured.

The lesson is clear: No matter what kind of trouble the economy finds itself in, recession or inflation, fiscal policy is a potential remedy.

MULTIPLIERS FOR FISCAL POLICY

Imagine an economy in the midst of a recession. The appropriate fiscal policy is to increase government spending or reduce taxes. Either of these changes in the government's budget will have a magnified effect on the overall economy. For instance, if the government increases spending by $20 billion, this change in spending will be subject to the multiplier phenomenon outlined in Chapter 16.

Specifically, if the MPC is 0.8 and government spending increases by $20 billion, then we can expect real GDP to increase by $100 billion.

Change in Real GDP = Initial Change in Spending × Multiplier
$100 billion   = $20 billion   × 5.0

Remember that the multiplier is equal to $1/(1 - MPC) = 5.0 \ (= 1/(1 - .8) = 1/.2)$.

The idea that real GDP increases by $100 billion when government spending increases by $20 billion is easily demonstrated in Figure 17.5.

The total spending line (C + I + G + X) shifts up by a distance equal to $20 billion. Real GDP, measured on the horizontal axis, increases by $100 billion.

However, real GDP will not rise by $100 billion if the government lowers taxes by $20 billion. This is because when consumers get their tax breaks totaling $20 billion they will initially increase spending by $16 billion, assuming once again that the MPC equals 0.8. Households save $4 billion of the tax cut.

Change in Real GDP = Initial Change in Spending × Multiplier
$80 billion   = $16 billion   × 5.0

In this case, real GDP increases by $80 billion.

The fact that a $20 billion dollar change in government spending has a slightly more powerful impact on real GDP than a $20 billion change in taxes has an interesting implication. What would happen if the government were to increase spending by $20 billion while simultaneously *increasing* taxes by $20 billion? The increase in government spending of $20 billion would cause a $100 billion increase in real GDP, while the $20 billion increase in taxes would reduce real GDP by $80 billion. The net effect is a $20 billion increase in real GDP.

If the government has a balanced budget so that spending equals tax revenues, it can maintain the balanced budget and still stimulate real GDP. This is because if spending and tax revenues were both raised by some amount, say $20 billion, then real GDP would increase by $20 billion.

Whenever the government changes spending and taxes so that the effects on the budget are neutral, this is known as a "balanced-budget" move. So an increase in government spending of $5 million and an increase in taxes of $5 million is a balanced-budget move. Similarly, a decrease in government spending of $4 billion and a decrease in taxes of $4 billion is a balanced-budget move.

In each of these cases, the change in government spending has a stronger impact than the change in taxes. Real GDP will be affected by the amount of the spending and tax change. For instance, when government increases spending by $5 million and taxes by the same amount, real GDP will increase by $5 million.

If government decreases spending by $4 billion and lowers taxes by the same amount, real GDP will decrease by $4 billion. You can arrive at this conclusion the long way: calculate the impact of the government spending change and the impact of the tax change. Then figure the net effect. Or you can take the shortcut: the balanced-budget multiplier is equal to 1. This means an increase in government spending of x dollars that is matched by an increase in tax revenues of x dollars results in an increase in real GDP of x dollars. Based on the same reasoning, a decrease in government spending of x dollars that is matched by a decrease in tax revenues of x dollars results in a decrease in real GDP of x dollars.

THE PHILLIPS TRADEOFF

Fiscal policy, however, has its drawbacks. We have already seen that a fiscal policy designed to remedy a recession will result in inflation. Similarly, a fiscal policy designed to combat inflation will result in declines in output and possibly a recession. It seems that fiscal policy cannot remedy both unemployment and inflation at the same time.

The idea that inflation and unemployment move in opposite directions was first noticed by a British economist, A. W. Phillips. Looking back over 100 years of British economic history he discovered that when inflation was high, unemployment was low. When inflation was low, unemployment tended to be high. The inverse relationship between inflation and unemployment became known as the Phillips tradeoff.

Phillips graphed the relationship between inflation and unemployment. The results were similar to Figure 17.6. A high inflation rate, such as point A, is associated with a low unemployment rate. A low inflation rate, such as point B, is associated with a high unemployment rate.

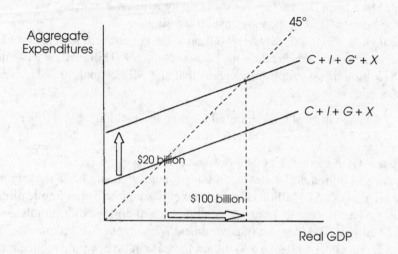

Fig. 17.5 An Increase in Government Spending

Phillips published his findings in 1958 and his relationship has been looked for in many economies over various time periods. For instance, it is well known that unemployment and inflation behaved according to the relationship in the United States in the 1960s, but the 1970s defied the Phillips tradeoff—both inflation and unemployment were high in the mid-1970s.

Economists are now able to explain why the Phillips relationship holds in some periods and not in others. Notice that when the aggregate demand curve shifts to the left, it results in the price level falling (lower inflation) and the quantity of output falling (higher unemployment). When the aggregate demand shifts to the right, just the opposite occurs—inflation rises and unemployment falls. All of this is in line with what Phillips discovered. This indicates that the aggregate demand curve must have been shifting about in the United States in the 1960s, while the aggregate supply curve remained stable.

Now consider what happens when the aggregate supply shifts left. Figure 17.7 depicts this event for the short run. The initial equilibrium is E1. Then the aggregate supply curve shifts left and the new equilibrium is E2. Prices are higher at E2 (inflation is up) and output is lower (unemployment is up). This goes against the Phillips relationship. Indeed, it is the worst of all situations with both inflation and unemployment rising. Economists call this *stagflation*.

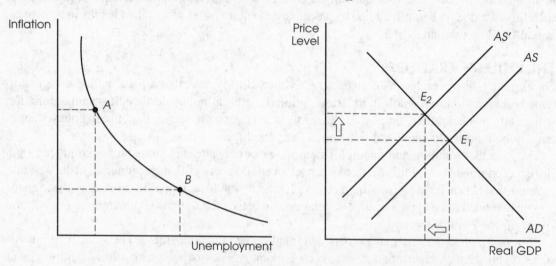

Fig. 17.6 The Phillips Curve   **Fig. 17.7 Stagflation**

STAGFLATION

Stagflation occurs whenever the aggregate supply curve shifts to the left. Since both inflation and unemployment are rising, this defies the Phillips relationship, which concludes that unemployment and inflation move in opposite directions.

Stagflation occurred in the 1970s in the United States when the supply of a very important resource, oil, was curtailed by the formation of an oil cartel. Notice that stagflation poses a special problem for fiscal policy. If both inflation and unemployment are high, should fiscal policy be used to fight the high unemployment or the high inflation? It cannot remedy both at the same time.

Figure 17.8 shows what would happen if fiscal policy were used to fight inflation during stagflation. The initial equilibrium is E1. Then the aggregate supply curve shifts to the left because resources are not as available. This results in stagflation and takes us to E2. Then the government runs a surplus by raising taxes and/or lowering spending. This shifts the aggregate demand curve to the left and we end up at E3. The price level is brought back down to its original level, but the quantity of output has fallen to new lows. The inflation has been cured but the recession has been made worse.

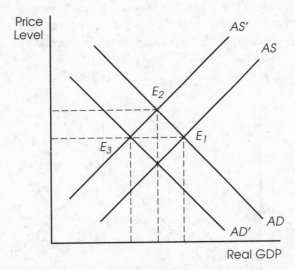

Fig. 17.8 Using Fiscal Policy to Fight Inflation During Stagflation

If fiscal policy is used to combat the recession during stagflation, then inflation will be taken to even higher levels. This is a major drawback of fiscal policy. It cannot cope with stagflation because it can remedy only one problem at the expense of another.

The true solution to stagflation is to get the aggregate supply curve to shift back to the right. This can be accomplished by making resources more available or a technological advance. There are no standard government policies that can accomplish this quickly and effectively. *Supply-side economics* is an attempt to shift the aggregate supply curve to the right to cure stagflation. Supply-side economists recommend special tax policies and less government regulation to accomplish the task. So far, however, these policies have not been effective.

In any event, the Phillips relationship poses a problem for advocates of fiscal policy. The relationship indicates that fiscal policy can remedy only one of the two economic evils at a time. When both inflation and unemployment rear their heads simultaneously, fiscal policy is not appropriate.

CROWDING OUT

Crowding out can render fiscal policy ineffective. Crowding out is the increase in interest rates and subsequent decline in spending that occurs when the government borrows money to finance a deficit.

To see how crowding out works, imagine an economy mired in a recessionary gap. Suppose the government implements the appropriate fiscal policy and runs a deficit. This means the government will need to borrow money. However, we have been ignoring the fact that if the government borrows a large portion of the funds available for lending, then interest rates would rise.

To understand this consider what would happen if you walked into a bank for a car loan just after the government had borrowed a good portion of the bank's loanable funds. They could give you the car loan, but probably at a higher rate of interest than before.

Now, you may decide that the monthly payments on the car and loan would be too high. You do not buy the car and hundreds of people make decisions similar to yours. The demand for cars drops and autoworkers are laid off.

Diagrammatically, crowding out is reflected in an aggregate demand curve that shifts back to the left after a fiscal policy has just shifted it to the right. This is shown in Figure 17.9. Originally the economy is in a recession at E1. An expansionary fiscal policy is used to shift the aggregate demand curve to the right. The new equilibrium is E2 and the recessionary gap is closed. However, interest rates rise because of the government borrowing associated with the fiscal policy. The higher rates of interest induce consumers and businesses to borrow and spend less than before. This drop in consumer and business spending shifts the aggregate demand curve back to its original position and the economy ends up back at E1 and in recession.

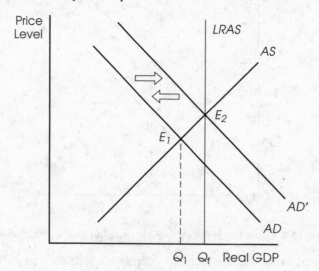

Fig. 17.9 Crowding Out

This is how crowding out can nullify the beneficial effects of fiscal policy. Crowding out is not always an issue. Sometimes there are plenty of loanable funds available and the government can borrow and deficit spend without an adverse effect on fiscal policy. Other times, the government borrowing raises interest rates, which chokes off consumer and business spending. The declines in consumer and business spending offset the increase in government spending and fiscal policy is ineffective.

RATIONAL EXPECTATIONS

In 1995 Robert Lucas of the University of Chicago won the Nobel Prize in economics "for having developed and applied the hypothesis of rational expectations, and thereby having transformed macroeconomic analysis and deepened our understanding of economic policy." This hypothesis is based on the idea that households and businesses will use all the information available to them when making economic decisions. This seems like a logical and harmless assumption, but carried to its logical conclusion, rational expectations implies that fiscal policy will be ineffective at changing the quantity of output.

Suppose the government tries to stimulate the economy through expansionary fiscal policy. The government deficit spends. People understand that such a policy results in higher prices. Even if they don't have the economic education to make this conclusion, others will, and they will read about it in the press: prices are expected to rise with expansionary fiscal policy. When households and firms expect prices to be higher in the future, they supply less labor and products right now. Why supply labor and products now when you can supply them next month at a higher price?

This reduction in supply nullifies the expansionary effect of the fiscal policy. Only prices rise because of the deficit spending by the government. The situation is illustrated in Figure 17.10.

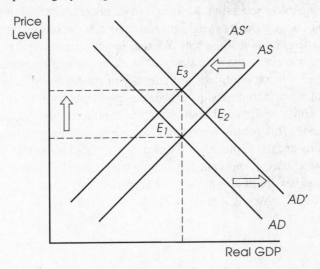

Fig. 17.10 Rational Expectations Nullifies Expansionary Fiscal Policy

Initially the economy is in equilibrium at E1. The government then deficit spends in order to increase the quantity of output. This shifts the aggregate demand curve to the right. Normally we would end up at E2 and that would be the end of the story. However, under rational expectations we never get to E2 because households and firms realize that the expansionary fiscal policy will result in higher prices. They are simply using the information in any economics text to reach this conclusion. Rational expectations are that people will use all the information available when making economic decisions.

Expecting higher prices for their labor and products, people and firms reduce their supply of labor and products right now. This causes the aggregate supply curve to shift to the left. The shift to the left of the aggregate supply curve occurs simultaneously with the shift to the right of the aggregate demand curve. The result is we move from E1 directly to E3. The quantity of output never increases; it remains unchanged. Only prices rise because of the fiscal policy.

The validity of the theory of rational expectations is still very much in question despite Professor Lucas having won the Nobel Prize for his development of it. However, the more people and firms in the economy use the information available to them, the less effective fiscal policy will be. Along with the Phillips curve and crowding out, rational expectations are one more reason to suspect that fiscal policy will not work to cure all recessions or inflations.

AUTOMATIC STABILIZERS
Automatic, or built-in, stabilizers are government policies already in place that promote deficit spending during recessions and surplus budgets during expansions. These policies prevent recessions from becoming depressions. They also help keep inflations from turning into hyperinflations.

Income taxes and antipoverty programs such as Temporary Aid to Needy Families (TANF) are examples of automatic stabilizers. Consider how income taxes are affected as the economy falls into a recession. More and more people become unemployed or make less income as the recession progresses. But when a household makes less income, it owes less in taxes. In other words, government tax revenues will automatically fall during a recession and this is exactly the type of fiscal policy called for to fight a recession.

Automatic stabilizers cannot prevent a recession because the drop in income is necessary for them to begin working. However, built-in stabilizers can prevent a recession from becoming a depression.

Let's consider how a program like TANF would work as an automatic stabilizer. Again, imagine an economy slipping into a recession. More and more households will qualify for TANF funds. Government spending on antipoverty programs automatically increases during a recession and a boost in government spending is just the sort of fiscal policy that is required to fight a recession.

Also notice that income taxes and TANF would work to prevent an expansion from becoming too exuberant. As the expansion continues, inflationary pressures build as households make more and more income. But more income means higher tax payments for households. Higher taxes are the appropriate fiscal policy to fight inflation. Also, fewer households will qualify for TANF funds as the economy expands. This means government spending on this program will be falling. Cuts in government spending are the appropriate fiscal policy to fight inflation.

Automatic stabilizers work to prevent business cycles from becoming too extreme in either direction. Many economists credit automatic stabilizers, not fiscal policy, for the decreased amplitude of business cycles since World War II.

Summary

- Fiscal policy is just one of several options policymakers can use to address economic concerns such as unemployment or inflation. The appropriate fiscal policy to combat unemployment and recessions is to have the government run a deficit by spending more and/or lower tax collections. To fight inflation, the government should run a surplus by cutting government spending and raising tax rates. These policies shift the aggregate demand curve to a more suitable position.
- Students may wonder why we have recessions and inflations if fiscal policy can be used against them. The answer is that fiscal policy has drawbacks and is not completely effective. One drawback of fiscal policy is that the same policies that fight recessions promote inflation. And if the economy is suffering from stagflation, recession, and inflation simultaneously, fiscal policy can address only one of these problems while making the other worse.
- Crowding out and rational expectations can make fiscal policy completely or partially ineffective. Crowding out refers to the rise in borrowing costs to firms and households after the government borrows to deficit spend. Higher borrowing costs can result in lower spending by households and firms that would offset the expansionary fiscal policy. Rational expectations assumes that people and firms will know that an expansionary fiscal policy will result in higher prices. Because prices are expected to be higher in the future, people work less and firms supply less right now. They would prefer to work and supply more later when wages and prices are higher. The reduction in supply offsets the expansionary fiscal policy.
- Yet another problem with fiscal policy is the fact that Congress and the President have to first realize the economy is in trouble, then design a fiscal policy to combat the recessionary or inflationary gap. All of this takes time. Fortunately, there are laws and programs already on the books that will work to fight recessions or inflations. These laws and programs are called automatic stabilizers. Tax laws and antipoverty programs are examples of built-in

stabilizers. Automatic stabilizers cannot prevent recessions or inflations, but they can prevent recessions from becoming depressions and inflations from becoming hyperinflations.

Terms

Automatic Stabilizers   government policies already in place that promote deficit spending during recessions and surplus budgets during expansions

Crowding Out   the increase in interest rates and subsequent decline in spending that occurs when the government borrows money to finance a deficit

Deficit   situation that exists when government spending exceeds tax revenues

Fiscal Policy   changes in government spending and taxes to fight recessions or inflations

Inflationary Gap   what occurs when the equilibrium quantity of output is above potential output

Phillips Tradeoff   the inverse relationship between inflation and unemployment

Rational Expectations   the idea that households and businesses will use all the information available to them when making economic decisions

Recessionary Gap   what occurs when the equilibrium quantity of output is below potential output

Stagflation   term used to describe the situation when the economy experiences inflation and a recession simultaneously

Surplus   spending by the government that is less than tax revenues

Formulas

Multiplier $= 1/(1 - \text{MPC})$

Change in Real GDP $=$ Initial Change in Spending $\times$ Multiplier

Multiple-Choice Review Questions

1. Fiscal policy refers to

   A. increases in taxes to fight recessions.
   B. decreases in taxes to fight inflations.
   C. changes in government spending and taxes to fight recessions or inflations.
   D. federal deficits.
   E. federal surpluses.

2. A federal deficit occurs when

   A. exports exceed imports.
   B. imports exceed exports.
   C. federal tax collections exceed spending.
   D. federal spending exceeds federal tax revenues.
   E. the federal government spends less than last year.

3. The appropriate fiscal policy to remedy a recession

   A. calls for the federal government to run a deficit.
   B. calls for the federal government to run a surplus.
   C. is increased taxes and government spending.
   D. is decreased government spending and taxes.
   E. is increased taxes and reduced government spending.

4. The appropriate fiscal policy to remedy inflation calls for

   A. the federal government to run a deficit.
   B. the federal government to run a surplus.
   C. increased taxes and government spending.
   D. decreased government spending and taxes.
   E. decreased taxes and increased government spending.

5. To close a recessionary gap

   A. the aggregate demand curve should be shifted to the right.
   B. the aggregate demand curve should be shifted to the left.
   C. the aggregate supply curve should be shifted to the right.
   D. the aggregate supply curve should be shifted to the left.
   E. prices should be raised.

6. To close an expansionary gap

   A. the aggregate demand curve should be shifted to the right.
   B. the aggregate demand curve should be shifted to the left.
   C. the aggregate supply curve should be shifted to the right.
   D. the aggregate supply curve should be shifted to the left.
   E. prices should be lowered.

7. One drawback of using fiscal policy to close a recessionary gap is that

   A. unemployment will rise.
   B. taxes will have to be raised.
   C. the equilibrium price level will rise.
   D. government spending on important programs will have to be cut.
   E. equilibrium output will fall.

8. Use the following three responses to answer the this question: Fiscal policy is not always effective because of

   I. crowding out.
   II. rational expectations.
   III. the balanced budget amendment.

   A. I only
   B. II only
   C. II and III
   D. I and II
   E. I, II, and III

9. Stagflation occurs when

   A. inflation falls and unemployment rises.
   B. inflation rises and unemployment falls.
   C. inflation and unemployment both rise.
   D. Inflation and output both rise.
   E. Inflation and output both fall.

10. Study the diagram below.

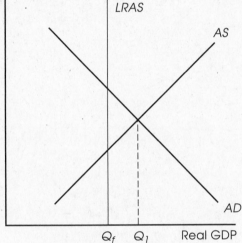

   A. It is incorrect since Qf can never be to the left of Q1.
   B. It is incorrect because AD should slope upward and AS should slope down.
   C. It portrays a recessionary gap.
   D. It portrays an inflationary gap.
   E. It portrays Phillips curves.

11. Crowding out

   A. is one reason fiscal policy is so effective.
   B. occurs when interest rates fall due to government borrowing.
   C. occurs when consumers and firms spend less offsetting expansionary fiscal policy.
   D. causes the aggregate demand curve to shift to the right.
   E. occurs when rising interest rates cause cuts in government spending.

12. The theory of rational expectations

   A. assumes that consumers and businesses anticipate rising prices when the government pursues an expansionary fiscal policy.
   B. implies that fiscal policy will be effective even during stagflation.
   C. supports the notion of a Phillips tradeoff.
   D. assumes that consumers and businesses do not use all the information available to them.
   E. was developed by Keynes as a remedy for the Great Depression.

13. Study the diagram below.

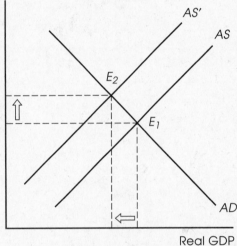

   A. It shows how fiscal policy can work to cure inflation.
   B. It shows how fiscal policy can work to close a recessionary gap.
   C. It portrays the Phillips tradeoff.
   D. It is incorrect because AD should slope upward and AS should slope down.
   E. It portrays stagflation.

14. Automatic, or built-in, stabilizers

   A. prevent inflation.
   B. prevent recessions from occurring.
   C. prevent inflation and recessions from occurring.

D. are government policies already in place that promote deficit spending during expansions and surplus budgets during recessions.

E. are government policies already in place that promote deficit spending during recessions and surplus budgets during expansions.

15. The Phillips curve

A. shows how government spending and tax collections are related.

B. is upward sloping from left to right.

C. indicates that inflation will be high when unemployment is low.

D. shows how the equilibrium price level is related to fiscal policy.

E. shows how output and prices are related.

MULTIPLE-CHOICE REVIEW ANSWERS

1. **C**	4. **B**	7. **C**	10. **D**	13. **E**
2. **D**	5. **A**	8. **D**	11. **C**	14. **E**
3. **A**	6. **B**	9. **C**	12. **A**	15. **C**

Free-Response Review Questions

I. Draw a diagram that portrays a recessionary gap. Be sure to label the axes of your diagram and the aggregate demand curve, the upward sloping aggregate supply curve, and the long run aggregate supply curve.

II. Describe the fiscal policy that would be appropriate to close the recessionary gap. On the diagram show how the fiscal policy works to close the recessionary gap.

III. Draw a Phillips curve. Be sure to label the axes of your diagram. An economy that is in recession would have a low inflation rate but a high unemployment rate. Mark such a point on your Phillips curve and label it "R". Suppose a fiscal policy is implemented and this policy closes the recessionary gap. Mark and label another point on the Phillips curve to demarcate the new inflation/unemployment combination and label it "AFP" for "after the fiscal policy." Explain how you concluded where AFP would be.

FREE-RESPONSE REVIEW ANSWERS

I.

A Recessionary Gap

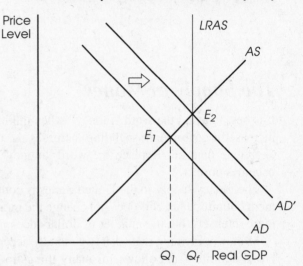

Fiscal Policy to Close a Recessionary Gap

be accomplished by the federal government increasing spending or by reducing taxes or both. Any of these policies will serve to increase aggregate demand. This is shown on the AS/AD model by a shift to the right of the aggregate demand curve.

III.

The Phillips Curve

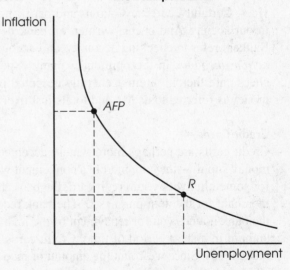

II. The appropriate fiscal policy to close a recessionary gap is for the federal government to run a deficit. This can

Beginning at point R, an expansionary fiscal policy would lower the unemployment rate but raise prices. After the fiscal policy the economy would have lower unemployment but higher inflation. This is the case at point AFP. Thus, an expansionary fiscal policy serves to slide the economy up the Phillips curve.

CHAPTER
18 Money and Banking

The Supply of Money

It is best to avoid the word "money" when talking about fiscal policy. It is incorrect to say that an increase in government spending increases the amount of money in the economy and, therefore, aggregate demand. Replace the word "money" with "income" in the previous sentence and it becomes correct.

The money supply in the United States is controlled by the Federal Reserve. When the government deficit spends, this does not change the money supply. The money in circulation may be used more intensely, but the number of dollars does not change with fiscal policy.

Money is anything that society generally accepts in payment for a good or service. This is a very broad definition and allows for many things to be counted as money. There have been societies that accepted beads and clamshells in exchange for goods and services.

Experts in the field of money and banking disagree on what should be included in the money supply because they disagree on what our society generally accepts in exchange for goods and services. Certainly, currency—coins and paper money—is the most widely accepted form of money in our society. And checks written on bank deposits are accepted almost as readily as currency. Bankers refer to checking accounts, and accounts that function like checking accounts, as *transaction accounts*. In the opinion of many experts, currency, transaction accounts, and travelers' checks are the only items generally accepted in payment in the United States. This definition of money is referred to as M1 and totals just over $1 trillion in 1999.

Credit Cards

Credit cards are perhaps more widely accepted than checks, but credit cards are not part of the money supply—they are merely a convenient way of taking out a loan from a bank. When you pay for something with your credit card, the bank that sponsors your credit card is actually paying the merchant for the item purchased. The bank records this transaction like a loan on its books. Then the bank hounds you for repayment of the loan and interest is charged if you do not pay the entire amount in a short period of time. Credit cards are one way banks use their depositors' money to make loans. Since we count the amount of money deposited into checking accounts as part of M1, it would be redundant to count credit cards also.

Savings Accounts and CDs

Many experts think that more than just the three items included in M1 should counted in the money supply. For instance, money in savings accounts might be part of the money supply. True, hardly any merchants will accept your passbook savings account and deduct from it when you make a purchase, but it is very easy to withdraw money from your savings account and make the purchase. Similarly, certificates of deposit are easily cashed (although there are stiff penalties for early withdrawal on these accounts), although no merchant will accept one for payment.

The issue here is liquidity—the ability to turn an asset into cash rapidly and without loss. Savings accounts and certificates of deposit are not generally accepted to pay for things, but they are very liquid and should, therefore, be counted as money. The definition of money known as M2 includes everything in M1 plus money deposited in savings accounts, certificates of deposit, and other sorts of accounts that are highly liquid.

TABLE 18.1
THE MONEY SUPPLY IN THE UNITED STATES (AS OF DECEMBER 1999) BILLIONS OF DOLLARS

M1		M2	
Currency	515.6	M1	1,123.8
Transaction accounts	599.9	Savings accounts	1,734.5
Travelers' checks	8.3	Certificates of deposit	955.0
Total	1,123.8	Other liquid assets	838.9
		Total	4,652.2

Source: Federal Reserve Bank of the United States

M1 and M2 are the most common definitions of money. However, there are several alternative definitions such as "M3" and "L". These alternative definitions of money include items that are less liquid such as stocks and bonds.

Fiat Money

There is a lot of gold in Fort Knox and an even bigger stash in the vault of the Federal Reserve Bank of New York, but none of this gold is used to back the money supply. The United States, and most nations of the world, use *fiat money*. This means that the coins and paper money have nothing standing behind them except the fact that they are *legal tender*.

Legal tender means that the coin or paper money must be accepted in exchange for goods or services by the decree of the government. Still, Confederate currency was legal tender during the Civil War and even die-hard Southerners wouldn't accept it. That is because far too much of it was supplied by the Confederate authorities. This reveals the key to understanding how fiat currency works—its supply must be kept relatively limited.

From 1873 until 1933 the United States was on some form of the gold standard. The money supply was backed by gold or gold and silver. The primary advantage of the gold standard is that the supply of money must be kept limited since the supply of gold is limited. However, this system can be too confining when an increase in the supply of money is warranted and there is not an increase in the amount of gold held by the government.

A fiat monetary system is more flexible in that the gold holdings of the government need not increase in order to expand the nation's supply of money. By the same token, nations that do not keep the supply of their fiat currency limited will see it diminish in value, sometimes to the point of becoming worthless.

WHAT IS MONEY GOOD FOR?
Most people think that money is good for only one thing—spending. True, textbooks refer to money as a "medium of exchange." Money is a much more efficient way to exchange goods and services than barter. Barter requires a double coincidence of wants; you have to find someone who

has what you want and wants what you have in exchange. Money obviates the need for this and allows us to spend our time more productively.

However, people use money in another way all the time: to make comparisons. Which corporation is bigger, Proctor and Gamble or Pfizer? The assets of Pfizer are worth about $170 billion, while the assets of Proctor and Gamble are worth $85 billion; Pfizer is twice the size of Proctor and Gamble. Notice that dollars figures were used to make this comparison. This is using money as a unit of account. Consider another example. Suppose you win a drawing and you can have the grand prize, a Ford Mustang, or $5,000. Most people would take the car based on the comparison that a new Ford Mustang is worth well over $10,000. Again, money is being used to compare things.

Finally, money also serves as a store of value. You can work hard for 40 years and stuff 20 percent of each paycheck under your mattress. After you retire you can live like a king. This is using money to store the value of your hard labor during your working years. Of course, money is a poor store of value during inflationary times. The $600,000 under mattress can buy less and less as prices rise. On the other hand, money is an excellent store of value during deflations. The $600,000 can buy more and more goods and services as prices fall.

TABLE 18.2
THE FUNCTIONS OF MONEY

- Medium of Exchange—money is used to buy goods and services
- Unit of Account—money is used to measure and compare
- Store of Value—money is used to accumulate wealth

The Federal Reserve System

To understand how the money supply can be changed, it is necessary to understand the Federal Reserve System, or FED, for short. The FED is the central bank of the United States. This means that it controls the money supply and supervises all the depository institutions within the country. All of the banks, savings and loans, credit unions, and mutual savings banks report to the FED each week. The FED can audit any of these institutions at any time and would have to approve any mergers and acquisitions.

The FED operates as the bank of banks. If you need a loan, you might go to a bank. If a bank needs a loan, it may borrow from the FED. If you feel uncomfortable carrying around a lot of cash, you might deposit some of that cash in your account at a bank. If a bank feels uncomfortable having a lot of cash in its vault, it may deposit some of that vault cash in its account at the FED.

Facts about The FED
1. There are 12 branches of the FED located in major cities throughout the nation. This makes it convenient for banks and other depository institutions to do their banking.
2. The main headquarters of the FED is in Washington, D.C.
3. The President of the United States appoints the seven members of the Board of Governors of the Federal Reserve System.
4. The President also appoints one of the members to be the chairman of the Board of Governors and another member to be the vice chairman.
5. All the members of the Board of Governors serve 14-year terms.
6. The Board of Governors makes the important decisions concerning the money supply. Should M1 and M2 be increased? Decreased? Held steady?

The FED is a quasi-governmental institution. The people working at the FED are paid by the federal government, but the FED is not part of the executive, legislative, or judicial branches of government. The Board of Governors makes decisions concerning the money supply in complete autonomy. The FED is not responsible to the President or Congress although it regularly reports to both on its operations and intentions for the money supply.

FRACTIONAL RESERVE BANKING

Banks and other depository institutions keep only a fraction of the money deposited with them on hand. Most of any given deposit is used to make loans or other investments. Nevertheless, banks have plenty of cash on hand to meet their withdrawal needs. A bank manager's worst nightmare is to run short of cash.

The FED's regulation D requires all depository institutions to keep 10 percent of the funds deposited in transactions accounts as reserves. Transactions accounts are checking accounts and other accounts that function as checking accounts, such as NOW accounts and share draft accounts. Reserves must be held against transactions deposits only. Savings accounts and certificates of deposit have no reserve requirement. Banks can hold their required reserves in their vault or in their account at the FED.

Many people think that the FED requires banks to keep aside 10 percent of the money deposited in transaction accounts to insure that there will be cash on hand to meet withdrawal needs. This is not true. As stated, bankers will make sure to have enough money on hand to meet withdrawal needs without any requirements from the FED. Reserve requirements, as we shall see below, help the FED control the money supply.

THE MONEY EXPANSION PROCESS

Imagine that a counterfeiter prints up $1,000 in phony bills and spends the fake money at a jewelry store. At the end of the day the jeweler deposits the counterfeit money into his bank. The bank, not detecting the phony bills, credits the jeweler's transaction account by $1,000. The bank must hold $100 of the $1,000 aside as required reserves. The remaining $900 can be used as the bank sees fit. Typically, excess reserves such as these $900 are used to make loans or buy investments since that is how the bank makes profits.

How suppose the bank loans the $900 to someone applying for a home improvement loan. The $900 ends up being spent on paint. The owner of the paint store deposits the $900 into a transaction account. Notice that this deposit is boosting transaction accounts by $900 and transaction accounts are part of the money supply as measured by M1 or M2. In other words, the money supply is increased when banks make loans with their excess reserves.

And this is not the end of the story. The bank that received the $900 deposit from the paint store must hold 10 percent of the deposit, or $90, as required reserves. The rest of the deposit is excess reserves and the bank can use these in any way they wish. Suppose the bank buys some real estate as an investment with the $810 in excess reserves. Whoever sold the real estate to the bank now has a check for $810. If this check is deposited into a transaction account, the money supply will be going up again, this time $810.

Again, this is not the end of the story. The bank that receives the deposit of $810 will hold 10 percent, or $81, aside as required reserves. The remaining $729 is excess reserves that the bank may use to make a loan or buy an investment.

When all is said and done, the original $1,000 in counterfeit money will have led to a $10,000 increase in the money supply. This is because of the money expansion process where banks create transaction account money by using their reserves to make loans or buy investments. Table 18.3 outlines the money expansion process for this example.

TABLE 18.3
THE MONEY EXPANSION PROCESS

	Deposits into transaction accounts	Required reserves	Excess reserves
Bank 1 (Counterfeiter's bank)	$1,000	$100	$900 (used to make a loan)
Bank 2 (Paint Store's bank)	900	90	810 (used to buy real estate)
Bank 3 (Real estate seller's bank)	810	81	729
Bank 4	729	72.90	656.10
.	.	.	.
	$10,000		

Remember that money deposited into transaction accounts is part of the money supply. When counterfeiters deposit $1,000 into their transaction account, the money supply ends up increasing by $10,000. This is because of all the subsidiary deposits that occur because of the original $1,000 deposit. The column labeled "deposits into transactions accounts" sums to $10,000.

Two formulas help us determine how much the money supply will increase because of a deposit from outside the system. The first formula is for the money multiplier:

Money Multiplier = 1 / reserve requirement

In our case the reserve requirement is 10 percent:

Money Multiplier = 1 / .10 = 10

This tells us that any deposit from outside the banking system, such as counterfeit money, will change the money supply by 10 times the amount of the deposit.

The second formula gives the change in the money supply because of the initial change in bank reserves:

Change in the Money Supply = Money Multiplier × Change in Bank Reserves

In our example the money multiplier is 10 and the initial change in bank reserves is the $1,000 in counterfeit money:

Change in the Money Supply = 10 × $1,000 = $10,000

If the reserve requirement was 5 percent and the counterfeiters deposited $4,000 in fake money, the change in the money supply would be:

Money Multiplier = 1 / .05 = 20

Change in the Money Supply = 20 × $4,000 = $80,000

POLICY TOOLS OF THE FEDERAL RESERVE

The previous examples illustrate why counterfeiting is considered to be such a serious crime. A small amount of counterfeit money can lead to a significant change in the money supply because of the monetary expansion process, but the examples also indicate how the FED could change the money supply.

The FED could print money and deposit it into a bank and the monetary expansion process would take over. The money supply would increase by a multiple of the FED's deposit. And what's more, the initial deposit isn't counterfeit.

As it turns out, there are several ways the FED could change the reserves of the banking system and, therefore, the money supply. These methods are the policy tools of the FED.

1. The FED could *raise or lower the reserve requirements* for depository institutions. If the reserve requirement was lowered, banks would have more excess reserves and could make more loans and investments. This would increase the money supply. To decrease the money supply the FED would raise reserve requirements.

2. Another policy tool involves the *discount rate*. The discount rate is the rate of interest the FED charges when it makes loans to depository institutions. Remember that if you want a loan you might go to a bank, whereas a bank that needs a loan may go to the FED. The FED charges banks a rather low rate of interest on the loans it makes, thus the name discount rate.

   If the FED lowers the discount rate, more banks are encouraged to borrow. These borrowings by banks from the FED increase bank reserves. The money supply will increase by a multiple of the borrowings from the FED.

   As an illustration, suppose the FED lowers the discount rate by half of a percentage point. Say that the lower discount rate encourages banks to borrow $12 million more than usual from the FED. Assuming a 10 percent reserve requirement, the money supply would then increase by $120 million:

   $$\text{Money Multiplier} = 1 \text{ / Reserve Requirement}$$

   $$\text{Money Multiplier} = 1 \text{ / } .10 = 10$$

   $$\text{Change in the Money Supply} = \text{Money Multiplier} \times \text{Change in Bank Reserves}$$

   $$\text{Change in the Money Supply} = 10 \times \$12 \text{ million} = \$120 \text{ million}$$

   If the Fed wanted to decrease the money supply, then the discount rate should be raised. Raising the discount rate discourages banks from borrowing from the FED, and banks, therefore, have less reserves. A decrease in reserves translates into a multiple decrease in the money supply.

3. The third and final policy tool available to the FED to initiate changes in the money supply is *open market operations*. Open market operations is when the FED buys and sells government securities in the secondary market. Government securities are IOUs that the government issues when it borrows money. They sometimes go by the names Treasury bills, bonds, or notes. The federal government of the United States has borrowed trillions of dollars from individuals and corporations, both foreign and domestic.

SECONDARY MARKET

When the government borrows money it issues a government security to the lender that states the amount of the loan, the rate of interest, and the length of the loan. However, the lender need not hold the government securities until it matures. At any time the lender may sell the government security to another investor. This is done in the *secondary market*.

Lenders wishing to sell government securities that have a relatively high rate of interest attached to them will experience a profit in the secondary market, while those with relatively low rates will experience a loss. But the FED does not buy and sell government securities in the secondary market with an eye toward making financial gains. The FED participates in the secondary market for government securities in order to change the money supply.

Imagine what happens when the FED buys government securities in the secondary market. The FED pays for the securities with a check that the seller deposits in a bank account. This deposit is an increase in bank reserves from outside the system. The money supply will increase by a multiple of this increase in bank reserves.

To take a specific example, if the reserve requirement is 10 percent and the FED wants to increase the money supply by $50 million, then the FED would buy $5 million worth of government securities in the secondary market.

$$\text{Money Multiplier} = 1 \,/\, \text{Reserve Requirement}$$

$$\text{Money Multiplier} = 1 \,/\, .10 = 10$$

$$\text{Change in the Money Supply} = \text{Money Multiplier} \times \text{Change in Bank Reserves}$$

$$\text{Change in the Money Supply} = 10 \times \$5 \text{ million} = \$50 \text{ million}$$

If the FED wanted to decrease the money supply, it would sell government securities in the secondary market. Persons or corporations that buy the securities will pay with a check. The FED cashes the check to draw the reserves out of the banking system and does not deposit proceeds of the sale back into the banking system. In this way bank reserves are depleted. The money supply falls by a multiple of the decline in bank reserves.

Specifically, if the FED sells $6 million worth of government securities in the secondary market, and the reserve requirement is 5 percent, then the money supply will fall by $120 million.

$$\text{Money Multiplier} = 1 \,/\, \text{Reserve Requirement}$$

$$\text{Money Multiplier} = 1 \,/\, .05 = 20$$

$$\text{Change in the Money Supply} = \text{Money Multiplier} \times \text{Change in Bank Reserves}$$

$$\text{Change in the Money Supply} = 20 \times -\$6 \text{ million} = -\$120 \text{ million}$$

Table 18.4 summarizes the policy tools of the FED.

TABLE 18.4
POLICY TOOLS OF THE FEDERAL RESERVE

Tool	Description	To Increase Money Supply	To Decrease Money Supply
Change Reserve Requirements	Change the percentage of each deposit that banks must hold aside.	Lower the reserve requirement	Raise the reserve requirement
Change the Discount Rate	Change the rate of interest the FED charges on bank borrowings.	Lower the discount rate	Raise the discount rate
Open Market Operations	Buy or sell government securities in the secondary market	Buy government securities	Sell government securities

Summary

- Money is anything generally accepted to pay for goods and services. Certainly, currency, transaction accounts, and travelers' checks are generally accepted. This definition of money is known as M1. Many experts think that other highly liquid assets should be considered money. These include savings accounts, certificates of deposit, and other liquid assets. Adding these three items to M1 gives M2, another prevalent definition of money.
- The money supply in the United States, like most nations, is not backed by gold or silver or any precious commodity. Fiat money is money because the government says it is money. Experience has shown that it is extremely important to keep the supply of a fiat money relatively limited if it is to function correctly.
- Money is good for spending (a medium of exchange), comparing things (a unit of account), and as an investment vehicle (a store of value). The United States is on a fractional reserve

system where depository institutions keep only a fraction of each deposit on hand. Most of the money deposited in a bank is used to make loans and buy investments.

- The Federal Reserve is the central bank of the United States and controls the money supply. It does this mostly with open market operations, but can also alter the discount rate or change reserve requirements. Any of these three techniques changes the reserves of the banking system. The money supply changes by a multiple of the change in bank reserves.

Terms

Certificate of Deposit   debt instrument that is similar to a savings account except the interest rate is slightly greater and the deposit cannot be drawn on without penalty

Currency   coins and paper money

Discount Rate   the rate of interest the FED charges when it makes loans to depository institutions

Excess Reserves   the amount of any deposit that does not have to be held aside and may be used to make loans and buy investments

Federal Reserve   the central bank of the United States

Fiat Money   money that is not backed by any precious commodity

Government Securities   IOUs that the government issues when it borrows money

Liquidity   the ability to turn an asset into cash rapidly and without loss

M1   currency, transaction accounts, and travelers' checks

M2   M1 plus savings accounts, certificates of deposit, and other liquid assets

Money   anything that society generally accepts in payment for a good or service

Money Multiplier   = 1 / reserve requirement, the multiple by which the money supply will change because of a change in bank reserves

Open Market Operations   activities in which the FED buys and sells government securities in the secondary market

Required Reserves   the amount of any deposit that must be held aside and not used to make loans or buy investments

Reserve Requirement   the percentage of any deposit that must be held aside and not used to make loans or buy investments

Savings Account   an account at a depository institution that earns interest while the funds are readily available but cannot be withdrawn with checks

Secondary Market   place where government securities that have already been issued may be bought or sold

Transaction Account   a checking account at a bank or a similar account at some other depository institution

Formulas

Money Multiplier = 1 / reserve requirement

Change in the Money Supply = Money Multiplier × Change in Bank Reserves

Multiple-Choice Review Questions

1. Which of the following is not included in M1?

   A. Coins.
   B. Paper money.
   C. Travelers' checks.
   D. Credit cards.
   E. Transaction accounts.

2. Which of the following is not included in M2?

   A. Currency.
   B. Travelers' checks.
   C. Certificates of deposit.
   D. Savings accounts.
   E. Credit cards.

3. Which of the following statements is true?

   A. Some of the things included in M2 are not as liquid as the things in M1.
   B. M2 is smaller than M1.
   C. M1 is backed by gold and M2 is backed by silver.
   D. The biggest component of M1 is currency.
   E. The biggest component of M2 is currency.

4. Fiat money

   A. is not backed by any precious commodity.
   B. can be exchanged for gold.
   C. is backed by gold, but cannot be exchanged for it.
   D. is not legal tender.
   E. can be backed by gold or silver.

5. The Federal Reserve is

   A. part of the legislative branch of government.
   B. the monetary authority for banks, but not other depository institutions.
   C. part of the judicial branch of government.
   D. in control of the money supply.
   E. in control of government spending.

6. Required reserves

   A. can be used by banks to make loans or buy investments.
   B. can be held in a bank's vault or its account at the FED.
   C. must be kept in a bank's vault.
   D. must be used to make loans.
   E. ensure that banks will have enough cash on hand to meet their withdrawals.

7. The secondary market for government securities is

   A. where used items are traded.
   B. located in smaller cities.
   C. where the government borrows money.
   D. where government securities that have already been issued may be bought or sold.
   E. where government securities are issued.

8. If the reserve requirement is 2 percent, then the money multiplier is

   A. 5
   B. 5 percent
   C. 50
   D. 50 percent
   E. one half

9. If the FED buys bonds in the secondary market

   A. the money supply will increase.
   B. the money supply will decrease.
   C. the money supply will not be affected.
   D. the discount rate would be affected.
   E. reserve requirements would have to be increased in tandem.

10. Which of the following would lead to an expansion of the money supply?

A. The FED raises the discount rate.
B. The FED buys government securities in the secondary market.
C. The federal government deficit spends.
D. The FED raises reserve requirements.
E. Taxes are reduced.

11. Assume the reserve requirement is 10 percent. If the FED sells $29 million worth of government securities in an open market operation, then the money supply can

A. increase by $2.9 million.
B. decrease by $2.9 million.
C. increase by $290 million.
D. decrease by $290 million.
E. increase by $26.1 million.

12. Assume the reserve requirement is 5 percent. If the FED buys $4 million worth of government securities in an open market operation, then the money supply can

A. increase by $1.25 million.
B. decrease by $1.25 million.
C. increase by $20 million.
D. decrease by $20 million.
E. increase by $80 million.

13. When the FED lowers the discount rate its intention is to

A. give depository institutions a break on their borrowings.
B. signal participants in financial markets that a recession is coming.
C. signal participants in financial markets that an inflationary period is coming.
D. lower prices in the economy.
E. encourage borrowing by depository institutions so that the money supply may expand.

14. Lowering reserve requirements would

A. force banks to hold more reserves and make more loans.
B. allow banks to make more loans and buy more investments thus decreasing the money supply.
C. allow banks to make more loans and buy more investments thus increasing the money supply.
D. allow banks more freedom to merge and acquire other businesses.
E. force banks to sell investments so that fewer funds are held in reserve.

15. The FED's Board of Governors has _____ members each serving _____ -year terms.

A. 14, 7
B. 7, 14
C. 8, 8
D. 50, 2
E. 8, 10

MULTIPLE-CHOICE REVIEW ANSWERS

1. D	4. A	7. D	10. B	13. E
2. E	5. D	8. C	11. D	14. C
3. A	6. B	9. A	12. E	15. B

Free-Response Review Questions

I. Assume the reserve requirement is 10 percent. If the FED buys $10,000 worth of government securities in the secondary market, will the money supply expand or shrink? By exactly how much?

II. Explain why the money supply changes when the FED buys $10,000 worth of government securities in the secondary market. Why is the change in the money supply not $10,000?

III. Suppose that depository institutions did not use all of their excess reserves to make loans and buy investments. For example, if the reserve requirement was 10 percent depository institutions would hold 20 percent of their deposits idle. How would this affect your answer to I. above?

FREE-RESPONSE REVIEW ANSWERS

I. If the FED buys $10,000 worth of government securities in the secondary market, the money supply expands. When the Fed pays for the securities the sellers will deposit their checks into the banking system. The reserves of the banking system will increase by $10,000. The money supply will increase by ten times that amount, or $100,000 because the money multiplier is 10 in this case. (Money multiplier = 1 / .10 = 10.)

II. The money supply increases because when the FED buys securities in the secondary market, this increases the reserves of banks where the checks are deposited. The reserves of these banks go up by $10,000. Now these banks are holding more reserves than they are required to by the FED's reserve requirements. The banks make loans and buy investments with these excess reserves and this serves to increase transaction accounts. Transaction accounts are part of the money supply.

III. If banks do not use all of their excess reserves to make loans and buy investments, then money expansion process is not as effective. When a bank makes a loan, this money ends up as a deposit elsewhere, usually at another bank. If banks prefer to hold extra reserves, then the loans will not be as large and the increase in the money supply because of the $10,000 increase in reserves also will not be as large. If banks have a 10 percent reserve requirement and hold 10 percent more in extra reserves, this means that the money multiplier is 5 (= 1 / .2) and the money supply will expand to only $50,000, not $100,000.

CHAPTER
19 Monetary Policy

Definition

Test your economic intuition by answering this question: If the economy is mired in a recession, should the money supply be increased or decreased? The correct answer is increased. Congratulate yourself for having good economic intuition if you answered correctly.

Here is a much more difficult, and less intuitive question: Why does an increase in the money supply stimulate a sluggish economy? After a moment of thought most people respond that an increase in the money supply would motivate spending. Not bad. But if households and corporations wanted to spend more, why don't they simply use the existing money supply more intensely? They could spend more without increasing the money supply if each dollar was turned over more often. If households and corporations don't want to increase spending, would an increase in the money supply force them to spend more?

You will be able to answer the more difficult questions posed above shortly. First, let's define monetary policy—changes in the money supply to fight recessions or inflations. The Board of Governors of the FED designs and executes monetary policy in the United States. Suppose the Board of Governors decides to increase the money supply. In Chapter 18 we saw that this could be accomplished with a decrease in reserve requirements, a decrease in the discount rate, or an open market purchase of government securities.

The Federal Open Market Committee (FOMC) helps the Board of Governors decide which tool to use. If the open market purchases are selected, then the FOMC plots out exactly how many government securities will be purchased at what time. The FOMC is comprised of twelve members. All seven of the members of the Board of Governors sit on the FOMC, as well as five of the presidents of the twelve FED regional banks.

Changes in The Money Supply

HOW CHANGES IN THE MONEY SUPPLY AFFECT THE ECONOMY—THE CLASSICAL VIEW

Classical economic analysis concludes that changes in the money supply have no effect on the equilibrium quantity of output; only prices and wages are affected. According to Classical theory, an increase in the money supply would increase aggregate demand, but the increase in aggregate demand would result in higher prices.

Workers would immediately realize that their wages could not buy as many goods and services at the higher prices and they would demand wage increases. When the dust settled, if the money supply was raised 10 percent, prices and wages would rise 10 percent and nothing else would be changed.

If the economy was in a recession and the unemployment rate was high, an increase in the money supply would not help. After the money supply was increased, prices and wages would be higher, but the unemployment rate would be unchanged.

The Classical view on how an increase in the money supply affects the economy is reflected in the aggregate supply/aggregate demand (AS/AD) model in figure 19.1. The increase in the money supply shifts the aggregate demand curve to the right. But suppliers respond to this increase in the demand for their products by raising prices from P1 to P2, but not output. Remember, the Classical aggregate supply curve is vertical. So the increase in aggregate demand has no effect on the quantity of output. Since output is unaffected, so is unemployment.

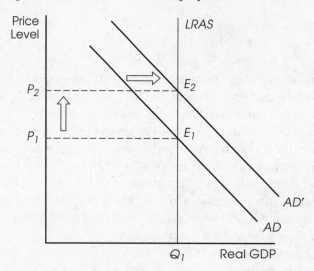

Fig. 19.1 An Increase in the Money Supply: Classical View

The Classical economists based their conclusions about how money affects the economy on the equation of exchange:

$$M \times V = P \times Q$$

Where M is the money supply
V is the velocity of money
P is the price level and
Q is the quantity of output or real GDP.

The money supply can be defined as M1 or M2. The velocity of money is the number of times the typical dollar of M1 or M2 is used to make purchases during a year. The price level is the average price of a good or service in the economy, the same as the vertical axis in the AS/AD model. The quantity of output can be measured with real GDP and is the same as the horizontal axis in the AS/AD model.

The equation of exchange is a *tautology*, meaning it is true by definition. No economist, Classical or not, disputes the fact that $M \times V = P \times Q$. But the Classical economists take this a step further and assume that V and Q are constant. If this is true, then the arithmetic of the situation tells us that if M increases 10 percent, P must also increase 10 percent.

The Classical economists referred to this result as *monetary neutrality*. A change in the money supply would result in a proportional change in prices. The quantity of output, real GDP, the rate of unemployment, and other real variables are unaffected. This analysis is in line with the Classical notion that the only things that can affect the quantity of output are resource availability and technology.

HOW CHANGES IN THE MONEY SUPPLY AFFECT THE ECONOMY—THE MONETARIST VIEW

It is easy to shoot down the Classical theory of monetary neutrality. The theory is based on the assumption that V and Q are constant. In the United States, the velocity of M1 was 3.6 in 1960 and 8.3 in 1999. Clearly, V is not constant. Similarly, Q, or real GDP, has increased 272 percent in the same time span. With a nonconstant V and Q, we can no longer conclude that a change in the money supply causes a proportional change in prices.

The Monetarist view on how a change in the money supply affects the economy is more realistic. The Monetarist view starts with the assumption that V and Q are stable, but not constant, in the short run. Now if the money supply is increased 10 percent, it is by no means definite that P will increase by 10 percent. Monetarists claim that both P and Q will increase and not necessarily by 10 percent.

According to the Monetarist view, a change in the money supply affects the economy in many ways. For one, interest rates will be affected and this will affect spending levels and, therefore, aggregate demand. For another, more money directly translates into more spending as households and firms try to spend and invest the increment in the money supply. And there are other channels through which a change in the money supply will affect the economy. They are "too numerous to enumerate," according to Milton Friedman a Nobel Prize-winning economist who is often called the father of monetarism.

On the AS/AD model, an increase in the money supply results in an increase in aggregate demand. This translates into an increase in the price level and the quantity of output. We get a different result than the Classical analysis because the aggregate supply curve is drawn upward sloping from left to right instead of vertical.

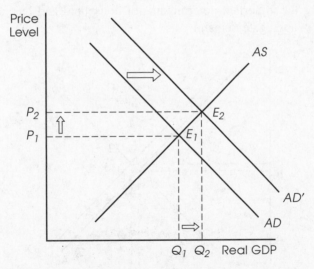

Fig. 19.2 An Increase in the Money Supply: Monetarist View

The Monetarist view on how a change in the money supply affects the economy, like the Classical view, is based on the equation of exchange. However, the Monetarist view is not as rigid. The Classical view maintains that V and Q are constant, so that an increase in M will have a proportional effect on P. Q is not affected. The Monetarist view is that V and Q are stable in the short run, but not constant. This means that both P and Q will be affected when M is increased. Indeed, the Monetarists assert that most of the fluctuations in Q over the years are the result of the FED changing M.

The Monetarists are highly critical of the FED. If changes in output are caused primarily by changes in the money supply, then all the FED need do is allow the money supply to increase at a reasonable constant rate, say 3 percent a year. When the FED undertakes monetary policies that reverse the direction of money growth, this results in the recessions and inflations we observe in the economy.

HOW A CHANGE IN THE MONEY SUPPLY AFFECTS THE ECONOMY—THE KEYNESIAN VIEW

A third perspective on how a change in the money supply affects the economy is that of the Keynesians. This view, like the monetarist view, is concerned with short run effects and uses an upward sloping aggregate supply curve. The difference is that the Keynesians believe that a change in the money supply affects the economy through one channel, not many—and that channel is the interest rate.

An increase in the money supply would lower interest rates, since more money is available to be borrowed. Lower interest rates encourage households and firms to take out loans in order to increase spending and investment in plant and equipment. This means more aggregate demand.

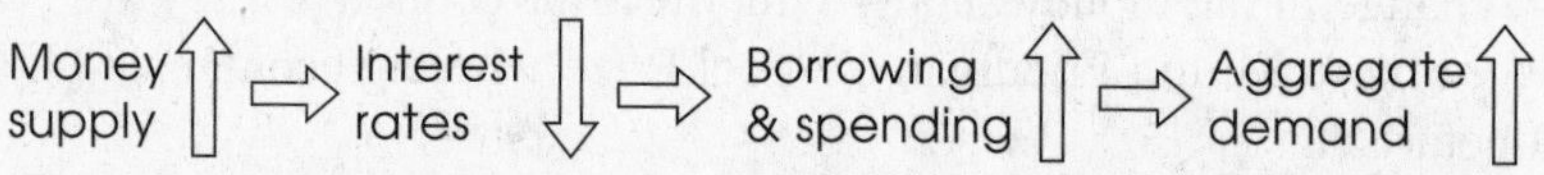

Money supply ⬆ ⇒ Interest rates ⬇ ⇒ Borrowing & spending ⬆ ⇒ Aggregate demand ⬆

Fig. 19.3 How an Increase in the Money Supply Affects the Economy: Keynesian View

However, Keynesians argue that the increase in aggregate demand will be small. This is because they believe that a decline in interest rates will not stimulate much spending. Keynesians feel that income and profits are the important determinants of household and business spending. Interest rates only mildly affect aggregate demand.

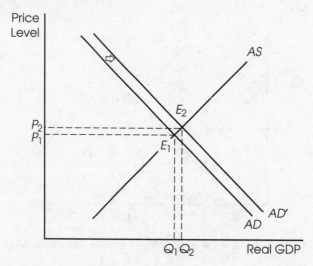

Fig. 19.4 An Increase in the Money Supply: Keynesian View

An increase in the money supply will shift the aggregate demand curve to the right, but only a small amount according to the Keynesian view. This is because a change in the money supply affects spending through only one channel—interest rates—not many channels as the Monetarists believe. Moreover, the interest rate channel does not result in major changes in spending when the money supply is changed. Keynesians argue that fiscal policy should be used to close recessionary and inflationary gaps. Monetary policy is not that effective in their eyes.

Summary

- The term "demand management policy" refers to both monetary and fiscal policy because, like fiscal policy, monetary policy shifts the aggregate demand curve. If the government decides to increase total spending in the economy, shifting the aggregate demand curve to the right, this could be accomplished by increasing the money supply, or increasing government spending, or reducing taxes.
- Most economists believe that a change in the money supply will affect both prices and output in the short run. Classical economic theory tells us that in the long run a change in the money supply will only affect prices. Only resources and technology can affect output in the long run, a change in the money supply cannot.
- Monetarists believe that changes in the money supply have a profound effect on the economy in the short run; for instance, a decrease in the money supply would result in lower prices and less output. Therefore, lowering the money supply would be a good way to fight inflation, but it could result in a recession since output decreases. The best thing the FED could do is forget about trying to close recessionary and inflationary gaps with monetary policy and instead, allow the money supply to grow at a steady, constant rate. This would result in an economy that grows at a steady, constant rate.
- The Keynesian economists disagree with the Monetarists on many points. A change in the money supply would affect the economy through just one channel, interest rates. And the effect would be mild since changes in interest rates do not have a profound effect on aggregate demand. Fiscal policy should be used to close recessionary and inflationary gaps. Monetary policy is ineffective.

TABLE 19.1
PERSPECTIVES ON THE MONEY SUPPLY

	Classical	Monetarist	Keynesian
A change in the money supply affects	the price level	the price level and output	the price level and output
through	many variables	many variables	the interest rate
The effect is	strong but limited to prices and wages	strong	weak
V and Q are	constant	stable	variable

At the outset of this chapter we asked if households and corporations don't want to increase spending, would an increase in the money force them to spend more? Hopefully at this point you can see that the answer is Yes, although "induce" may be a better word than "force." Monetarists think that a significant amount of spending would be induced by an increase in the money supply. Keynesians disagree.

Terms

Board of Governors   executive board of the FED that makes major monetary policy decisions

Demand Management Policy   monetary and fiscal policy

Equation of Exchange $M \times V = P \times Q$; the money supply times its velocity equals the price level times output

Federal Open Market Committee (FOMC)   a committee within the FED that designs and executes the particulars of monetary policy

Monetarist   one who believes that changes in the money supply have a profound effect on the economy

Monetary Neutrality   policy in which a change in the money supply would result in a proportional change in prices while real variables, such as the unemployment rate, would be unaffected

Monetary Policy   changes in the money supply to fight recessions or inflations

Velocity of Money   describing the number of times the typical dollar of M1 or M2 is used to make purchases during a year

Formulas

Equation of Exchange: $M \times V = P \times Q$

Multiple-Choice Review Questions

1. The Federal Open Market Committee

   A. advises the President of the United States.
   B. is part of the Federal Reserve System.
   C. has seven members.
   D. promotes free trade.
   E. is part of the legislative branch of government.

2. According to Classical economic theory, a decrease in the money supply would

   A. raise the price level and output in the economy.
   B. lower the price level and output in the economy.
   C. raise the price level in the economy.
   D. lower the price level in the economy.
   E. raise the price level and lower output in the economy.

3. According to monetarist analysis, a decrease in the money supply would

   A. raise the price level and output in the economy.
   B. lower the price level and output in the economy.
   C. raise the price level in the economy.
   D. lower the price level in the economy.
   E. raise the price level and lower output in the economy.

4. According to Keynesian analysis, a decrease in the money supply would

   A. raise the price level and output in the economy.
   B. lower the price level and output in the economy.
   C. raise the price level in the economy.
   D. lower the price level in the economy.
   E. raise the price level and lower output in the economy.

5. In the equation of exchange

   A. M stands for the money supply and Q stands for quality.
   B. V stands for the velocity of GDP and Q stands for quality.
   C. P stands for the price level and Q stands for quarter.
   D. P stands for the price level and V stands for the velocity of money.
   E. P stands for population and V stands for the velocity of money.

6. The velocity of money

   A. cannot be calculated for an actual economy.
   B. is how fast money can be transferred.
   C. is required to calculate the money multiplier.
   D. is the number of times a typical dollar changes hands.
   E. is the number of times a typical dollar is used to make a purchase in a year.

7. In the equation of exchange, if V and Q are constant, then

   A. changes in the price level must be proportional to changes in the money supply.
   B. changes in the money supply have no effect on the price level.
   C. changes in the price level have no effect on the money supply.
   D. the equation is invalid.
   E. the money supply must be zero.

8. In the United States over the years, V and Q

A. have not changed significantly.
B. are perfectly constant.
C. have decreased significantly.
D. have increased significantly.
E. changed once since World War II.

9. According to Monetarist theory, when the money supply is changed, the economy is affected

A. only because a change in the money supply affects interest rates.
B. in several ways.
C. because interest rates change and so do many other factors that affect spending.
D. because many factors that affect spending change, but not interest rates.
E. but only insignificantly.

10. According to Keynesian theory, a decrease in the money supply would

A. lower interest rates, which would encourage borrowing and, therefore increase spending.
B. raise interest rates, which would discourage borrowing and, therefore, increase spending.
C. raise interest rates, which would discourage borrowing and, therefore, reduce spending.
D. lower interest rates, which would discourage borrowing and, therefore, reduce spending.
E. raise interest rates, which would encourage borrowing and, therefore, reduce spending.

11. Which of following could cause the aggregate demand curve to shift to the left?

A. An increase in the money supply.
B. Contractionary demand management policies.
C. Expansionary demand management policies.
D. An increase in government spending.
E. There is more than one correct answer here.

12. According to Monetarist theory,

A. the FED should actively conduct monetary policy.
B. changes in the money supply do not have significant effects.
C. fiscal policy is the preferred way of shifting the aggregate demand curve.
D. the FED should allow the money supply to grow at a constant rate.
E. the FED should randomly change the money supply.

13. According to Keynesian theory,

A. the FED should not conduct monetary policy.
B. changes in the money supply have significant effects.
C. fiscal policy is the preferred way of shifting the aggregate demand curve.
D. the FED should allow the money supply to grow at a constant rate.
E. the FED should randomly change the money supply.

14. Milton Friedman

A. never won a Nobel Prize despite his contributions to economic analysis.
B. is a Monetarist.
C. is a Keynesian.
D. won a Nobel Prize for his contributions to Classical economic analysis.
E. never won a Nobel Prize despite his contributions to Monetarist analysis.

15. Monetarists believe that V and Q are
   A. constant.
   B. stable.
   C. variable.
   D. not critical for understanding how money affects the economy.
   E. unstable.

MULTIPLE-CHOICE REVIEW ANSWERS

1. **B**	4. **B**	7. **A**	10. **C**	13. **C**
2. **D**	5. **D**	8. **D**	11. **B**	14. **B**
3. **B**	6. **E**	9. **C**	12. **D**	15. **B**

Free-Response Review Questions

I. Suppose the money supply is increased. What would happen to the equilibrium price level, the equilibrium quantity of output, and the unemployment rate according to
A. Classical economic theory?
B. Monetarist theory?
C. Keynesian theory?

II. Explain why the three schools of economic thought in Part I. reach different or similar conclusions concerning how an increase in the money supply will affect the economy.

FREE-RESPONSE REVIEW ANSWERS

I. If the money supply were increased then

A. according to Classical economic theory the equilibrium price level would increase and the equilibrium quantity of output would remain unchanged. Since the quantity of output is unchanged, the unemployment rate is unchanged.

B. according to Monetarist theory the equilibrium price level would increase and the equilibrium quantity of output would increase as well. Since the quantity of output increased, the unemployment rate would fall.

C. according to Keynesian theory the equilibrium price level would increase slightly and the equilibrium quantity of output would increase slightly as well. Since the quantity of output increased slightly, the unemployment rate would decrease slightly.

II. All three schools of thought agree that an increase in the money supply will raise the equilibrium price level. However, the Keynesians believe that the price level will only rise slightly. This is because they believe that an increase in the money supply will stimulate only a small amount of extra spending. Another way of saying this is that the Keynesians feel that an increase in the money supply will shift the aggregate demand curve to the right, but only by a small amount.

Similarly, the Keynesians feel that the equilibrium level of output will increase only slightly because total spending is not that sensitive to changes in the money supply. Therefore, unemployment falls modestly. The Monetarists, on the other hand, believe that an increase in the money supply has a significant impact on the economy. The equilibrium quantity of output rises substantially because spending is boosted by the increase in the money supply. Therefore, unemployment falls significantly.

Only the Classical thinkers believe that the equilibrium level of output and the unemployment rate will be completely unaffected by the increase in the money supply. This is because of the Classical emphasis on the long run effects of any change in the economy. The amount of output that an economy can generate depends on the amount of resources available and the state of technology. An increase in the money supply affects neither of these and so the Classical conclusion is that output is not affected by an increase in the supply of money. It only serves to raise prices.

CHAPTER
20 Economic Growth

Living Standards

In 1948 real GDP per capita (in 1996 dollars) in the United States was $10,641. By 1999 it had risen to $32,447. These figures indicate that the standard of living has roughly tripled in those 52 years. Real GDP per capita represents how much was produced, per person in the nation. When more goods and services are produced, this implies more material wealth. This is the essence of economic growth—increments in material wealth. The percentage change in real GDP, or real GDP per capita, is the customary measure of economic growth.

Of course, not all growth is good. Some bemoan the congestion, pollution, and loss of simplicity that sometimes accompany economic growth. Nevertheless, generally speaking, more output per person implies higher living standards. Life is more harsh in Tanzania, where GDP per capita is less than $1,000, than in Australia where GDP per capita is over $20,000.

In the United States since World War II, real GDP typically grows about 3 percent a year. Real GDP per capita has an average growth rate of just under 2 percent for the same period. This means that American citizens enjoy a standard of life that improves just under 2 percent a year.

Even small differences in the rate of growth can add up over the years. Imagine two economies, both with a real GDP per capita of $30,000. If real GDP per capita grows by 1 percent a year in the first economy and 2 percent a year in the second, then in 25 years the first economy will have a real GDP per capita of $38,500, while in the second it will rise to $49,200.

This brings us to the "rule of 70." It will take 10 years for GDP, or any variable, to double if it grows by 7 percent a year. More generally, a variable will double in 70/x years, where x is the annual growth rate of the variable. So if the standard of living grows at 5 percent a year, we can expect the standard of living to double in 14 (= $^{70}/_5$) years.

It is well known that the fruits of economic growth are not shared equally among the population in America. Since income is unequally distributed, so is the economic bounty. In fact, America has one of the more skewed distributions of income in the industrialized world. Roughly half of all the income goes to 20 percent of the families. The poorest 20 percent of the population earns only 5 percent of all the income. Growth theorists argue about what can be done about disparities in living standards within a nation. Some see the disparity as a natural consequence of growth, while others insist that economic growth need not result in economic inequality.

The Determinants of Economic Growth

The production possibilities frontier can be used to summarize the factors that cause an economy to grow. Our previous analysis indicated that two factors could cause the production possibilities frontier to shift outward: (1) an increase in the amount of resources, and, (2) a technological advance that increases productivity.

Figure 20.1 illustrates how an increase in a particular resource, labor, would affect the production possibilities frontier. If the economy was producing at point A before the increase in the amount of labor in the economy, it could now produce at a point such as B, where more guns and butter are consumed.

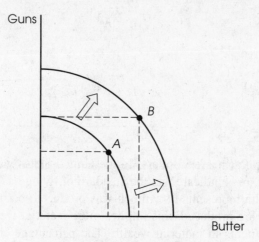

Fig. 20.1 An Increase in Labor Force

Figure 20.2 shows a how a technological advance in butter production would affect the production possibilities frontier. Apparently the technological advance has no application in gun production because the intersection of the frontier on the vertical axis has not changed. Nevertheless, the economy can consume more guns and butter after the technological advance. This can be seen by comparing points A and B in Figure 20.2.

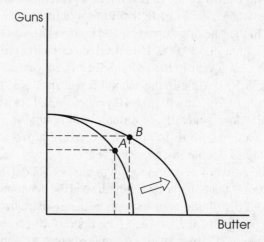

Fig. 20.2 A Technological Advance in Butter Production

The aggregate demand/aggregate supply (AS/AD) model can also illustrate economic growth. If the long run aggregate supply curve is used, then shifts in aggregate demand have no effect on the equilibrium quantity of output. Only a shift to the right of the long run aggregate supply curve can increase equilibrium output. This is shown in Figure 20.3.

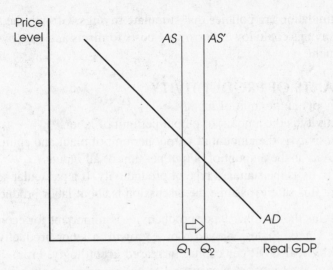

Fig. 20.3 An Increase in Long Run Aggregate Supply

The only question that remains is, what can cause the long run aggregate supply curve to shift to the right? Readers with good retention will remember that there are two factors that could cause the long run aggregate supply curve to shift to the right: (1) an increase in the amount of resources, and (2) a technological advance that increases productivity. These are the same two factors that can cause the production possibilities frontier to shift outward.

Our investigation of the production possibilities frontier and the AS/AD model indicates that there are two general factors affecting economic growth: (1) resource availability, and (2) the productivity of those resources. To dig deeper, we now ask what can affect resource availability and productivity.

THE DETERMINANTS OF RESOURCE AVAILABILITY

Recall that resources are classified into three categories—land, labor, and capital. One way to promote economic growth is to promote the availability of each of these classes of resources. For instance, you might think that the amount of natural resources, what economists call land, is strictly limited, but that is not true. New deposits of oil, natural gas, and minerals are continually being discovered. Also, advances in agriculture and irrigation can make more land available for farming. Discoveries of mineral deposits and the creation of arable fields are examples of natural resources becoming more readily available. This results in more production and, therefore, economic growth.

The availability of labor is primarily based on demographic factors. These demographics are a major concern in Russia. It is expected that the labor force in Russia will shrink due to a decline in the birth rate. A smaller labor force means an important resource is less available. This will have a negative impact on economic growth in Russia.

But the supply of labor is not only affected by demographic factors. Government-subsidized child care could increase the supply of labor as could education and training programs. Both these policies have been suggested as ways to encourage the supply of labor and economic growth.

Capital is the term economists use to indicate plant and equipment. An expansion of the amount of plant and equipment in the economy would shift the production possibilities frontier outward or the long run aggregate supply curve to the right. In either case, the result is economic growth. Economists have advocated a variety of policies that would promote spending on plant and equipment. Tax breaks for businesses that expand their capital stock have been tried as a means to spur investment spending. Lower interest rates may also help. What would lower interest rates? Expansionary monetary policy, for one thing. Another idea for lowering interest rates and promoting capital accumulation are policies that stimulate savings. Growth theorists have long realized that increased savings could lower borrowing costs for firms and thereby encourage spending on plant and equipment.

THE DETERMINANTS OF PRODUCTIVITY

- Productivity is output per unit of input.
- Labor productivity is the amount of output per unit of labor.
- Capital productivity is the amount of output per unit of plant and equipment.
- Total productivity is the amount of output per unit of all inputs.
- Labor productivity is the standard type of productivity. If a particular sort of productivity is not mentioned, it is safe to assume the discussion is about labor productivity.

Table 20.1 highlights the fact that labor productivity is important for economic growth. From 1948 until 1973 the United States enjoyed robust growth in labor productivity and living standards, as measured by real GDP per capita, increased accordingly. From 1973 until 1999, the growth rate of labor productivity has slowed and so has economic growth.

TABLE 20.1
LABOR PRODUCTIVITY AND THE STANDARD OF LIVING IN THE UNITED STATES

Period	Average Growth Rate of Labor Productivity (%)	Average Growth Rate of Real GDP Per Capita (%)
1948–1973	2.9	2.1
1973–1999	1.6	1.4

Source: U.S. Bureau of Labor Statistics; Bureau of Economic Analysis; U.S. Bureau of the Census

What determines the productivity of labor? One of the most important factors is the amount of capital relative to the amount of labor. An increase in the amount of plant and equipment per worker will increase labor productivity.

Also, technology can affect the productivity of labor. The innovations that brought a personal computer to almost every office worker's desk undoubtedly raised productivity.

Another factor affecting productivity is the skill level of work force. Education and training can raise labor productivity. Economists call attempts to improve the quality of the labor force investments in "human capital." Human capital is the skill and knowledge embodied in the labor force. A labor force with high levels of human capital is more productive.

Summary

- Economic growth is defined as the growth of output usually as measured by real GDP or real GDP per capita. In the United States, real GDP per capita has grown about 2 percent a year since World War II; however, economic growth was higher than 2 percent from 1948 until 1973 and has averaged about 1.5 percent since then. And the fruits of economic growth are not shared equally by all Americans. The top 20 percent of families garner 50 percent of all the income earned.
- Economic growth is the result of increased resource availability or increased productivity. Long run output can increase only if more resources are on hand or those resources are more productive; however, there are a variety of factors that can impact resource availability and productivity. Table 20.2 delineates these factors.

TABLE 20.2
DETERMINANTS OF ECONOMIC GROWTH

Increased Resource Availability
- Discovery of new natural resources
- Growth of the labor force
- Growth of the capital stock

Increased Productivity
- More capital per unit of labor
- Technological progress
- Better educated and trained work force

- Finally, economists recognize that economic growth has its price. Economic growth can degrade the environment, cause congestion, and lead to more hectic lifestyles. Still, most people would prefer to live where real GDP per capita is high than where it is low.

Terms

Capital   plant and equipment

Capital Productivity   the amount of output per unit of plant and equipment

Economic Growth   growth of output usually measured by the percentage change in real GDP or real GDP per capita

Human Capital   the skill and knowledge embodied in the labor force

Labor Productivity   the amount of output per unit of labor

Productivity   output per unit of input

Total Productivity   the amount of output per unit of all inputs

Formulas

Rule of 70   Years it takes a variable to double = 70/the annual growth rate of the variable

Multiple-Choice Review Questions

1. Economic growth is

   A. measured by the number of businesses in the economy.
   B. shared equally among the population.
   C. critical in determining the standard of living in a nation.
   D. measured by the amount of government spending.
   E. measured by the unemployment rate.

2. The standard of living is measured by

   A. GDP.
   B. GDP per capita.
   C. Real GDP per capita.
   D. Actual GDP per capita.
   E. the unemployment rate.

3. Which of the following will result in economic growth?

   A. A decrease in the unemployment rate.
   B. An increase in the unemployment rate.
   C. An increase in the size of the labor force.
   D. A decrease in the population.
   E. A change in political leadership.

4. Which of the following will promote economic growth?

   A. Government regulation.
   B. A new production technique that lowers costs.
   C. Increased taxes.
   D. More strict pollution standards for corporations.
   E. Reduced taxes.

5. Which of the following will promote economic growth?

   A. An increase in the amount of capital.
   B. Lower wages.
   C. Price controls that keep prices low.
   D. Increased government spending.
   E. A decrease in the money supply.

6. If real GDP per capita was $10,000 in 1990 and $15,000 in 2000, then the amount of economic growth is

   A. 0.5 percent.
   B. 5.0 percent.
   C. 50 percent.
   D. 3.3 percent.
   E. More information is required to determine the amount of economic growth.

7. If real GDP per capita was $20,000 in 1980 and $21,000 in 1990, then we conclude that the standard of living has increased

   A. 0.5 percent.
   B. 5.0 percent.
   C. 50 percent.
   D. 3.3 percent.
   E. More information is required to determine the amount of economic growth.

8. The standard of living will increase if

   A. everyone works harder.
   B. the population grows.
   C. GDP increases.
   D. real GDP increases.
   E. real GDP increases at a greater rate than the population.

9. Output in country A is 1,200 units and its population is 100 persons. Output in country B is 2,400 units and its population is 400 persons.

   A. Country A has a higher standard of living than country B.
   B. Country A has a lower standard of living than country B.
   C. Country A and B have identical living standards.
   D. Country A is less productive than country B.

E. More information is needed to determine which country has the higher standard of living.

10. Output in country X is 30,000 units and there are 3,000 persons working, while country Z has an output of 40,000 units and 8,000 workers.

A. The productivity of labor in country Z is 33 percent higher than in country X.
B. The productivity of labor in country Z is 25 percent higher than in country X.
C. The productivity of labor in country X is 33 percent higher than in country Z.
D. The productivity of labor in country X is 25 percent higher than in country Z.
E. The productivity of labor in country X is twice as much as country Z.

11. The government can promote economic growth by

A. setting a minimum wage.
B. regulating industry.
C. taxing firms that waste resources.
D. job training programs.
E. restricting imports.

12. Private industry can promote economic growth by

A. implementing innovative production techniques.
B. offering products at artificially low prices.
C. giving a significant amount of profits to charity.
D. hiring workers who are not really needed.
E. adhering to environmental standards.

13. The size of the labor force in Japan is expected to shrink beginning in 2010 as a large segment of its population retires. This will

A. affect labor productivity more than economic growth.
B. affect economic growth more than labor productivity.
C. not have a major effect on economic growth or labor productivity.
D. affect labor productivity and economic growth equally.
E. shift Japan's aggregate supply curve to the right.

14. If the standard of living increases, we can conclude that

A. output must have increased.
B. population must have increased.
C. output and population must have increased.
D. population must have decreased.
E. output must have increased proportionally more than population.

15. If real GDP per capita grows at a rate of 10 percent a year, then we can expect the standard of living to double in

A. 10 years.
B. 9 years.
C. 8 years.
D. 7 years.
E. 5 years.

MULTIPLE-CHOICE REVIEW ANSWERS

1. C	4. B	7. B	10. E	13. B
2. C	5. A	8. E	11. D	14. E
3. C	6. C	9. A	12. A	15. D

Free-Response Review Questions

I. Use the production possibilities frontier to illustrate the effects of a very successful government policy to train the labor force so that workers became more productive. Be sure to label the axes of your diagram.

II. A. Use the AS/AD model to show the effects of a decrease in the availability of timber due to a depletion of the supply of trees. Be sure to use a long run aggregate supply curve and label the axes of your diagram.

B. Now suppose the government reduced taxes while the supply of timber was depleted. What effect would this have?

FREE-RESPONSE REVIEW ANSWERS

I. The effects of a more productive labor force due to training.

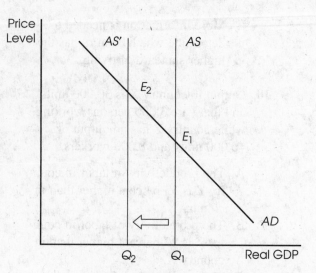

B. If the government reduced taxes while the supply of timber was depleted, this would shift the aggregate demand curve to the right. The equilibrium quantity of output would still fall to Q2, but the equilibrium price level would be higher than if the government did not reduce taxes.

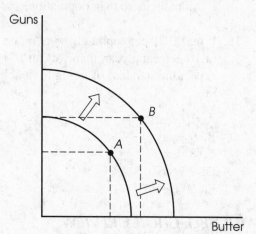

II. A. A decrease in the supply of timber shifts the aggregate supply curve to the left. This will raise the equilibrium price level and lower the equilibrium quantity of output.

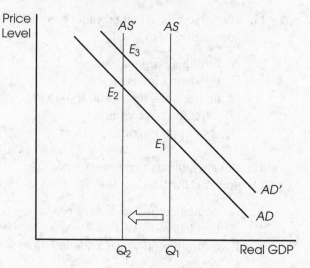

21 International Trade and Exchange

The Balance of Trade

In 1999 the United States was the world's largest exporting nation, shipping almost a trillion dollars worth of goods and services abroad. However, in that same year, the United States imported $1.25 trillion worth of goods and services. The fact that our imports exceeded our exports by $250 billion is troubling to some people. Don't foreigners want our products? We buy their products, but they don't buy as many of ours. Won't this have adverse economic effects? Will we owe foreign nations money? Doesn't this cost American jobs?

A nation's balance of trade is equal to its exports minus its imports. Earlier we called this figure net exports. For the United States in 1999, the balance of trade was negative $250 billion (= $1 trillion − $1.25 trillion). When the balance of trade is negative it can be referred to as a *trade deficit*. The last time America had a trade surplus was 1975. Are these chronic trade deficits a problem, and what, if anything, can be done about them?

Trade deficits can indeed be symptomatic of underlying economic problems. For instance, if a nation's exports are of inferior quality or cost too much relative to the competition, then it may experience a trade deficit. Or a country might rely heavily on imports just to meet its subsistence needs while it has nothing to export. This dire situation would result in a trade deficit as well. Finally, a nation's currency may be overpriced for one reason or another. This would make it expensive for foreigners to buy their products. A trade deficit could be the result.

But there is a more likely explanation for the chronic trade deficits in the United States: We have higher incomes than our trading partners. We are doing so well that we can afford the best of everything no matter where in the world it might be produced. This makes America's imports swell. Unfortunately, many other countries are not doing as well. They cannot afford to buy our exports and our trade balance suffers. If this idea about the origin of our trade deficits is correct, then we should see smaller deficits, or even surpluses, when our economy is experiencing a recession. During the 1991–92 recession the trade deficit shrunk to $20 billion. The last trade surplus in the United States was in 1975 on the tail end of a severe 16-month recession.

Trade Restrictions

ARGUMENTS FOR TRADE RESTRICTIONS

Even if our trade deficits spring from the high standard of living we enjoy, they may still be problematic. When we buy foreign textiles, that means there is less demand for domestic textile workers. Imported textiles could mean unemployment for domestic textile workers.

Barriers to free trade across nations have been erected for a variety of reasons. One argument is to protect jobs from foreign competition. However, there is a steep price to pay for this protection. Everyone who buys textiles will be paying more for them because competition was thwarted. We know from our earlier analysis of comparative advantage that free trade enables the countries involved to consume more than under restricted trade.

Other reasons for trade restrictions include the infant industry argument, the diversity argument, and dumping. Infant industries are those that are just getting started. At this point they are in no condition to compete with foreign industries that have all the advantages of being well established. The argument is that these infant industries will be able to compete after they have developed. At that point, the trade restrictions could be dropped.

Another reason to protect an industry from foreign competition is for the sake of diversity. A nation should not rely too heavily on others. What if a war broke out? Do you think our enemies would continue to export to us? We need to encourage some industries despite their inefficiencies because diversity is healthy. Trade barriers can promote diversity.

Dumping is a technical term in international trade. It describes a situation where foreign producers are selling a product in the domestic market for less than it cost to produce it. The foreign firms would like to establish a foothold in our markets, so they are willing to absorb the loss. Domestic producers argue that prices will soon rise once the foreign firms have put them out of business. Trade barriers can be used to prevent dumping.

TABLE 21.1
ARGUMENTS FOR TRADE RESTRICTIONS

- Promote domestic employment
- Infant industry argument
- Diversity of production
- Prevent dumping

INSTITUTING TRADE RESTRICTIONS

There are a variety of ways to discourage or prevent imports from coming into a country. Quotas, tariffs, and licensing requirements are the most common.

1. An import quota is a limit on the amount of a product that can be imported. When the import quota is set at zero, domestic producers are completely protected from foreign competition. Figure 21.1 shows the effects of an import quota on the domestic market for rice.

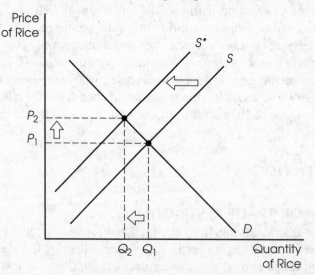

Fig. 21.1 A Quota on Rice Imports

The quota on rice restricts the supply shifting of the supply curve to the left. The more restrictive the quota, the further to the left the supply curve shifts. After the quota is imposed the price of rice will rise and the amount of rice bought and sold will fall.

2. An import tariff is a tax on the specified imported product. The tariff serves to raise the price of the imported product in the eyes of domestic consumers. This gives the edge to domestic producers. Figure 21.2 shows the effects of an import tariff.

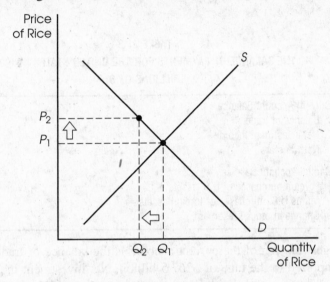

Fig. 21.2 A Tariff on Imported Rice

The price of rice would be P1 except that the tariff raises it to P2. The higher price causes a decrease in the quantity of rice demanded and the amount actually bought and sold is now lower (Q2). The tariff, like the quota, raises the domestic price of rice and lowers the amount bought and sold. These higher prices and reduced amounts of consumption are the costs of trade restrictions.

3. Clever administrators can stifle trade in many ways aside from quotas and tariffs. Arcane rules and regulations are often developed with no other purpose in mind than to discourage competition. Governments may require businesspersons to obtain a license granting them the right to import a specific product. The government need only limit the number of licenses it grants and the amount to be imported by each license holder in order to restrict trade. The effects of licensing agreements and rules and regulations that stifle trade are shown in exactly the same manner as the import quota diagram in Figure 21.1.

TABLE 21.2
TRADE RESTRICTIONS

- Quotas
- Tariffs
- Licensing requirements

Economists are generally against any trade restrictions. Comparative advantage suggests that free trade allows nations to consume more goods and services than if trade was restricted. Moreover, the arguments for trade restrictions are dubious while the costs in terms of higher prices and less consumption are more definite.

The Balance of Payments

The balance of payments is comprised of the *current account* and the *capital account*. The current account is made up of the trade balance, net investment income, and net transfers. The capital account consists of foreign purchases of U.S. assets minus U.S. purchases of foreign assets, plus the change in official reserves. Table 21.3 delineates the balance of payments for the United States in 1999.

TABLE 21.3
THE BALANCE OF PAYMENTS FOR THE UNITED STATES IN 1999
(BILLIONS OF $)

Current Account Balance	−338.9
Balance of trade	−276.5
Net investment income	−24.8
Net transfers	−46.6
Capital Account Balance	+338.9
Foreign purchases of U.S. assets	711.4
Minus U.S. purchases of foreign assets	−381.2
Change in official reserves	8.7

By far the largest portion of the current account is the balance of trade. In 1999 we exported more than we imported to the tune of $267.5 billion. Net investment income is how much U.S. citizens earned as interest and dividends from abroad minus how much we paid foreigners in interest and dividends. In 1999 we paid foreigners more than they paid us. The difference was $24.8 billion. Net transfers are how much money our government and citizens send as gifts or aid to foreigners minus how much foreigners send to us in gifts and aid. We sent more to them than they sent to us by a difference of $46.6 billion. Totaling all three negative numbers gives −$338.9 billion for the current account in 1999.

The capital account is comprised of foreign purchases of assets in the United States ($711.4 billion in 1999) minus our purchases of foreign assets ($381.2 billion) plus the change in official reserves ($8.9 billion). Official reserves are our government's holdings of foreign currencies.

Notice that the current account and the capital account sum to zero. This is an accounting necessity. When the current account is negative, as it was in 1999, this means that we have been spending more abroad than foreigners have been spending here, whether it is on goods and services, or investment payments, or gifts and aid. This excess spending abroad puts dollars in foreign hands. What does a Dane do with dollars when kroner are required for spending in Denmark?

The capital account accounts for those dollars that were put in foreign hands. The capital account for 1999 indicates that most of the dollars that wound up in foreign hands were used to buy assets in the United States. Had foreigners not wanted to use their dollars to buy investments in the United States, our government would have been forced to draw down its official reserves and use its holdings of foreign currencies to trade for all the dollars that foreigners held.

The capital account must be positive by the same magnitude that the current account is negative. This is because all the dollars that wind up overseas must be accounted for. Nevertheless, economists still speak of balance of payments deficits and surpluses. What they are referring to is the change in official reserves. If official reserves are increasing, it is a balance of payments surplus. A balance of payments deficit exists if official reserves are falling. Therefore, in 1999 the United States managed a small balance of payments surplus despite a large balance of trade deficit.

Exchange Rates

The exchange rate is the value of one country's currency in terms of another's. Exchange rates are determined, as we shall see, by supply and demand. Table 21.4 shows selected exchange rates.

TABLE 21.4
SELECTED EXCHANGE RATES ON JUNE 19, 2000

One U.S. dollar equals:
1.66	Australian dollars
1.47	Canadian dollars
7.75	Danish kroner
6.82	French francs
2.03	German marks
44.85	Indian rupees
2,012.34	Italian lire
105.74	Japanese yen
9.91	Mexican pesos
0.66	British pounds

Let us consider the exchange rate between the U.S. dollar and the French franc. One dollar was worth about 7 francs in June 2000. This implies that one franc is worth about $\frac{1}{7}$ of a dollar or 15 cents. Why isn't the franc worth more or less? Because the supply and demand for francs intersected at 15 cents per franc. This is illustrated in Figure 21.3.

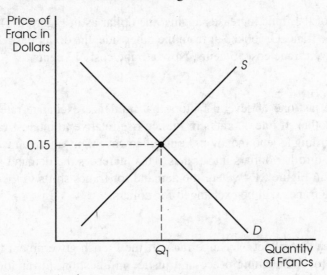

Fig. 21.3 The Supply and Demand for Francs

The demand for francs in the international market is downward sloping, which implies that the quantity of francs demanded will be greater when the dollar price is lower. This makes sense: More people and firms would want to acquire francs if they could get a lot of them for each dollar. The supply curve for francs is upward sloping, which implies that the quantity of francs supplied will be greater when the dollar price is higher. Again, this makes sense: More people would be willing to part with their francs if they could get more cents for each one.

Changing Rates

The exchange rate between the franc and the dollar is changing constantly because the supply and the demand for francs in terms of dollars are shifting constantly. If Americans began to appreciate

French wine more, then the demand for francs would increase. That's because importers of French wine would have to place bigger orders and pay for those orders in francs.

When the demand for francs increases, the demand curve for francs shifts to the right as shown in Figure 21.4. The result is a rise in the dollar value of the franc and an increase in the amount of francs exchanged.

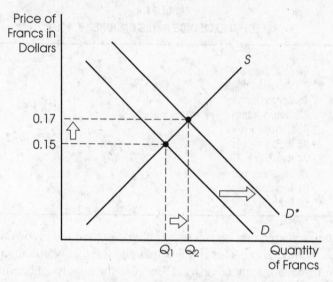

Fig. 21.4 An Increase in the Demand for Francs

When the value of the franc increases against the dollar as in Figure 21.4, this is known as an "appreciation" of the franc. Or looked at from the other side, the dollar has "depreciated" vis-à-vis the franc. Previously, a franc cost 15 cents. Now a franc costs 17 cents.

Interest Rates

Changing tastes are just one of several factors that influence exchange rates between countries. Interest rates are another. If interest rates in France rise relative to interest rates in America, then it will be more rewarding to lend money in France. However, an American wanting to lend money in France must first turn her dollars into francs. This increases the demand for francs. The result will be the same as in Figure 21.4 where the demand for francs shifts to the right. The franc will appreciate and more francs will be exchanged for dollars.

Political Stability

Political stability can also affect exchange rates. If the French government finds itself in turmoil with its credibility for maintaining peace and justice in question, fewer foreigners will want to invest in France. The demand for francs would fall even if interest rates were relatively higher in France. This would shift the demand for francs to the left. Moreover, French citizens will want to store more of their wealth abroad. Who knows what might happen to bank accounts and financial assets in a country where the government is losing control? When French citizens want to place some of their wealth in America, they typically start by trading their francs for dollars. This is reflected in a shift to the right in the supply of francs.

So political instability in France would decrease the demand for francs and increase the supply. This is shown in Figure 21.5. The result is a significant depreciation of the franc.

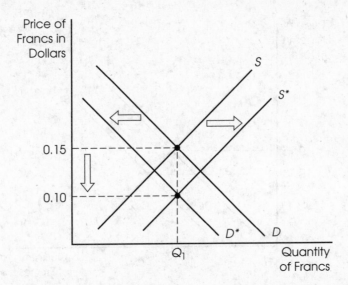

Fig. 21.5 An Decrease in the Demand and an Increase in the Supply of Francs

Relative Levels of Income

The relative levels of income in France and America will influence the exchange rate between dollars and francs. If America is better off than France in terms of income, Americans will be able to afford more of the finer things France has to offer. And France will not be able to enjoy America's exports to the same extent because of her relatively lower standard of living. So if the standard of living in America advanced while France slipped into a recession, the situation would be just the opposite of that portrayed in Figure 21.5—the demand for francs would increase because Americans could afford French exports. The supply of francs would fall, not increase, since the French would not be demanding as many American exports as before the recession.

Relative Prices

Relative prices in France and America can also impact exchange rates. If prices rise in France while they hold steady in America, the value of the franc will depreciate. This is because some Americans will balk at purchasing French products because of the higher prices, thus reducing the demand for francs. And French citizens will buy more American products since the prices of these items has held steady. This will increase the supply of francs. The situation is just as depicted in Figure 21.5.

Astute readers may take the analysis a step further. Once the value of the franc depreciates, the higher-priced French products will appear cheaper to Americans and the lower-priced American products will appear more expensive to the French. This is because the currencies must be exchanged to obtain each other's products. If you reasoned this way, congratulate yourself—you have outlined the theory of purchasing power parity. This theory states that the same product, say, a pencil, will cost the same if it is bought domestically or imported because exchange rates change to erase any price differential that may exist. It's an interesting theory, but the real world abounds with counterexamples.

Speculators have an important impact on exchange rates. Individuals and institutions buy and sell currencies with an eye toward making a profit. As with all financial transactions, these speculators want to "buy low and sell high." If it is expected that the franc will depreciate in the near future, speculators will try to sell their francs now before the price falls. In Figure 21.6, this would increase the supply of francs, shifting the supply curve to the right. Notice that the result is a depreciation of the franc from 15 cents to 13 cents. Speculation often results in self-fulfilling prophecies.

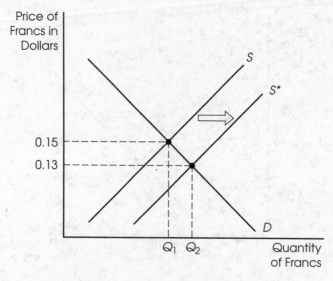

Fig. 21.6 An Increase in the Suppy of Francs

TABLE 21.5
DETERMINANTS OF EXCHANGE RATES

- Demand for a nation's exports (tastes)
- Relative interest rates
- Political stability
- Relative level of income
- Relative prices (theory of purchasing power parity)
- Speculation

EXCHANGE RATE REGIMES

Before the Great Depression, most of the large economies of the world were on a gold standard. Essentially, the gold standard kept exchange rates between countries fixed. Since the dollar was worth a certain amount of gold and the franc was worth a given amount of gold, the value of the dollar versus the franc would be established. If the value of the franc appreciated vis-à-vis the dollar, someone could use their dollars to buy gold and then use that gold to buy francs, and then use those francs to buy more dollars than they started with.

Arbitrage of this sort kept exchange rates between nations fixed, but the gold standard was not without flaws. If tastes changed and Americans clamored for French products, the exchange rate did not rise to choke off some of this foreign demand. In such a situation the United States would develop a balance of payments deficit as French citizens and institutions piled up dollar holdings. Many historians and economists point to balance of payment crises caused by the gold standard as one of the central causes of the Great Depression.

Modern international exchange is no longer based on gold. The Bretton Woods regime replaced the fixed exchange rate system based on gold in 1944. In the Bretton Woods system the dollar was as good as gold. Countries pegged the value of their currencies to the dollar and the United States stood ready to trade any dollar holdings of foreign governments to gold at $35 an ounce. This system broke down in 1971 when the United States, running chronic trade deficits, could no longer support the $35 an ounce price of gold.

Managed Float

The current system for determining international exchange rates is referred to as a *managed float*. Supply and demand determine exchange rates between currencies as outlined above. But if exchange rates change in a manner deemed to be detrimental, nations will intervene. Intervention involves coordinated buying and selling of currencies in order to adjust their equilibrium values determined by supply and demand.

For example, because the United States runs chronic trade deficits there is an abundant supply of dollars in international markets. This tends to depress the value of the dollar. A depreciated dollar would lower America's demand for foreign products. This would help with our chronic trade deficits, but it would hurt the countries that export to us. If governments decide to support the dollar, they would intervene by buying dollars. This results in the dollar appreciating in value.

A managed float allows supply and demand to determine exchange rates within a range of values. Once exchange rates exceed that range, governments use their currency holdings to intervene.

Monetary and Fiscal Policy in an Open Economy

Monetary and fiscal policy can be used to fight inflation or recession. However, our previous discussion of these policies ignored their effects on the exchange rate and the balance of trade. The impacts of monetary and fiscal policy in the context of an open economy are more complicated.

An expansionary monetary policy still stimulates the economy in the short run by increasing the quantity of output and putting upward pressure on prices. This will worsen the balance of trade since the increase in output means an increase in income. Rising incomes tend to drive imports, worsening the balance of trade. And rising prices tend to discourage exports, again, worsening the balance of trade.

Policymakers need to keep in mind the effects of monetary policy on imports and exports. In a closed economy, an increase in the money supply stimulates output and income in the short run. In an open economy these effects will be dampened because imports will rise. That is to say, some of the stimulatory effect will be spent overseas, and exports will fall because of the inflation resulting from the increase in the money supply.

The effects of an expansionary fiscal policy are tempered in the same way in the context of an open economy. An increase in government spending and a reduction in taxes will increase output and income in the short run, while putting upward pressure on prices. Higher levels of income tend to raise imports while higher prices tend to discourage exports. This worsens the balance of trade and implies that the effects of the fiscal policy will not be as pronounced.

Also notice that monetary and fiscal polices will affect exchange rates because these policies alter incomes and prices. Remember that exchange rates are impacted by the relative level of income and the relative level of prices in a nation.

Summary

- The United States has been importing more than it has been exporting since the mid-1970s. However, our trade deficits are more a symptom of how well off we are relative to our trading partners than a cause for alarm. Most economists agree that trade restrictions, such as import tariffs, quotas, and licensing agreements, are harmful. Free trade, where countries specialize according to the law of comparative advantage, benefits consumers in the countries involved.

- Nevertheless, most nations restrict trade in one way or another. The arguments for trade restrictions vary from promoting employment to preventing dumping. Infant industries and the benefits of a diverse manufacturing base are two more reasons put forward to justify trade restrictions. However valid the reason, economic analysis shows that the cost of restricting trade is higher prices to the consumer.

- A nation's balance of payments accounts for the funds that flow into and out of the country. If there is a deficit in the current account, there must be a corresponding surplus in the capital account. Still, people speak of balance of payments surpluses and deficits. What is being referred to is a specific entry, change in official reserves, in the capital account. If the nation's central bank is experiencing a reduction in the amount of foreign currency it holds, the balance of payments is said to be in a deficit. On the other hand, if the central bank's official reserves are increasing, a balance of payments surplus exists.

- The exchange rate is the price of one nation's currency in terms of another. In today's world, exchange rates are determined by the supply and demand for a nation's currency—up to a point. Occasionally, nations will intervene in the market by supplying more or less of a particular currency or demanding more or less. Nations use their official reserves during these interventions in order to prop up or devalue a given currency. In other words, countries can adjust the position of the supply and demand curves for a currency, but only if they have the cooperation of the major trading nations. Without cooperation no single nation has enough reserves to make much of an adjustment to the supply or demand curves of most currencies. This international monetary system, where supply and demand determine exchange rates with the occasional intervention by a consortium of trading partners is known as a managed float.

- Exchange rates, therefore, are free to float about where supply and demand might take them. Just so long as they don't go too far and cause an intervention. Anything that can affect the supply or the demand for a nation's currency will affect its exchange rate. The demand for a nation's exports affects the demand for its currency, as do relative interest rates. Relative prices and income also affect exchange rates. And speculation can play a role. If market participants expect a particular currency to appreciate in the near future, they will try to buy as much as they can now. As we have seen, this increases the demand for the currency, which, in turn, causes it to appreciate, the fulfillment of a self-fulfilling prophecy.

- Exchange rates are affected when a country pursues monetary and fiscal policy because, in the short run, these policies affect income and prices. Moreover, the balance of trade will be affected by monetary and fiscal policy because imports and exports are impacted by changes in income and prices as well. The short run effects of monetary and fiscal policy are not as pronounced in an open economy.

Terms

Appreciation   the increase of the value of a currency in terms of another currency

Balance of Payments   an accounting of the funds that flow into and out of a country comprised of the capital account and the current account

Balance of Trade   a nation's exports minus its imports

Capital Account - a portion of the balance of payments comprised of foreign purchases of U.S. assets minus U.S. purchases of foreign assets, plus the change in official reserves

Closed Economy   a hypothetical economy with no foreign trade

Current Account   a portion of the balance of payments comprised of the trade balance, net investment income, and net transfers

Depreciation   the decrease of the value of a currency in terms of another currency

Dumping   the practice of foreign producers selling a product in the domestic market for less than it cost to produce it

Exchange Rate   the value of one country's currency in terms of another's

Gold Standard   a unit of currency that is equivalent to a stated amount of gold

Import Quota   a limit on the amount of a product that can be imported

Import Tariff   a tax on a specified imported product

Infant Industries   those industries that are just getting started, perhaps requiring trade restrictions

Intervention   situation in which a nation or group of nations uses their official reserves to supply or demand a currency in order to alter the exchange rate

Managed Float   an exchange rate regime where supply and demand determine exchange rates with occasional intervention when warranted

Net Investment Income   amount U.S. citizens earned as interest and dividends from abroad minus how much was paid to foreigners in interest and dividends

Net Transfers   money our government and citizens send as gifts or aid to foreigners minus how much foreigners send to us in gifts and aid

Official Reserves   government's holdings of foreign currencies

Open Economy   an economy with foreign trade

Trade Deficit   excess of a nation's imports over its exports

Trade Surplus   excess of a nation's exports over its imports

Formulas

Balance of Payments = Current Account + Capital Account

Multiple-Choice Review Questions

1. When a country has a balance of trade deficit

   A. it must make up the difference by shipping gold to its creditors.
   B. its exports exceed its imports.
   C. its currency will appreciate.
   D. corrective actions must be taken.
   E. its imports exceed its exports.

2. A balance of trade surplus can be the result of

   A. a loose monetary policy.
   B. foreigners having no taste for this country's products.
   C. an appreciation of the country's currency.
   D. low levels of income relative to other nations.
   E. high domestic prices.

3. One strategy a corporation may use to gain market share in a foreign market is

   A. raising the price of its product.
   B. convincing its government to put an import tariff on the product.
   C. convincing its government to place a quota on the product.
   D. cornering.
   E. dumping.

4. Tariffs and quotas

   A. result in higher domestic prices.
   B. promote trade between nations.
   C. do not necessarily affect domestic prices.
   D. affect domestic prices: the former raises them while the latter lowers them.
   E. are one way to fight inflation.

5. Tariffs and quotas

   A. result in lower domestic prices.
   B. sometimes raise and sometimes lower the amount of the product sold domestically.
   C. lower the amount of the product sold domestically.
   D. raise the amount of the product sold domestically.
   E. do not affect domestic prices or quantities.

6. Which of the following is NOT an argument for restricting trade?

   A. To protect infant industry
   B. To promote employment
   C. To fight inflation
   D. To promote a diversity of industries
   E. To prevent dumping

7. A balance of payments deficit means that a country has

   A. imported more than it has exported.
   B. exported more than it has imported.
   C. taken in more money than it has sent abroad.
   D. lowered its official reserve position.
   E. lost gold to foreign nations.

8. If a country has a negative value on its current account, then it must

   A. pay that amount to its trading partners.
   B. have a positive value of equal magnitude on its capital account.
   C. depreciate its currency.
   D. appreciate its currency.
   E. send gold abroad.

9. With a managed float

   A. countries occasionally intervene in foreign exchange markets.
   B. countries never have to intervene in foreign exchange markets.
   C. countries must constantly intervene to maintain the value of their currencies.

D. exchange rates are fixed.

E. each currency is worth a stated amount of gold.

10. An expansionary monetary policy tends to

A. improve the balance of trade.

B. have no effect on imports.

C. worsen the balance of trade.

D. have no effect on exports.

E. have an ambiguous effect on the balance of trade.

11. In the balance of payments, the trade balance

A. is ignored.

B. appears in the capital account.

C. appears in the current account

D. is included in the official reserves.

E. is counted as part of "net transfers."

12. If interest rates rise in the United States relative to other nations, then

A. the value of the dollar will tend to appreciate.

B. the value of the dollar will tend to depreciate.

C. exchange rates will be affected but not the value of the dollar.

D. the exchange rate will not be affected.

E. the balance of trade will tend toward a surplus.

13. If prices rise in the United States relative to other countries, then

A. the value of the dollar will tend to appreciate.

B. the value of the dollar will tend to depreciate.

C. exchange rates will be affected but not the value of the dollar.

D. the exchange rate will not be affected.

E. the balance of trade will tend toward a surplus.

14. If the demand for dollars rises while the supply of dollars falls, then the

A. dollar will appreciate.

B. dollar will depreciate.

C. exchange rates will be affected but not the value of the dollar.

D. exchange rate will not be affected.

E. balance of trade will tend toward a surplus.

15. If the demand for our exports rises while our tastes for foreign goods falls off, then

A. the value of the dollar will tend to appreciate.

B. the value of the dollar will tend to depreciate.

C. exchange rates will be affected but not the value of the dollar.

D. the exchange rate will not be affected.

E. the balance of trade will tend toward a surplus.

MULTIPLE-CHOICE REVIEW ANSWERS

1. E	4. A	7. D	10. C	13. B
2. D	5. C	8. B	11. C	14. A
3. E	6. C	9. A	12. A	15. A

Free-Response Review Questions

I. Assume that exchange rates between nations are fixed and do not change. Now suppose that people around the world develop a taste for the products of country A. What will happen to the balance of trade in country A? Explain how this will change in tastes affecting the official reserve position of country A.

II. Now assume that exchange rates between nations are perfectly flexible. Again, suppose that people around the world develop a taste for the products of country A. Do you expect the currency of country A to appreciate or depreciate? Explain why. Will the balance of trade react differently now exchange rates no longer fixed? Explain. What will happen to the official reserve position of country A in this case?

FREE-RESPONSE REVIEW ANSWERS

I. Since people around the world will purchase more products from country A the exports of country A will increase. There is no reason why country A will import more at this point in time. Therefore, the balance of trade in country A will improve. Specifically, if there was a trade deficit, it will diminish now that tastes have changed.

The official reserve position of Country A will also strengthen. In order to purchase products from country A, foreigners have to obtain the currency of country A. They offer their own currencies in exchange. Eventually, these foreign currencies end up swelling the official reserves of country A.

II. The currency of country A will appreciate in value as people across the globe clamor for its currency in order to purchase its exports. The demand for the currency of country A will increase and this raises the value of its currency. The balance of trade in country A should still improve with exports increasing and imports remaining unchanged. However, since the currency of country A appreciated, its products will appear more expensive to foreigners. This should choke off some of the demand for the products of country A and its exports will not increase as much as in the case where the exchange rate is fixed. Therefore the balance of trade will not improve as much as the case where exchange rates are fixed.

Similarly, the official reserve position of country A will improve with the balance of trade. People around the world will need the currency of country A in order to buy its products. They offer their own currencies in exchange. But with an appreciated currency in country A, some foreigners will balk at purchasing its products and this means that the official reserve position of country A will not strengthen as much as when exchange rates were fixed.

MODEL ADVANCED PLACEMENT EXAMINATION IN MACROECONOMICS

Answer Sheet

1. Ⓐ Ⓑ ⓒ Ⓓ Ⓔ	16. Ⓐ Ⓑ ⓒ Ⓓ Ⓔ	31. Ⓐ Ⓑ ⓒ Ⓓ Ⓔ	46. Ⓐ Ⓑ ⓒ Ⓓ Ⓔ
2. Ⓐ Ⓑ ⓒ Ⓓ Ⓔ	17. Ⓐ Ⓑ ⓒ Ⓓ Ⓔ	32. Ⓐ Ⓑ ⓒ Ⓓ Ⓔ	47. Ⓐ Ⓑ ⓒ Ⓓ Ⓔ
3. Ⓐ Ⓑ ⓒ Ⓓ Ⓔ	18. Ⓐ Ⓑ ⓒ Ⓓ Ⓔ	33. Ⓐ Ⓑ ⓒ Ⓓ Ⓔ	48. Ⓐ Ⓑ ⓒ Ⓓ Ⓔ
4. Ⓐ Ⓑ ⓒ Ⓓ Ⓔ	19. Ⓐ Ⓑ ⓒ Ⓓ Ⓔ	34. Ⓐ Ⓑ ⓒ Ⓓ Ⓔ	49. Ⓐ Ⓑ ⓒ Ⓓ Ⓔ
5. Ⓐ Ⓑ ⓒ Ⓓ Ⓔ	20. Ⓐ Ⓑ ⓒ Ⓓ Ⓔ	35. Ⓐ Ⓑ ⓒ Ⓓ Ⓔ	50. Ⓐ Ⓑ ⓒ Ⓓ Ⓔ
6. Ⓐ Ⓑ ⓒ Ⓓ Ⓔ	21. Ⓐ Ⓑ ⓒ Ⓓ Ⓔ	36. Ⓐ Ⓑ ⓒ Ⓓ Ⓔ	51. Ⓐ Ⓑ ⓒ Ⓓ Ⓔ
7. Ⓐ Ⓑ ⓒ Ⓓ Ⓔ	22. Ⓐ Ⓑ ⓒ Ⓓ Ⓔ	37. Ⓐ Ⓑ ⓒ Ⓓ Ⓔ	52. Ⓐ Ⓑ ⓒ Ⓓ Ⓔ
8. Ⓐ Ⓑ ⓒ Ⓓ Ⓔ	23. Ⓐ Ⓑ ⓒ Ⓓ Ⓔ	38. Ⓐ Ⓑ ⓒ Ⓓ Ⓔ	53. Ⓐ Ⓑ ⓒ Ⓓ Ⓔ
9. Ⓐ Ⓑ ⓒ Ⓓ Ⓔ	24. Ⓐ Ⓑ ⓒ Ⓓ Ⓔ	39. Ⓐ Ⓑ ⓒ Ⓓ Ⓔ	54. Ⓐ Ⓑ ⓒ Ⓓ Ⓔ
10. Ⓐ Ⓑ ⓒ Ⓓ Ⓔ	25. Ⓐ Ⓑ ⓒ Ⓓ Ⓔ	40. Ⓐ Ⓑ ⓒ Ⓓ Ⓔ	55. Ⓐ Ⓑ ⓒ Ⓓ Ⓔ
11. Ⓐ Ⓑ ⓒ Ⓓ Ⓔ	26. Ⓐ Ⓑ ⓒ Ⓓ Ⓔ	41. Ⓐ Ⓑ ⓒ Ⓓ Ⓔ	56. Ⓐ Ⓑ ⓒ Ⓓ Ⓔ
12. Ⓐ Ⓑ ⓒ Ⓓ Ⓔ	27. Ⓐ Ⓑ ⓒ Ⓓ Ⓔ	42. Ⓐ Ⓑ ⓒ Ⓓ Ⓔ	57. Ⓐ Ⓑ ⓒ Ⓓ Ⓔ
13. Ⓐ Ⓑ ⓒ Ⓓ Ⓔ	28. Ⓐ Ⓑ ⓒ Ⓓ Ⓔ	43. Ⓐ Ⓑ ⓒ Ⓓ Ⓔ	58. Ⓐ Ⓑ ⓒ Ⓓ Ⓔ
14. Ⓐ Ⓑ ⓒ Ⓓ Ⓔ	29. Ⓐ Ⓑ ⓒ Ⓓ Ⓔ	44. Ⓐ Ⓑ ⓒ Ⓓ Ⓔ	59. Ⓐ Ⓑ ⓒ Ⓓ Ⓔ
15. Ⓐ Ⓑ ⓒ Ⓓ Ⓔ	30. Ⓐ Ⓑ ⓒ Ⓓ Ⓔ	45. Ⓐ Ⓑ ⓒ Ⓓ Ⓔ	60. Ⓐ Ⓑ ⓒ Ⓓ Ⓔ

Model Advanced Placement Examination in Macroeconomics

Two hours are allotted for this examination: 1 hour and 10 minutes for Section I, which consists of multiple-choice questions; and 50 minutes for Section II, which consists of three mandatory essay questions.

Section I—Multiple-Choice Questions

Time—1 hour and 10 minutes
Number of Questions—60
Percent of Total Grade—66⅔

DIRECTIONS
Each of the questions or incomplete statements beginning on page 288 is followed by five suggested answers or completions. Select the one that is best in each case and then fill in the corresponding oval on the answer sheet.

1. Command economies

   A. have no advantages over capitalism.
   B. are superior to market economies.
   C. are generally more equitable than market economies.
   D. are generally more efficient than market economies.
   E. create incentives that are lacking in market economies.

2. When the price of product X decreases this encourages

   A. suppliers to increase the supply of product X since consumers buy more at the lower price.
   B. consumers to conserve on product X.
   C. entrepreneurs to supply more of product X in order to make up for lost profits.
   D. consumers to buy products that are close substitutes for product X.
   E. suppliers to decrease the quantity supplied of product X.

3. Which of the following is NOT included in GDP?

   A. Federal government purchases of goods and services
   B. Imports
   C. State and local government purchases of goods and services
   D. Exports
   E. The change in business inventories

4. If the CPI increases from 110 to 115, then the cost of living has increased

   A. 4.3 percent.
   B. 4.5 percent.
   C. 15 percent.
   D. 5 percent.
   E. 115 percent.

5. Given the diagram below, what can be expected when the level of income in the economy is $2,000?

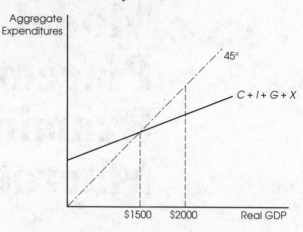

   A. Inventories are accumulating and savings are falling.
   B. Inventories are accumulating and savings are rising.
   C. Inventories are dwindling and savings are falling.
   D. Inventories are dwindling and savings are rising.
   E. Inventories are constant and savings are zero.

6. The diagram below

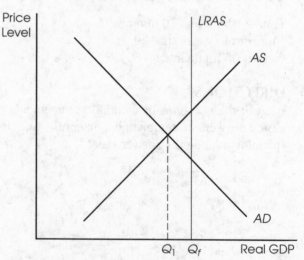

   A. is incorrect since Qf can never be to the right of Q1.
   B. is incorrect because AD should slope upward and AS should slope down.

C. portrays a recessionary gap.
D. portrays an inflationary gap.
E. portrays Phillips curves.

7. A rise in the price level lowers total spending because

   I. consumers' incomes cannot go as far now that prices have risen.
   II. foreigners buy less.
   III. higher prices result in higher interest rates which lower spending.

A. Only I is correct.
B. I and II are correct.
C. I and III are correct.
D. II and III are correct.
E. I, II, and III are correct.

8. Assume the reserve requirement is 5 percent. If the FED sells $10 million worth of government securities in an open market operation, then the money supply can

A. increase by $200 million.
B. decrease by $200 million.
C. increase by $50 million.
D. decrease by $50 million.
E. increase by $150 million.

9. According to Classical economic analysis, a change in the money supply results in

A. a proportional change in the quantity of output.
B. a slight change in the quantity of output.
C. a dramatic change in the quantity of output.
D. no change in the price level.
E. a proportional change in the price level.

10. A country that experiences a depreciation of its currency can expect its

A. imports to rise.
B. exports to fall.
C. balance of trade to worsen.
D. balance of trade to improve.
E. balance of trade to be unaffected.

11. Given the table below which statement is true?

Country	Labor hours needed to produce a unit of	
	Wine	Cheese
France	40	80
Belgium	15	60

A. France has the absolute advantage in both products.
B. France should specialize in and export wine while Belgium should specialize in and export cheese.
C. France has the comparative advantage in cheese.
D. France has the absolute advantage in cheese.
E. Belgium has the comparative advantage in both products.

12. Suppose country Z increases its production of automobiles without decreasing its production of any other goods or services. This

A. implies that the opportunity cost of producing cars is zero.
B. cannot occur in the real world.
C. defies the law of increasing costs.
D. cannot occur without a technological advance.
E. can occur if country Z was initially producing at a point inside its production possibilities frontier.

13. You buy 100 shares in the XYZ corporation on the internet and your broker charges you $29.95.

A. This will increase the investment component of GDP and therefore GDP.
B. This has no effect on GDP.
C. This will increase GDP by $29.95.
D. This will increase GDP by the cost of the shares minus $29.95.
E. This will increase GDP by the cost of the shares plus $29.95.

14. The inflation rate

   I. is the percentage change in the CPI.

  II. is the rate at which prices are rising.

 III. measures how fast the economy is expanding.

  A. Only I is true.

  B. I and II are true.

  C. I and III are true.

  D. II and III are true.

  E. I, II, and III are true.

15. In the short run, an increase in taxes can be expected to

  A. decrease real GDP and prices.

  B. increase real GDP and prices.

  C. increase real GDP and decrease prices.

  D. decrease real GDP and increase prices.

  E. decrease real GDP and not affect prices.

16. The appropriate fiscal policy to remedy a recession is to

  A. increase government spending and taxes.

  B. reduce government spending and taxes.

  C. increase government spending and reduce taxes.

  D. decrease government spending and increase taxes.

  E. increase the money supply.

17. If the federal government collects more in tax revenues than it spends, then

  A. it is running a deficit.

  B. this would be the correct fiscal policy to fight a recession.

  C. this would be the correct monetary policy to fight a recession.

  D. this would be the correct fiscal policy to remedy inflation.

  E. this would be the correct monetary policy to remedy a recession.

18. Which of the following would lead to a decrease in the money supply?

  A. The FED lowers the discount rate.

  B. The FED sells government securities in the secondary market.

  C. The federal government spends less money.

  D. The FED lowers reserve requirements.

  E. Taxes are reduced.

19. The velocity of money is

  A. constant according to the Keynesians.

  B. the speed by which money can be transferred between accounts.

  C. stable according to the Monetarists.

  D. stable according to the Keynesians.

  E. how long it takes a change in the money supply to affect the economy.

20. If interest rates rise relatively more in country A than in country B, then the value of country A's currency will

  A. appreciate.

  B. depreciate.

  C. remain unchanged.

  D. change indeterminately.

  E. depreciate by the difference in interest rates.

21. A shift to the left of the production possibilities frontier

  A. could result from a technological advance.

  B. could result from an increase in resources in the economy.

  C. could result from a decline in resource availability.

  D. is not possible.

  E. is the result of increased productivity.

22. Which of the following will not cause a change in demand for a particular product?

    A. A change in the price of the product.
    B. A change in the prices of substitute products.
    C. A change in income.
    D. A change in the prices of complementary products.
    E. A change in the expected future price of the product.

23. You order a carpet from Turkey.

    A. This will increase the GDP of the United States.
    B. This will decrease the GDP of the United States.
    C. This will have no effect on the GDP of the United States.
    D. This will reduce the GDP of Turkey.
    E. Both A and D are correct.

24. If nominal GDP equals $9,000 and real GDP equals $6,000, then the GDP deflator equals

    A. 150
    B. 1.5
    C. 667
    D. 0.667
    E. 20

25. According to Classical economic theory, an increase in the money supply could be expected to

    A. increase output and decrease prices.
    B. decrease output and increase prices.
    C. increase output and prices.
    D. increase output and not affect prices.
    E. not affect output and increase prices.

26. The aggregate demand curve indicates that if the price level rises

    A. total demand for goods and services will not be affected.
    B. aggregate supply will fall.
    C. aggregate supply will rise.
    D. the quantity demanded of goods and services will increase.
    E. the quantity demanded of goods and services will decrease.

27. Suppose an economy is in equilibrium at full employment and the government cuts taxes. This will

    A. have no effect on real GDP or the price level.
    B. raise real GDP and the price level in the short run.
    C. raise real GDP and the price level in the long run.
    D. raise the price level, but not real GDP in the short run.
    E. raise real GDP in the long run.

28. Open market operations are

    A. the basis for capitalism.
    B. used on occasion by the government to control prices.
    C. when the Federal Reserve trades government securities in the secondary market.
    D. when the government borrows money to finance a deficit.
    E. used to police securities markets.

29. In order to close a recessionary gap, Keynesians recommend

    A. monetary policy.
    B. fiscal policy.
    C. the gold standard.
    D. tax increases.
    E. a money supply that grows at a steady predetermined rate.

30. According to the theory of purchasing power parity, if prices in a country rise relative to other countries, then its

   A. balance of trade will improve.
   B. currency will appreciate.
   C. currency will depreciate.
   D. official reserves will grow.
   E. its balance of payment position will improve.

31. Points outside the production possibilities frontier

   A. do not require efficient resource use.
   B. do not require full resource use.
   C. are unobtainable at this point in time.
   D. are unavoidable.
   E. are undesirable.

32. What will happen to the equilibrium price and the equilibrium quantity of good A when consumers expect the price of good A to be higher in the near future?

   A. The equilibrium price will rise and the equilibrium quantity will fall.
   B. The equilibrium price will fall and the equilibrium quantity will rise.
   C. The equilibrium price and the equilibrium quantity will both rise.
   D. The equilibrium price and the equilibrium quantity will both fall.
   E. There is not enough information to answer definitely.

33. Which of the following events would not affect GDP?

   A. You buy dinner at a restaurant.
   B. You buy groceries.
   C. You have your hair cut at the salon.
   D. You have a professional do your taxes.
   E. You buy your friend's car.

34. The GDP deflator

   A. does not account for changes in the prices of imported goods and services.
   B. is more accurate than the CPI.
   C. is calculated for each month.
   D. can be used to calculate the CPI.
   E. is derived from the CPI.

35. If the marginal propensity to consume equals .75 and government spending increases by $100 million, then overall real GDP can be expected to _____ by _____.

   A. decrease ; $133.33 million
   B. increase ; $133.33 million
   C. decrease ; $400 million
   D. increase ; $400 million
   E. increase ; $75 million

36. Which of the following would NOT result in a shift to the left of the aggregate demand curve?

   A. An increase in taxes.
   B. An increase in the money supply.
   C. A decrease in foreign preferences for our products.
   D. A decrease in consumer spending to bleak expectations about future job prospects.
   E. A decrease in resources.

37. The theory of rational expectations

   A. implies that consumers use common sense when making economic decisions.
   B. assumes people use all the information available when making economic decisions.
   C. implies that fiscal policy will be effective even during stagflation.
   D. supports the notion of a Phillips tradeoff.
   E. was developed by Keynes as a remedy for the Great Depression.

38. Money is

A. currency.
B. only good for acquiring goods and services.
C. anything that a society generally accepts in payment.
D. anything with intrinsic value.
E. always backed by some precious commodity.

39. Monetarists advocate

A. fiscal policy.
B. monetary policy.
C. the gold standard.
D. a constant money supply.
E. a money supply that grows at a steady predetermined rate.

40. According to the "rule of 70," a variable such as GDP that grows at 5 percent a year will double in

A. 70 years.
B. 35 years.
C. 350 years.
D. 70.5 years.
E. 14 years.

41. Macroeconomics is primarily concerned with

A. money.
B. whether the world is making the most out of its resources.
C. whether a family is making the most out of its income.
D. whether firms are maximizing their production levels.
E. whether a nation is making the most out of its resources.

42. Which of the following will increase the supply of a particular product?

A. An increase in the product's price.
B. A decrease in the product's price.
C. An increase in the expected future price of the product.

D. A decrease in the price of one of the main factors used to produce the product.
E. A decrease in the productivity of workers making the product.

43. Which of the following is NOT included in GDP?

A. Proprietors' income.
B. Transfer payments.
C. Depreciation of plant and equipment.
D. Rental income.
E. Wages and salaries.

44. Inflation

A. hurts creditors who do not anticipate it.
B. hurts creditors who anticipate it.
C. hurts debtors.
D. benefits debtors.
E. both A and D are correct.

45. Which of the following persons is considered to be unemployed?

 I. Mary who has quit her job to look for another.
 II. John who fulfilled his dream by retiring from work at age 45.
 III. Diane who works part-time but would like to work full time.

A. I only.
B. II only.
C. III only.
D. I and III.
E. II and III.

46. Business cycles are

A. regular and persistent.
B. irregular.
C. easy to predict.
D. no longer operating in capitalist economies.
E. based on Say's Law.

47. Figure the dollar amount represented by the distance A-B in the diagram below. Assume the MPC = 0.8.

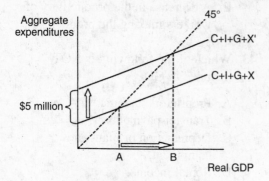

A. $10 million.
B. $8 million.
C. $25 million.
D. $20 million.
E. $12.5 million.

48. Which of the following is NOT included in M1?

A. Coins.
B. Savings accounts.
C. Transaction accounts.
D. Travelers' checks.
E. Paper money.

49. Which is the appropriate policy to slowdown an economy that is producing above its long run potential?

A. Increase the money supply.
B. Decrease the money supply.
C. Increase government spending.
D. Decrease taxes.
E. Run a deficit.

50. The population of country X is exactly the same as country Y, but country X produces twice as much output as country Y. We can conclude that

A. the people of country X are smarter than the people of country Y.
B. the people of country X enjoy a standard of living twice as much as country Y.

C. the people of country Y enjoy a standard of living twice as much as country X.
D. the people of country Y work twice as hard as the people of country X.
E. country X is bigger than country Y.

51. Economics is

A. a social science that studies how resources are used.
B. a field in business that studies how wealth is accumulated.
C. a social science that studies how the government can make better laws.
D. split into two fields: household and global economics.
E. a social science that is primarily concerned with international competitiveness.

52. Which of the following would cause the demand curve for a particular product to shift to the left?

A. An increase in the price of the product.
B. A decrease in the price of a substitute product.
C. A decrease in the price of a complimentary product.
D. An increase in the price of the product.
E. People's tastes change so that they prefer the product more than before.

53. The term "investment" is used by economists to mean

A. retirement savings.
B. buying shares in a corporation.
C. lending money through a financial intermediary.
D. business spending on plant and equipment.
E. business spending on plant and equipment plus the change in business inventories.

54. People who quit a job to look for another one are

A. not counted as unemployed.
B. not counted in labor force.
C. frictionally unemployed.
D. structurally unemployed.
E. cyclically unemployed.

55. If nominal GDP equals $5,000 and the GDP deflator equals 150, then real GDP equals

A. $33.33.
B. $3,333.
C. $7,500.
D. $5,150.
E. $750,000.

56. If the marginal propensity to consume equals .8, then the multiplier is

A. undefined.
B. 5.
C. 1.25.
D. less than 1.
E. 4.

57. If the government of country Z increases spending by $12 million dollars and raises tax collections by the same amount, then what will be the overall impact of these moves on real GDP in country Z?

A. Real GDP will increase by $6 million.
B. Real GDP will decrease by $6 million.
C. Real GDP will remain unchanged.
D. Real GDP will increase by $12 million.
E. Real GDP will decrease by $12 million.

58. Suppose you observe an economy where prices are falling and real GDP is rising. This may have been caused by

A. stagflation.
B. an advance in technology.
C. an increase in government spending.
D. a decrease in government spending.
E. an decrease in the money supply.

59. If the reserve requirement is 8 percent, then the simple money multiplier is

A. 8
B. 92
C. 1.25
D. 12.5
E. 125

60. Which of the following would reduce economic growth?

A. The destruction of a portion of the capital stock due to war.
B. An increase in the unemployment rate.
C. A technological advance.
D. An increase in the labor force.
E. An increase in the savings rate.

Section II—Free-Response Questions

Planning Time—10 minutes
Writing Time—50 minutes
Percent of Total Grade—$33\frac{1}{3}$

DIRECTIONS

You have 50 minutes to answer all three of the following questions. It is suggested that you spend approximately half your time on the first question and divide the remaining time equally between the next two questions. In answering the questions, you should emphasize the line of reasoning that generated your results; it is not enough to list the results of your analysis. Include correctly labeled diagrams, if useful or required, in explaining your answers. A correctly labeled diagram must have all axes and curves clearly labeled and must show directional changes.

Students should consider doing a "sketch" (main points, quick graph, etc.) of the answer before actually answering the free-response questions. Good luck! When you use graphs on the free-response questions, label the axes and make direct references to any symbols, e.g., MR, P, output, on the graphs when you respond to questions.

> **Note**: Recent Advanced Placement examinations require *three* questions. Some of the questions may be based on material covered in the common chapters, such as production possibilities frontier or curve when applied to international trade. For these questions, please refer to those chapters.

1. Country X is a closed economy experiencing increasing unemployment and falling real GDP. The leaders of Country X have decided to use a fiscal policy to remedy the situation.

   A. Should taxes be increased or decreased in this situation?
   B. Draw an aggregate supply/aggregate demand diagram and show how the change in taxes would remedy the economic problems in Country X. Be sure to label the axes and curves in your diagram. Be clear about which curve(s) is (are) shifting which way. State what will happen to real GDP and unemployment because of the tax change.
   C. What will happen to the price level in Country X because of the tax change? Refer to your diagram in your response.
   D. Now suppose Country X is an open economy. Describe how the tax change would affect the balance of trade and the exchange rate.
   E. Does the tax change have a different effect on real GDP and unemployment when Country X is open? Explain.

2. Explain how Monetarists come to the conclusion that

   (a) the Federal Reserve should allow the money supply to grow at a pre-stated amount of 2 or 3 percent a year.
   (b) fiscal policy is ineffective.

3. Suppose the Federal Reserve buys bonds from the private sector.

   (a) In the short run, explain how this open market purchase by the Federal Reserve will affect output, income, employment, and prices.
   (b) How will your answer change if it is assumed that households and firms have rational expectations?

ANSWERS AND ANSWERS EXPLAINED

MULTIPLE-CHOICE QUESTIONS— MODEL EXAM (MACROECONOMICS)

1. C	13. C	25. E	37. B	49. B
2. E	14. B	26. E	38. C	50. B
3. B	15. A	27. B	39. E	51. A
4. B	16. C	28. C	40. E	52. B
5. B	17. D	29. B	41. E	53. E
6. C	18. B	30. C	42. D	54. C
7. D	19. C	31. C	43. B	55. B
8. B	20. A	32. C	44. E	56. B
9. E	21. C	33. E	45. A	57. D
10. D	22. A	34. A	46. B	58. B
11. C	23. C	35. D	47. C	59. D
12. E	24. A	36. B	48. B	60. A

Answers Explained

1. C (Chapter 3) Command economies typically have a more equal distribution of income than capitalist economies.

2. E (Chapter 3) Suppliers are not induced to provide more of a product when its price falls and consumers do not conserve on relatively low priced products. The Law of Supply indicates that the quantity supplied will decrease when the price of the product decreases.

3. B (Chapter 14) Consider the equation GDP = C + I + G + X. X is exports minus imports. So exports are included in GDP but imports are subtracted out. G is federal, state, and local government purchases; I is business spending on plant and equipment plus the change in business inventories.

4. B (Chapter 15) (115 − 110)/110 = 0.045 = 4.5%

5. B (Chapter 16) Since real GDP is $2,000, income must be $2,000. But spending (aggregate expenditures) is less than $2,000 because the C + I + G + X line lies below the 45 degree ray when real GDP = $2,000. If spending is less than income, then inventories must be accumulating and savings are rising.

6. C (Chapter 17) A recessionary gap occurs when equilibrium real GDP (Q1) is to the left of full-employment real GDP (Qf).

7. D (Chapter 16) When the price level rises, so does total income in the economy. Therefore I. is not correct. However, foreign incomes do not rise so foreigners buy less of our products. II. is correct. III. is a statement of Fisher's Hypothesis and is also correct.

8. B (Chapter 18) If the reserve requirement is 5 percent then the money multiplier is 20 (= 1/.05). Bank reserves fall by $10 million because of the open market operation. The money supply falls by $200 million (= $10 million × 20).

9. E (Chapter 19) The Classical notion of monetary neutrality is based on the idea that the money supply and the price level are proportionally related.

10. D (Chapter 21) When a nation's currency becomes cheaper its exports look lower-priced to foreigners and its imports look more expensive to domestic buyers. This promotes exports and discourages imports and therefore improves the balance of trade.

11. C (Chapter 2) Since Belgium can produce both wine and cheese with less labor hours than France,

Belgium has the absolute advantage in both products. The opportunity cost of cheese in Belgium is 60/15 = 4 wine; the opportunity cost of cheese in France is 80/40 = 2 wine. France has the lower opportunity cost of producing cheese and therefore the comparative advantage in cheese production.

12. **E** (Chapter 2) D is close but not correct because an increase in resources could have caused the increased automobile production without a decline in production elsewhere. E is correct because if Country Z was producing inside the production possibilities frontier then it was not using its resources fully or efficiently. By using its resources fully or more efficiently it can produce more automobiles without producing less of any other products.

13. **C** (Chapter 14) Financial transactions are not counted in GDP, but brokerage services are counted.

14. **B** (Chapter 15) One way to measure inflation is to take the percentage change in the CPI. This gives the rate at which prices are rising, but it says nothing about how fast the economy is growing or expanding.

15. **A** (Chapter 16) An increase in taxes shifts the aggregate demand curve to the left. This will decrease real GDP and the price level if the aggregate supply curve is upward sloping as it is in the short run.

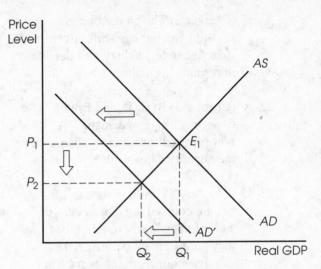

16. **C** (Chapter 17) Increasing government spending and reducing taxes stimulate aggregate demand and fight recessions. Increasing the money supply does this as well, but that is monetary policy.

17. **D** (Chapter 17) Running a surplus shifts the aggregate demand curve to the left which is the appropriate fiscal policy to fight inflation.

18. **B** (Chapter 18) When the FED sells securities in the secondary market they get paid with checks drawn on bank accounts. Bank reserves fall and the money supply falls by a multiple of the decline in bank reserves.

19. **C** (Chapter 19) In the equation of exchange ($M \times V = P \times Q$), if V is constant, then all of the Monetarist assertions are valid. For instance, GDP ($= P \times Q$) will be closely tied to the money supply (M).

20. **A** (Chapter 21) When interest rates in country A rise people from country B will want to place loans there. People from country B will need to obtain the currency of country A in order to do this. The demand for country A's currency rises. This causes it to appreciate.

21. **C** (Chapter 2) The production possibilities frontier can shift left from a decline in technology or a decline in resource availability.

22. **A** (Chapter 3) B, C, D, and E will cause a "change in demand." A, however, will result in a "change in the quantity demanded."

23. **C** (Chapter 14) Imports such as this rug are counted in GDP as consumer expenditures (C), but then they are taken out because net exports subtracts out imports. The overall effect is no effect.

24. **A** (Chapter 15) (9,000/6,000) × 100 = 150

25. **E** (Chapter 16) an increase in the money supply raises prices but has no effect on real GDP (output) with a Classical aggregate supply curve.

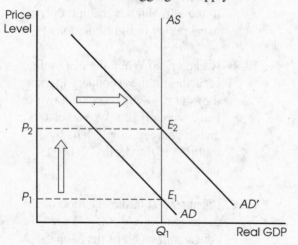

26. **E** (Chapter 16) The aggregate demand curve slopes upward to show that when the price level rises the quantity of goods and services demanded will decrease.

27. **B** (Chapter 17) The diagram below shows an economy in equilibrium at full employment at E1. The tax cut shifts the aggregate demand curve to the right. The new equilibrium, E2, occurs at a higher price level

and higher real GDP. This is what happens in the short run making B the correct response. In the long run, the aggregate supply curve shifts to the left and E3 is the long run equilibrium. In the long run only the price level rises because of the tax cut.

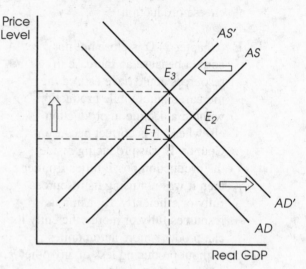

28. **C** (Chapter 18) This is the definition of an open market operation.

29. **B** (Chapter 19) Keynesians think that fiscal policy is more effective than monetary policy.

30. **C** (Chapter 21) The theory of purchasing power parity states that exchange rates will change so that prices for a given product will appear the same whether the product is bought domestically or imported. Therefore, if a country's prices rise its exchange rate must fall so that its products appear to be the same price to someone importing them.

31. **C** (Chapter 2) The production possibilities frontier shows all the combinations of two goods that an economy can produce using all of its resources fully and efficiently. Points outside the frontier represent combinations beyond the economy's capabilities.

32. **C** (Chapter 3) When consumers expect the price of good A to be higher in the future, they demand more right now. The demand curve shifts to the right. This causes the equilibrium price and quantity to rise.

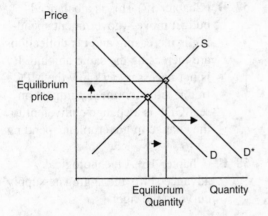

33. **E** (Chapter 14) Second hand sales are not counted in GDP. A, B, C, and D are examples of consumer spending which is counted.

34. **A** (Chapter 15) Since imports are subtracted out of GDP, the GDP deflator (which is based on GDP) does not account for changes in the prices of imported goods and services.

35. **D** (Chapter 16) If the marginal propensity to consume is .75, then multiplier is 4 (= 1/(1 − .75)). The increase in government spending gets multiplied by 4 to determine the overall increase in spending and therefore real GDP. 4 × $100 million = $400 million.

36. **B** (Chapter 16) An increase in the money supply shifts the aggregate demand curve to the right.

37. **B** (Chapter 17) Rational expectations is the idea that households and businesses will use all the information available to them when making economic decisions.

38. **C** (Chapter 18) This is the general definition of money. D is incorrect. United States currency has no intrinsic value.

39. **E** (Chapter 19) According to Monetarist theory, the growth rate of GDP is closely tied to the supply of money. If the supply of money grows at a steady, predetermined rate, then so will GDP.

40. **E** (Chapter 20) The rule of "70" applies here. 70/5 = 14.

41. **E** (Chapter 2) C and D are microeconomic issues; B is international or global economics; A is not correct because money is not the PRIMARY concern of macroeconomics.

42. **D** (Chapter 3) An increase in supply occurs when the prices of the inputs required to make the product fall. A is not correct since this would cause an "increase in the quantity supplied," not an "increase in supply."

43. **B** (Chapter 14) Consider table 14.3 which indicates that proprietors' income, depreciation, rental income, and wages and salaries are included in the income approach to calculating GDP. Transfer payments are not.

44. **E** (Chapter 15) Inflations hurts lenders because they are repaid in dollars that are not worth as much. Some lenders, however, anticipate this and demand higher rates of interest when the loan is made. Borrowers, or debtors, like inflation because they get to repay loans with dollars that are worth less.

45. **A** (Chapter 15) Mary is frictionally unemployed. Retired persons presumably are not looking for work

so they are not part of the labor force. People who work part-time are counted as employed even if they would like to work full-time.

46. **B** (Chapter 16) Business cycles are difficult to forecast because they are irregular in duration and severity even though they are recurrent.

47. **C** (Chapter 17) The $C + I + G + X$ line has shifted up by $5 million. The multiplier in this case is 5 $(= 1/(1 - MPC) = 1/(1 - .8) = 1/.2)$ So real GDP must have increased by $25 million $(= 5 \times \$5$ million$)$.

48. **B** (Chapter 18) Savings account deposits are counted in M2.

49. **B** (Chapter 19) Contractionary monetary policy is the only policy listed here that will shift the aggregate demand curve to the left.

50. **B** (Chapter 20) The standard of living depends on real GDP per capita. Country X has twice the output per person as country Y.

51. **A** (Chapter 2) Economics is a social science and its main concern is the efficient use of resources.

52. **B** (Chapter 3) If the price of a substitute product falls, then the quantity demand of that substitute will rise. There will be less demand for this product, shifting the demand curve to the left. D would not shift the demand curve but result in movement up the given demand curve.

53. **E** (Chapter 14) Economists use the term investment in a peculiar way.

54. **C** (Chapter 15) Frictional unemployment occurs when people change jobs.

55. **B** (Chapter 15) $(5,000/150) \times 100 = 3,333.33$

56. **B** (Chapter 16) The multiplier $= 1/(1 - MPC) = 1/(1 - .8) = 1/.2 = 5$

57. **D** (Chapter 17) This is a balanced-budget move—government spending is increasing and tax collections are increasing the same amount. It is not necessary to know the MPC. In this situation the net impact on real GDP is a change equivalent to the change in government spending.

58. **B** (Chapter 16) A technological advance shifts the aggregate supply curve to the right.

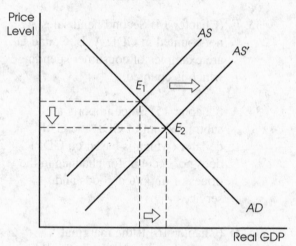

The answer is the same if you use the long run aggregate supply curve.

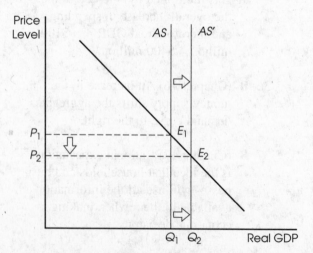

59. **D** (Chapter 18) $1/.08 = 12.5$

60. **A** (Chapter 9) Economic growth depends heavily on the amount of resources and the state of technology. War destroys resources. Notice that unemployment does not destroy resources. It only implies that they are not being used fully.

FREE-RESPONSE ANSWERS—MODEL EXAMINATION (MACROECONOMICS)

1. (a) Taxes in Country X should be decreased. Decreasing taxes is a fiscal policy that stimulates aggregate demand by placing more disposable income in the hands of households.

(b)

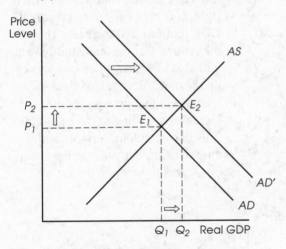

The decrease in taxes causes an increase in aggregate demand. The government is not spending less but households have more disposable income and presumably spend at least a portion of it. The aggregate demand curve shifts to the right. The result is an increase in real GDP from Q1 to Q2. Since more is being produced, more workers are required and the unemployment rate falls.

(c) The price level in Country X will rise. This is shown by the movement from P1 to P2 in the diagram. The increase in output is not enough to match the spending increase and prices are forced upward.

(d) If Country X is an open economy, the rise in real GDP and the increase in the price level will affect the balance of trade and the exchange rate. The increase in spending and income implied by the increase in real GDP means that the imports of Country X will be increasing. Citizens of Country X are spending more and some of that is on products from abroad. And the rise in prices in Country X also implies more imports as these will appear to be a better bargain than before. Moreover, the exports of Country X will diminish since they have risen in price. Imports up and exports down means the balance of trade will deteriorate. Imports up and exports down also implies a depreciation of the currency of Country X. Eventually, this depreciation may mitigate against the balance of trade worsening.

(e) The tax change has a similar effect on real GDP and unemployment when Country X is open. The aggregate demand curve shifts to the right and real GDP increases which implies that the unemployment rate will fall. However, the effect is not as pronounced as when the economy was closed because some of the fiscal thrust is spent overseas. Diagrammatically, the aggregate demand curve does not shift as far to the right when the economy is open.

2. (a) Monetarists conclude that it is best for the FED to allow the money supply to grow at a prestated amount of 2 or 3 percent a year. This conclusion is based on the equation of exchange and certain assumptions about its variables. The equation of exchange states that $M \times V = P \times Q$.

The money supply times the velocity of money equals the price level times output. The Monetarists believe that V and Q are stable in the short run. Therefore, if M increases, then P will increase almost proportionally. However, it is realistic to assume that Q, output, will increase 2 or 3 percent each year in the United States as technology advances and we obtain more resources. If Q grows 2 or 3 percent a year, then M can grow the same percent without putting any upward pressure on prices. Monetarists disagree with the FED implementing discretionary monetary policy. All the FED needs to do is allow the money supply to grow at the same rate as our potential output.

(b) The Monetarists feel that fiscal policy is ineffective mainly because of crowding out. When the government spends more or taxes less to stimulate the economy, it must borrow to make up the difference. This borrowing raises interest rates because it uses up a portion of the pool of loanable funds. These higher interest rates, in turn, discourage consumer and business spending because the borrowing costs involved to finance some of these expenditures has just risen. In the end, government spending has gone up but consumer and business spending has gone down. The overall effect is no change in spending making the fiscal policy ineffective.

3. (a)

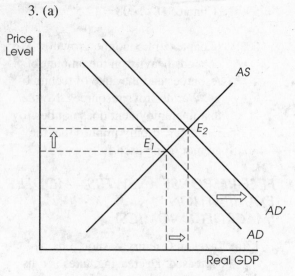

The FED buys bonds from the private sector and this increases the money supply. This shifts the short run aggregate demand curve to the right. It is now easy to see that real GDP (output) will increase. This means that income and employment will also be rising. Prices, as shown on the vertical axis, also rise. An increase in the money supply increases spending in the economy. This boosts output, income, and employment, but some of the spending serves to increase prices.

(b)

If households and firms in the economy have rational expectations this means that they use all the information available to them before making decisions. Presumably most of these households and firms understand economics. When the FED increases the money supply, everyone knows that real GDP and prices will rise. Expecting higher prices for their labor and products in the near future, people reduce their supply of labor and firms reduce their supply of products right now. This causes the aggregate supply curve to shift to the left. The shift to the left of the aggregate supply curve occurs simultaneously with the shift to the right of the aggregate demand curve. The result is we move from E1 directly to E3. The quantity of output never increases. It remains unchanged. Only prices rise because of the increase in the money supply. Increases in the money supply are highly inflationary under rational expectations.

INDEX